THE THINGS OUR FATHERS SAW

VOLUME IV:
THE UNTOLD STORIES OF THE
WORLD WAR II GENERATION
FROM HOMETOWN, USA

UP THE BLOODY BOOT:
THE WAR IN ITALY

MATTHEW A. ROZELL
WOODCHUCK HOLLOW PRESS
Hartford · New York

Copyright © 2018, 2023 by Matthew A. Rozell. Rev. 3.28.24 LARGE PRINT. All rights reserved. No part of this publication may be reproduced, distributed, or transmitted in any form or by any means without the prior written permission of the publisher.

Information at matthewrozellbooks.com

Maps by Susan Winchell.

Front Cover: A machine gunner and two riflemen of Co K, 87th Mountain Infantry, 10th Mountain Division, cover an assault squad routing Germans out of a building in the background. Sassomolare Area, Italy, on March 4, 1945. Credit: Public Domain, U.S. Army Signal Corps photograph. Layout by Emma Rozell.

Back Cover: U.S. infantrymen pushing toward Itri, Italy, during Operation DIADEM, May 18, 1943. Credit: Public Domain, U.S. Army Signal Corps photograph.

Any additional photographs and descriptions sourced at Wikimedia Commons within terms of use, unless otherwise noted.

Publisher's Cataloging-in-Publication Data

Names: Rozell, Matthew A., 1961-
Title: The things our fathers saw : the untold stories of the World War II generation, volume IV: up the bloody boot, the war in Italy / Matthew A. Rozell.
Description: Hartford, NY : Woodchuck Hollow Press, 2018. | Series: The things our fathers saw, vol. 4.
Identifiers: LCCN 2018908489 | ISBN 978-1-948155-47-2 large print pbk. | ISBN 978-1-948155-01-4 (pbk.) | ISBN 978-1-948155-08-3 (hbk.) | ISBN 978-1-948155-00-7 (ebook)
Subjects: LCSH: United States. Army--Biography. | World War, 1939-1945--Campaigns--Italy. | World War, 1939-1945--Campaigns--Africa, North. | World War, 1939-1945--Personal narratives, American. | Military history, Modern--20th century. | BISAC: HISTORY / Military / Veterans. | HISTORY / Military / World War II.
Classification: LCC D810.V42 U673 2018 (print) | LCC D810.V42 (ebook) | DDC 940.54/8173--dc23.

matthewrozellbooks.com

Created in the United States of America

To the memory of

The World War II Generation

and

Al Havens and Skip Gordon

THE THINGS OUR FATHERS SAW IV

THE STORYTELLERS

(IN ORDER OF APPEARANCE):

PETER DEEB
EDWIN ISRAEL
THOMAS COLLINS
JAMES BRADY
ELIZABETH BRADY
HAROLD ERDRICH
FRED CROCKETT
FLOYD DUMAS
ABBOTT WILEY
ANTHONY BATTILLO
FREDERICK VETTER
CARL NEWTON
ARTHUR THOMPSON
HAROLD WUSTERBARTH
WILLIAM MILLETTE

THE THINGS OUR FATHERS SAW IV

TABLE OF CONTENTS

AUTHOR'S NOTE _____ 9

'THE MUDDY, BLOODY BOOT' _____ 21

   THE CONTEXT OF THE MEDITERRANEAN
   CAMPAIGN _____ 26
   PERSPECTIVE _____ 29
   NORTH AFRICA _____ 31
   OPERATION TORCH _____ 32
   SICILY _____ 35
   SALERNO _____ 37
   THE GUSTAV LINE AND ANZIO _____ 38
   ON TO ROME _____ 39
   TO THE GOTHIC LINE AND THE ALPS _____ 40

THE RANGER _____ 49

   TRAINING _____ 55
   'RANGERS LEAD THE WAY' _____ 58
   'BLACK DEATH' _____ 62
   'NO TIME TO REST' _____ 66
   SICILY _____ 72
   THE INVASION OF ITALY _____ 82
   CISTERNA _____ 86
   WOUNDED _____ 89
   'DARBY'S THERE' _____ 93

THE SCOUT — 95
Invasion — 97
The German Soldier — 101
D-Day — 104
Responsibility — 106

THE ARTILLERY MAN — 111
On the Line — 114
The Guns — 116
Surrender — 125
Home — 127
Thoughts — 128

THE CAPTAIN AND THE NURSE — 129
The Rapido River — 133
Monte Cassino — 136
The Hospital — 139
The Fight — 141

THE MORTAR MAN — 147
Monte Cassino — 156
France and Germany — 158
Dachau — 159
The Clothing Store — 163

THE DOG MAN — 167
The Messenger Dogs — 177
A Sunday Evening in the Po Valley — 181

THE END OF THE WAR	183
THE ESCAPEE	**191**
REPLACEMENT	194
TAKEN PRISONER	197
CINECITTÀ	201
ESCAPE	202
ROME	208
HARASSING THE GERMANS	218
LIBERATION	221
HOME	224
THE BATTERY COMMANDER	**229**
'YOU'RE ALL GODDAMN YANKEES'	231
'I DON'T WANT TO BE AN OFFICER'	234
OVERSEAS	240
THREE STRIKES	243
STRAFED	246
SHELLED	248
MONEY	253
PEACH PIE	256
ON THE ROAD	260
NEW OFFICERS	265
'A COLUMN OF GERMAN INFANTRY'	268
NO FLAGS	270
RANK	272
THE MAP MAKER	**277**

Breakout	285
Rome	286
The Po Valley	293
The Duffel Bag	294
Senator Lodge	298

MOUNTAIN MEN — 305

THE MEDIC — 315

Mountain Equipment	318
A Red Cross	325
Officers	326
The Climb on Riva Ridge	327
Mount della Torraccia	331

THE BAR MAN — 339

Training	341
First Action on Riva Ridge	348
Counterattacked	350
The Artillery Observer	354
'The Little Things'	357

THE SQUAD LEADER — 361

Riva Ridge and Mount Belvedere	368
The Po Valley	370
War's End	373

THE PLATOON LEADER — 379

| Mules | 384 |

ATTU AND KISKA	388
SHIPPING OUT	392
RIVA RIDGE AND MOUNT BELVEDERE	397
'WE ARE GOING TO BE SLAUGHTERED'	399
THE MINEFIELD	402
SHOES	407
THE CANNONEER	**411**
PACK MULES	417
THE TUNNELS	420
LAGO DEL PREDIL	421
CIVILIANS	424
EPILOGUE	**429**
ABOUT THIS BOOK/ACKNOWLEDGEMENTS	**449**
NOTES	**455**

U.S. infantrymen pushing toward Itri, Italy, May 18, 1943.
Credit: U.S. Army photograph, Public Domain.

Author's Note

I turned down the dirt road, winding my truck past maples and oaks, deeper and deeper into the lakeside hills to an old camp where I remembered coming as a young boy with my father and the family. It was late in the morning on an early summer day, and I found the camp once more, feeling like a blind man navigating by the senses. I knocked on the door of the cottage, the lake now in full view below, where we fished and swam the summer hours away, not a care in the world. But this Saturday I was paying a visit to an older couple who had made their annual pilgrimage up north from their home in Long Island to spend a couple of weeks at this beloved camp, as they had done for decades. I'd known my dad's sister and her husband for all my life but didn't know anything about their wartime experiences. I was there to piece it all together, to make some sense of their time in Italy, where Aunt Liz was an Army nurse, and Uncle Jim was an Army captain, and where they met and began a relationship that would last over 60 years.

Jim called me into the kitchen, shook my hand, and told me to sit down as he lit his pipe. Aunt Liz gave me a hug and a kiss and insisted on pouring coffee and slicing a piece of her chocolate cake, which I dug into as I told them about a project I had started with our high schoolers. For years we had been collecting, videotaping, and transcribing the stories of our World War II veterans. I had an interest, and I found the stories fascinating, and I channeled this passion to my students. The fall semester after this 2003 interview with my aunt and uncle, I created a formal elective history course at the high school for our seniors, to encourage them to go out into the community to interview their elders; in fact, I used this videotape I had recorded with them in class, to get them primed, and to introduce to them the war in Italy.

Jim Brady: 'I was lying in the hospital, and I heard this awful roar—what the hell is that? I look up, out the tent flaps; I never saw so many planes in my life! There were probably more at Tarawa, but I'd never seen so many planes; they bombed the abbey! All you could see was this big smoke, and dust; they just wiped out the abbey. There were many, many casualties at Monte Cassino... because the Germans were so good, and also with the onset of trench foot. With trench foot, you'd get an infection, and gangrene set in; the only way to cure it was to cut off your foot! I had two or three friends—I saw them down in Naples later on, after I got off the line—and they were all smiling. 'I'm going home; I lost my leg, but I'm going home!'—and they were happy as hell! 'I've got one foot left, but I'm going home!' That's the way they felt about it, you know?'

Elizabeth: 'When I was there I had a very sad ward, because most of the boys were paralyzed and had wounds, you know, spinal injuries; it was sad. We had to do everything for them, write letters and things, and really it was a big awakening for me of what I was getting into, when I saw that. It was still 1943, 'See the world with Uncle Sam,' you know, but by that time I had also met Jim in Naples. We had another ward that had German prisoners. I felt so sorry for them, because they had some men, old men, who really weren't able to fight. They had ulcers; they had a great many physical deformities. But they put them in the German army anyway. They were scared to death, because on the same ward we had two SS men. We knew who they were. They scared the other ones so bad! In fact, one time one *of the German prisoners knifed one of the SS men in the lavatory.'*

*

Fifteen years have passed since I sat with them, but my memory of those few hours around the kitchen table remains clear. Aunt Liz and Uncle Jim are gone now, and the day is fast approaching when no one with firsthand memory of World War II will be alive. Most will have gone the way of the World War I and Civil War generation without ever having told the tale outside of their own brothers and sisters who experienced it with them. So, thank you for buying this book; it's the culmination of a mission that for me turns out to have been lifelong. If you actually read it to the end, you will have done something important—you will have remembered a person who may be now long dead, a veteran who may have lived out his or her final days wondering if it was all worth it. And if you don't make it to the end of this book, then that's on me. I'm not a professional historian, though at one time I was on that track; I was an ordinary schoolteacher who recognized the extraordinary achievements of the witnesses and survivors of the most tumultuous period in the annals of mankind. And these people were our teachers and coaches, shopkeepers and carpenters, millworkers and mechanics, nurses and stenographers, lawyers and loggers, draftsmen and doctors, people from every walk of life, high school dropouts and college graduates. They were the World War II generation, and there was a time when sixteen million of them were in uniform.

As a teacher of history, I felt a responsibility to make what for many kids was the dullest subject come to life. So early in my career, I took it upon myself to devote more than the 'suggested' hour or two for the study of World War II in the classroom. It began when I assigned kids to take home a two-page survey I made up to start them asking questions of their grandparents or relatives. And I felt no shame in bribing them with 'extra credit'; I was more interested in what I would get back. The simple forms were almost always completed by the 'elder partner', but the connection between the generations had been made, and the spark would follow.

Over the years I became well-versed in the story of World War II, mainly from the American perspective because I had to be able to understand our interviewees' stories in the proper context. I also taught my students the skills of critical questioning and post interview analysis and follow-up, corroborating events and incidents wherever possible. That is not to say that a broad multi-national grounding in the history was secondary to my research. In my travels as a young man, I was brought to stand before the gates of Leningrad at the massive Piskaryovskoye Memorial Cemetery, where nearly a half-million people lay buried in 186 mass graves, killed in just 900 days. As an American traveling in the Soviet Union during the Cold War, it was a required, and sobering, stop, made all the more dramatic when I recognized that in this one place—in just one Soviet city—lay more World War II dead than the number of American military dead in every theater of the United States' three years, eight months, and twenty-two days at war. When one really delves into it, the history of World War II can be so overwhelming as to be staggering; in my talks on trying to grasp the magnitude of the Holocaust, I've likened it to entering a room with a dozen doors. Open one, and you find yourself in another room, with another dozen doors to enter.

I suppose I entered into my very first 'room' in junior high school, walking up the block to Moran's Newsroom to feast my eyes on the latest *Sgt. Rock* comic books, parting with my hard-earned quarters to follow the soldiers of 'Easy Company' as they fought out of one carefully laid 'Kraut' ambush to the next. Books followed, including the title that would go on to shape my life in ways I could not possibly imagine: Studs Terkel's 1984 *The Good War: An Oral History of World War II*. That book later became assigned reading for many of my students and was the model for this series. My journey into preserving the oral histories of World War II also led me to become an authority on the teaching of the Holocaust, the greatest crime in the history of the world perpetrated under the aegis of the world's most catastrophic war. I've studied at the feet of the world's foremost Holocaust scholars and have traveled to the authentic sites of mass murder, where sheer evil still has a palpable presence at now tranquil places, but where also the survivors and liberators have returned to mark the triumph of life over death. It's been a heavy road, all an outgrowth of my collecting of stories, but it's also been a journey that has culminated in nearly 300 Holocaust survivors being reunited with their actual American soldier-liberators.

Almost all the first-person interviews my students and I collected over the years were deposited in the New York State Military Museum for future generations to learn from—over a hundred to date. As one of the most active contributors to their program, I also leaned on them for some of the interviews I edited with a loving hand for this book. My friends Wayne Clarke and Mike Russert, the workhorses of the NYS Veterans Oral History Program, traversed the state for several years gathering these stories under the leadership of Michael Aikey; they well know the feeling of bonding with these extraordinary men and women. In bringing these stories back to life, I hope I did a service to them as well as to the general public.

A final note. Whenever I did an interview, I was always interested in getting our veterans' opinions on current events, and I always encouraged my students to ask. Some readers have taken me to task for 'injecting politics' into the narrative, but I am unrepentant; most of the old soldiers' commentaries on our nation's engagements at the time of their interviews have proven prophetic, and I consider those frank observations part of their gift to posterity. I wish I could find a book of Revolutionary War or Civil War veteran reminiscences that offered the same.

So back to the book you hold in your hands. When I began *The Things Our Fathers Saw* series, I began in the Pacific Theater and worked my way through the stories of that war, from Pearl Harbor to Tokyo Bay. Most of the veterans hailed from an area surrounding Glens Falls, New York, that *Look Magazine* renamed 'Hometown, USA' and devoted six wartime issues to illustrating patriotic life on the home front.[1] That book was well received, and a nationwide readership clamored for more. The

---

[1] *Most of the veterans hailed from an area surrounding Glens Falls, New York, that Look Magazine renamed 'Hometown, USA'*-In keeping with the hometown theme, the series title remains the same for this book. Some of the veterans have a direct connection to 'Hometown, USA', and others a more circuitous one, but most hailed from New York hometowns bound together by the simple hope that the boys would return. Many did, and many did not.

second and third volumes highlighted the men who fought in the skies over Europe. This volume takes the reader through the early days of the liberation of Europe, beginning in the Mediterranean and North Africa and continuing to Sicily and Italy.

*

The war in the Mediterranean, and particularly the Italian Campaign, is one that for many Americans is shrouded in mystery and murkiness. Yet it was here that the United States launched its first offensive in the west on enemy soil, and it was here that Allied forces would be slogging it out with a tenacious enemy fighting for its life in desert passes, against fortified beachheads, across swollen and angry rivers, up and over punishing mountain ridges, and through mud-rutted valleys in the longest single American Campaign of World War II. Here men would be asked to do the impossible, and get it done.

Matthew Rozell
Washington County, New York
Father's Day 2018

The War in Italy. Map by Susan Winchell, after Donald L. Miller.

CHAPTER ONE

'The Muddy, Bloody Boot'

On December 7, 1941, I was rabbit hunting off Ridge Street in Queensbury with my oldest brother. We had a radio in the car and we heard about the attack on Pearl Harbor as we were coming home that afternoon. We thought it was quite devastating. My brother enlisted in the Marines a few weeks later, in the first part of 1942. I had another brother who enlisted in the Army, and we lost him over at the Anzio beachhead in 1944. That's the perils of war... —World War II veteran Donald Rowell

Nearly forty miles south of Rome in the hills outside of Anzio, seventy-seven well cared for acres are set aside, shaded by gentle Roman pines and haunting Italian cypresses. Twenty-three sets of brothers repose here, as do several nurses killed by an exploding shell as they cared for the wounded in the heat of the battle for the beachhead. An entire American bomber crew, killed at the same instant, rest side by side in perpetual comradeship, a fraction of the American war dead who lay beneath 7,860 white marble headstones. In the chapel to the south of the central mall, a wall of Carrara marble is inscribed with the names of 3,095 of the missing, though some have since been properly identified through the miracles of modern science.

Most of the men and women interred at the World War II Sicily-Rome American Cemetery and Memorial were killed in the invasion of Sicily and the mainland at Salerno and Anzio. In the 27-acre North Africa American Cemetery and Memorial in Tunisia, over 6,500 American dead or missing are interred or remembered. At the Florence American Cemetery, 4,399 Americans lay, most killed in the final push from Rome to the Alps, including almost forty percent of the American Fifth Army's dead.[2] Less than a year had passed since the first Japanese torpedo at Pearl Harbor to the invasion of North Africa. More than 900 bloody days would follow.

Step ashore, young Americans, to the land of the classical civilizations, of Roman roads and olive groves, of rugged hills sloping to kiss the sparkling seas. Step ashore, young men; see Naples, and die.

*

Napoleon once remarked that the Italian peninsula was like a boot that had to be entered from the

---

[2] *Most of the men and women interred-* Since the end of World War I, more than 218,000 Americans are buried or memorialized in stately resting places overseas. Since 1923, the American Battle Monuments Commission has been administering and maintaining military cemeteries throughout the world. One might wonder why the families of the deceased would choose not to have the remains of their loved ones repatriated. The reason is twofold. The obscenely high death and identification rates made it logistically difficult to ship all bodies home in a 'timely' fashion. In fact, by the end of the 1940s, when families were still being notified about the recovery of their loved ones' remains, forty percent opted for the object of their grief to repose in the land where he or she fell. Many families had deemed it more proper for their loved ones to lie with their comrades who had made the ultimate sacrifice beside them. This evolved into a conspicuous expression of the heavy price paid by the United States of America in the far-flung corners of the free world today, though most of the ABMC cemeteries are in Europe. Source: American Battle Monuments Commission. https://www.abmc.gov.

top, a nearly impossible feat he had undertaken in crossing the Alps with an army in 1800 to prove the point, as Hannibal the Carthaginian had done millennia earlier. Nearly one hundred and fifty years later, that was not in the realm of possibility for the Allies looking to take Italy, but to fight from the bottom up would prove to be no less of a strategic and logistical nightmare.

The American Fifth Army of General Mark Clark fought the entire campaign trudging from south to north in the mountains of Italy against heavily fortified German positions on the high ground. For this it was awarded twenty percent of the Medals of Honor received in any branch in World War II. The British Eighth Army, fighting for much of the campaign up the opposite coast, would pay a heavy price too—together the Allies suffered over 300,000 casualties, and the Germans would lose more than 430,000 killed and wounded.[1]

One is given to wonder, then, why it is that so many Americans know so little of this campaign today. Aside from competing educational agendas and a relative indifference to an in-depth study of this period of our nation's history in our schools, one should understand that even as the Italian Campaign unfolded, not much of it was known back home. A year and a half into the fight, a delegation of visiting congressmen was stunned by egregious battlefield conditions and demanded to know who was responsible for the 'cover-up.' One reporter commented that the press simply could not put into words the combat conditions that men fought and died in for the good folks back home. Others felt that aside from Allied censorship, perhaps the press was reluctant to criticize commanders in the field while the boys were fighting and dying. And the simple fact remained that America was essentially fighting two full-blown wars at once, one in the Pacific and this one in Europe. There was a lot going on at the same time, and today that is easy to overlook. There's also the propensity to teach and learn the history as if the way things turned out was somehow preordained, as if it was a foregone conclusion that Americans and their allies were destined to win the war from the outset. Rick Atkinson, the author of the highly recommended epic *Liberation Trilogy* chronicling America's involvement in World War II in Europe, points out that none of this was inevitable, but in North Africa and Italy is where the United States cut its teeth and began to act like a great power.[2] These campaigns were to be a giant leap for a nation that on the eve of World War II lagged behind Bulgaria as the 18th placeholder for the largest army in the world.[3]

The Context of the Mediterranean Campaign

While many American planners had expected war at some point, few expected it to begin first in the Pacific. As ships were being torpedoed and strafed at Pearl Harbor, the Axis jackboot had trampled through eastern and western Europe and down into North Africa. Vichy France collaborated with Hitler as Great Britain and the Soviet Union struggled for survival. Indeed, by 1942, the German army had soldiers spread over a vast area on three fronts—France, Russia, and North Africa—with two-thirds of the troops based in Russia following the largest invasion in history on June 22, 1941, involving three million men along a three-thousand-mile front. Hitler's invasion of the Soviet Union in the east had started very strong, and in the months before Pearl Harbor, German forces had Leningrad surrounded and were knocking on the gates of Moscow. On December 6, 1941, the Soviets launched a massive winter counteroffensive against the Germans at Moscow. Hitler's death grip on Stalin's throat loosened, but with over a half-million square miles still occupied by nearly 200 German divisions, Mother Russia was nearing her breaking point, bearing the furious brunt of Hitler's ideological and economic war of extermination in the east. Soviet armies were being bled white, and Stalin was imploring Churchill and Roosevelt to open a second front to staunch the flow. Something would have to be done to relieve the pressure on the Soviet Union, and fast.

This was an important fixation for British Prime Minister Winston Churchill, for if the Soviet Union collapsed, all bets on thwarting the complete Axis domination of the continent, and probably Britain herself, were off. His vision of an Italian Campaign would have British and British Empire troops, few French forces and the United States striking the Axis empire first through what he erroneously termed 'the soft underbelly of Europe.' It would also necessitate a postponement of the primary invasion at Normandy. The U.S. Army Chief of Staff, General George C. Marshall, vigorously opposed this idea, arguing that it would draw off too many men and resources rather than placing all efforts into defeating the enemy directly through the primary offensive plan, the cross-channel invasion to establish a straightforward base of operations and supply in northern France. Churchill countered that it was better to harass and harry the enemy through indirect means, recalling the horrors of the World War I bloodletting in the trenches of the Western Front. It might also hasten the downfall of Mussolini, whose military and political fortunes by this point were turning into fiascos. Additionally, the oil refineries of Romania and industrial targets in southern Germany would be more accessible for Allied air power flying out of Italian bases. President Roosevelt was won over; Churchill would have his way.

Perspective

As the Mediterranean Campaign opened for the United States in early November 1942, the Marines were mopping up the six-month campaign on the Guadalcanal offensive and engaging the Japanese in New Guinea. U.S. troops would soon be attacking the Japanese at Attu in the Aleutian Islands. The Battle of the Atlantic was winding down with the crippling of the German U-boat threat. Stalingrad on the eastern front was holding on by a thread, but by February 1943 the Germans were dealt a crippling loss of their Sixth Army. American and British heavy bombers began the saturation bombing of German cities. U.S. troops continued their island-hopping march through the Central Pacific, fighting horrific battles for Tarawa, Makin in the Gilbert Islands, and moving steadily through the Marshall, Caroline, and Marianas Islands before enduring more horror at Saipan, Guam, Peleliu, and the Philippines. The long-range bombing of Tokyo and other Japanese cities commenced as planners forged ahead for landings at Iwo Jima and Okinawa.

While most of this was unfolding, Allied strategists continued to plan the most ambitious amphibian invasion in history, the cross-channel attack on Hitler's Fortress Europe on the Normandy coast. The American Fifth Army's capture of Rome on June 4, 1944, made bold headlines as the first Axis capital fell, only to be relegated to the back pages as Operation Overlord unfolded in the early morning hours of D-Day two days later. That summer of 1944, all eyes were on the beaches and the battlefields in France. Back in Italy, the mud, the mountains, the rain, and the rivers remained, and the men slogged ahead the only way they knew, terrified more of letting down their fellow sufferers than for any long-quashed vision of glory.

*

The Italian campaign of 1943-45 would become the main event in the American involvement in the Mediterranean Theater, but first North Africa had to be secured. It was a confusing landscape with a thousand-mile coastline, rugged mountains and primordial passes, blazing desert sands and barren wadis, and of Italian, German, and Vichy French adversaries.

North Africa

The fight in North Africa long preceded American involvement in the war and would go on for three years. The collaborationist Vichy French government of Marshal Pétain had French troops and ships in North African ports; just how they would respond to Allied intervention on their colonial soil was a complex open question. For both the Allies and the Axis powers, control of the Suez Canal was vital. For the British, it was the lifeline to their far flung eastern empire, and a conduit for resources. Naturally, it was just as vital for the Axis to disrupt it and co-opt any oil from the Middle East or other raw materials for themselves. Mussolini had invaded Ethiopia in 1936, but Italian troops had met disaster in their attempts to consolidate any semblance of empire in Africa or in their ill-fated attempts on Greece and in the Balkans, for which Hitler had to bail them out. In March 1941, General Rommel and his Afrika

Korps attacked the Allies in Libya, pushing them to the brink at Tobruk. In June 1942, Tobruk fell, with 35,000 Allied troops taken prisoner. British General Harold Alexander was put in overall command, and General Bernard Law Montgomery was put in charge of the British Eighth Army. 'Monty' took time to consolidate his forces, and by October 1942, he had 230,000 men and 1,400 tanks to Rommel's 80,000 men and 500 tanks. The Battle of El Alamein became a turning point, commencing on October 23, 1942, with a massive bombardment of German lines by 800 big guns, followed by aerial bombing before the tanks were sent into battle; after furious action, Rommel was forced to withdraw his forces from the battlefield in early November.

Operation Torch

On November 8, 1942, the joint British-American invasion of French North Africa began under the command of Lieutenant General Dwight D. Eisenhower, his first battle command. 'Operation Torch' commenced literally days after the Battle of El Alamein, with 65,000 troops landing at

Casablanca in Morocco and Oran and Algiers in Algeria, with the plan of advancing by land and sea to Tunisia while Montgomery's Eighth Army pressed in from the east. It was hoped that the Vichy French would come over to the Allies, but negotiations broke down. The Germans responded by sending reinforcements from Sicily and Italy and beefed up fortifications as Hitler immediately ordered the occupation of all of France. At Casablanca in French Morocco, Roosevelt and Churchill held high-level talks with their commanders to formulate policy and operations, targeting Sicily and Italy next and reiterating the call for Germany's unconditional surrender. But the Germans would have other plans. Rommel decided to attack the untested American II Corps commanded by General Lloyd Fredendall at the Kasserine Pass, dealing a setback in the Atlas Mountains in west-central Tunisia. Frantic American efforts and overwhelming air support kept Rommel from overrunning his next objective, and he withdrew to his defenses two weeks later, leaving behind 6,000 American dead and wounded in the first major engagement between American and Axis forces in World War II.

Hard lessons were being learned by these young Americans. Allied struggles in North Africa forced serious contemplation over where efforts had fallen short, and invigorated leadership initiated changes to improve battlefield performance. There had to be a renewed emphasis upon air superiority, proper command, and cover in this new desert landscape, including a strategic emphasis on positioning units to be more effective in working together in tandem. General George S. Patton was now given command of the western II Corps.[4]

Ultimately, Rommel was trapped between the British forces in the east and the Allied forces advancing westward along the Algerian coast. Rommel had decided to evacuate troops, but Hitler expressly forbade it. Falling ill, the Desert Fox was flown out of North Africa; by May 3, 1943, the war in North Africa was over, with nearly a quarter-million Axis troops captured, killed, or wounded at the cost of 75,000 Allied casualties. Eisenhower remarked that American ground forces had now come of age, and the stage was set for the invasion of Sicily.[5]

Sicily

On July 10, 1943, in the largest amphibious operation in the history of the world to that date, 160,000 troops were landed by 3,000 ships covered by more than 4,000 aircraft in Operation Husky.[6] High winds and early morning darkness hampered efforts to regroup once deployed. Gliders crashed, and paratroops landed in the sea; only 12 of 147 gliders landed on target.[7] Landing craft missed their marks, dropping heavily loaded men into water still well over their heads. Others got lost, and initial resistance was much heavier than expected. Yet out of the confusion, soldiers rallied around their leaders, and vital targets such as Sicily's main airfield were secured. Allied manpower swelled to nearly half a million; thirty-eight days after the invasion began, Sicily was secured for the Allies. The Italians suffered tremendous losses, with nearly 40,000 casualties and over 150,000 missing in action or taken prisoner. The Allies sustained about

20,000 killed or wounded, and the Germans in Sicily suffered around 18,000, with another 10,000 being taken prisoner, but over 100,000 German troops escaped to mainland Italy across the Strait of Messina.

*

A few weeks before the fall of Sicily, Mussolini presented the Fascist Grand Council with an enfeebled plan to defend Italy, but only in the north. He was immediately dismissed by the king and taken into custody; the new government met secretly to begin armistice negotiations with the Allies.

German Field Marshal Albert Kesselring was now placed in overall command in southern Italy. He had argued to Hitler that in the event of Italy dropping out of the war, he could hold the Allies off for two years, commanding the high ground in chain after chain of mountain defenses, culminating in the vaunted 'Gothic Line' in the Apennines north of Rome. He was not far off the mark in his assessment; before the Gothic Line was breached, eighteen months and 200,000 lives would be spent.[8]

Salerno

The invasion of Italy and the capture of Rome began with three main landings: the toe across the Strait of Messina, the heel at Taranto, and the Gulf of Salerno. On September 3, British and Canadian forces landed and pushed from the toe inland without too much friction. Five days later, just before the landings at Salerno, the Italian government surrendered, defecting to the Allies one month after that. But the opening of the mainland Italian Campaign at Salerno would not be that easy. The coastal plain was split by a river, and mountain passes threw up obstacles on the road to Naples, the next objective.[9] Kesselring masterfully prepared for this, and in German counterattacks nearly threw General Mark Clark's American Fifth Army back into the sea over the next week before veteran reinforcements from North Africa and Sicily helped turn the tide. Kesselring then ordered the immediate German occupation of the entire peninsula and a withdrawal to the Volturno River and the Gustav Line south of Rome; the Germans tore up infrastructure and laid mines all along the invaders' path, then settled in for the long, terrible winter to welcome the Allies to their new battlefront.

*

The Gustav Line and Anzio

The Germans withdrew to fortify the formidable terrain in the mountains between the Allies and Rome along the narrowest point on the peninsula between the Tyrrhenian and Adriatic Seas. Fifteen German divisions manned defenses they described as a 'string of pearls,' with Monte Cassino as the anchor and the Rapido River as a 'natural moat' before the town of Cassino and the fifteen-hundred-year-old Benedictine monastery that commanded views of the Liri Valley and the highway north to Rome.[10] Here the Allied advance ground to a halt as winter rain and snow, raging rivers and streams, plummeting temperatures and blasting winds pummeled men into exhaustion as they attempted to break through during the first half of 1944.

Eighty miles north of the Gustav Line, Operation Shingle commenced on January 22, 1944, in an attempt to flank German positions, but the invasion was dependent on the element of surprise and getting off the beaches quickly, especially since the surrounding terrain included low-lying marshland scored with irrigation ditches hemmed in by the rising mountains. American general John P. Lucas, wary of his position and preferring to consolidate his forces and anchor the harbor before breaking out, did not capitalize on successfully catching the Germans off guard; Field Marshal Kesselring took advantage of the delay and ordered every available unit to the high ground overlooking the beachhead, and flooded the irrigation ditches and canals with salt water. The back-and-forth fighting pitted both sides in a deadly four-month stalemate that claimed over 40,000 casualties on each side, and again nearly pushed the Allies back into the Tyrrhenian Sea before the breakout.

On to Rome

Ten months had passed since the invasion of Sicily. A final concentrated push along a twenty-mile section between the sea and Cassino at last broke the Gustav Line and ended the stalemate at Anzio. Free now to pursue and cut off the retreating German Tenth Army, American general Mark Clark broke orders and instead advanced to Rome, which the Germans had declared an open city and had now abandoned. On June 4, 1944, the first formerly Axis capital fell to the Americans; on the five-month push from Cassino to Rome, 100,000 Americans had been killed or wounded, even as now the Germans were essentially allowed to escape to inflict many more Allied casualties in the coming months.

To the Gothic Line and the Alps

Not long after the first celebratory bottles of wine were emptied on the streets of Rome, the Allied cross-channel invasion in the early hours of June 6 knocked Mark Clark's Fifth Army off the front pages. Overnight, the conquest of Italy became a sideshow; for over a year the needs of Operation Overlord had siphoned off top commanders, men, and materiel, but the fight had not ended with the fall of Rome. For the Germans, it was essential to guard the passes leading northward into the Greater Reich, and they would continue to offer fierce resistance.

The Gothic Line in the northern area of the Apennine Mountains was the next string of defenses. The British and Commonwealth Eighth Army committed troops from 10 nations, beginning in August 1944 and lasting through the following spring and almost all the way to the end of the war in Europe. Supreme Commander Harold Alexander's plan was to envelop the Germans in a giant pincer movement, with the British in the east and the Americans in the west. Control of the skies had long been ceded to the Fifteenth Air Force, by now dropping 1,200 tons of bombs a day at industrial targets in Romania, Austria, and Germany itself. But a few weeks before the launching of 'Operation Olive,' Operation Dragoon, the second amphibious landing on the French coast (this time at the Riviera in the south) was simultaneously put into action, drawing down Allied resources in northern Italy even further. Kesselring succeeded in his attempt to stave off the inevitable before the next winter closed in, and the Allied offensive was again forced to fight through the bitter cold, rain, mud, and snow in the mountains of Italy.

As the spring sun grew warmer and the Allies raced the Germans to the alpine passes, every American soldier was rattled to the bones in learning about the sudden passing of President Roosevelt on April 12, 1945. Yet the end was near. The 442nd Regimental Combat Team, an all-Nisei unit whose parents, in many cases, were interned back home behind barbed wire, had joined the offensive and fought valiantly, becoming one of the most decorated units in U.S. Army history. The all-black 92nd Infantry Division was also deployed to fight here, and the last of World War II's American divisions to arrive in Europe, the 10th Mountain Division, was about to make their reputation in alpine combat by scaling cliffs in the dead of night, to the startled amazement of mountaintop enemy defenders.

Italian partisans also were very active in liberating their country from the fascist yoke; by 1945, they numbered nearly 50,000 in the north. Near Lake Como on April 28, 1945, they ambushed a convoy of trucks and found Mussolini himself disguised as a German soldier trying to get out of Italy.[11] Il Duce had been rescued only a few weeks after his arrest in a daring SS glider mission and had returned to Italy on Hitler's orders to attempt to organize Fascist resistance, to no avail. He and his mistress were executed a day later, and their bodies were strung up upside-down in a Milan public square for all to see. It was a sight that many GIs witnessed and recalled for the rest of their lives.

The war in Italy ended on May 2, 1945, though for many it ended well before that. For others, the memories of friends and loved ones left behind would be cherished, not to be forgotten, but honored so long as the living breath remained with the survivors.

'We have never, ever, ever forgotten these people who we lost over there; there's a huge cemetery in Florence where they're buried. We have the division association that goes back to Italy every two or three years, and it's always a stop at the Florence cemetery. We have a memorial service. Whenever we gather the group, they're always remembered. And I think World War II made me appreciate more of what life is all about.'

44 | THE MUDDY, BLOODY BOOT

*

The War in North Africa. Map by Susan Winchell, after Donald L. Miller.

CHAPTER TWO

The Ranger

Peter Deeb was born in March 1919 in Tonawanda, New York. He was one of the original members of the 1st Ranger Battalion of the U.S. Army, an American commando force that traced its heritage back to the legendary Major Robert Rogers and his intrepid hit-and-run Ranger companies of the French and Indian War, who scouted and struck enemy positions with stealth in the wilds of frontier America two decades before the American Revolution. Drawing on that heritage, Darby's Rangers became the precursor to today's U.S. Army Rangers.

As the Allies opened the dramatic Mediterranean series of campaigns that would stretch over 900 days in North Africa, Sicily, and Italy, Darby and his hand-picked men would live up to their motto, 'Rangers Lead the Way.' They spearheaded the infiltration of enemy *coastlines with grit and determination by knocking out heavy gun batteries and enemy observation outposts, taking crucial airfields, and cracking open the defenses of vital ports.*

After their successful raids in North Africa, the 3rd and 4th Ranger Battalions would be added, and later, an even larger composite force with elements of attached units was created, but like Major Rogers' force almost 200 years before them, bad intelligence and overwhelming enemy firepower would almost completely wipe them out after a string of stunning successes.

Sitting on a leather couch in a New York armory building a few months after his 82nd birthday in 2001, Peter Deeb gave a no-nonsense account of his time in the Rangers that underscored his love and respect for his commanding officer, William O. Darby, his disdain for bureaucracy and red tape, and his perception of the unwillingness of the Army brass to listen to the fighting man.

'When we first got overseas, we didn't have a single military idea, we didn't even have a single [artillery] gun that could compete with the Germans. They had panzers and they had these storm troops. We didn't have anything to compare with that, understand? We were practically helpless...

[The Rangers] did everything at night; we didn't fight in the daytime if we could help it—at nighttime *you go and within the first three hours, between 11:00 p.m. and 2:00 in the morning, you've got to accomplish your mission, still under darkness, or get the hell out of there.'*

Peter Deeb

I was drafted in the Army, I think, in July of 1941. I went to Fort Niagara for induction, Fort Belvoir for my basic training, and was assigned to the 1st Armored Division at Fort Knox.

I was in the artillery. I took engineer training, and they assigned me to the artillery. You know how it is. I was just a regular gunner, you know what I mean? They rotate the guys, put the guns in, clean them up. Stuff like that. That's all, just routine.

We got overseas about June '42, first to Ireland. From Ireland, I heard about going into the Commandos, so I volunteered for it. What happened is the British Commandos needed extra men, and the United States Army didn't have any liaison troops for the British Commandos. Originally, we were supposed to be the liaison from the U.S. Armored Division artillery, right? Just go to Scotland and learn about the Commandos, and then we would come back and train others in doing liaison work with the Commandos. That was the original overall plan, but that wasn't what happened.

Colonel Darby happened to be a native out of Arkansas, and he was perhaps one of the most knowledgeable men on Rangers that we ever had. He went through West Point and he still insisted that Rangers were going to be what he wanted [to create]. So, when he got over there, he engineered a way around the system.

When we first got overseas, we didn't have a single military idea, we didn't even have a single [artillery] gun that could compete with the Germans. They had panzers and they had these storm troops. We didn't have anything to compare with that, understand? We were practically helpless. We couldn't use the Marines. United States Marines did not fight in Europe; we had to use them in the Pacific. Understand? I mean, so that's the background.

*

Colonel Darby wanted to show the British Commandos [what we could do], and he was authorized to do this at Casablanca. The President of the United States and General Marshall, and all the rest, said, 'Yes, it's a good idea to have a comparative unit with the Commandos.' But they didn't know that when you went through the Commandos, you had to become an independent fighting outfit, just like the British Commandos were.

Army Chief of Staff General George C. Marshall had toured the British Commando proving ground in Scotland in 1942, and the idea was planted that an American Commando-type force should be raised. The name would be taken from the legendary Robert Rogers and his Rangers of the French and Indian War. Rogers' forces were the eyes and ears of the regular army, a scouting and intelligence-gathering operation trained to travel lightly and swiftly behind the lines, sabotaging enemy stocks, setting ambushes, gathering prisoners for interrogation, and conducting far-flung raids into enemy lines, in all seasons and weather conditions. Lord Louis Mountbatten was then the chief of the British Combined Operations Headquarters, set up to coordinate army and naval raids to harass the Germans, and he agreed to have the new American force train with his British Commandos.[3]

General Lucian Truscott was charged with raising the new American commando unit and placed Lieutenant Colonel William O. Darby in charge. Darby, a charismatic 31-year-old West Point graduate from Arkansas, was ready for action. Notices were placed in the American camps in Northern Ireland encouraging GIs to sign up, if they had what it took for this new and exciting venture.[12]

Colonel Darby connived to make a Ranger Battalion, which is what he had in mind all along. We got to a place called Carrickfergus, Northern Ireland, and 1,500 men [volunteered] out of 50,000 troops at that time. They took the select of all those who they thought could withstand the training, and Darby engineered the idea of cutting us down to 500 and becoming part of the first American Commandos. That was the overall pitch. Well, that resonated with the United States Army.

---

[3] *Lord Louis Mountbatten was then the chief of the British Combined Operations Headquarters-* Perhaps not so ironically, Rogers and his American rangers were indeed fighting for king and country as British subjects against the common French and Indian threat in the intercontinental Seven Years' War, twenty years before the American Revolution, which some term the world's 'First World War.'

At the time, they thought that we would be the first American Commandos and we'd come back into the military service. But Darby knew that it was damn near impossible to have a Commando-type unit back under [regular] military command. He knew that there was no way that this thing was going to work [under regular military control]. See, after Dunkirk, [it was clear that Commando units needed to be formed].[4] There was no damn sense having us under a military command because they couldn't understand what the hell is going on. What are you going to do? Listen to them? You can't. So they set the Commandos aside, and they set us Rangers aside.

Training

Then we went to Scotland for training up at Achnacarry Castle.[5] Ranger training in Scotland

---

[4] *after Dunkirk-* After the disastrous Battle of France and subsequent emergency evacuation of the British Expeditionary Force in May 1940 at Dunkirk, British Prime Minister Churchill called for 'a force to be assembled and equipped to inflict casualties on the Germans and bolster British morale'; that they 'must be prepared with specially trained troops of the hunter class who can develop a reign of terror down the enemy coast.'

[5] *Achnacarry-*'The Commando Basic Training Centre at Achnacarry, Scotland, was regarded as one of the finest of all the Allied special training centers

was identical with the British Commando training; it was live fire ammunition. They took actual examples of warfare in Europe and infused it in our training command. They had men in there with two to three years' combat training in desert warfare. They had guys in there from the [Royal] Air Force, all the branches of service, and they were forming into one Commando unit.

So we picked up all our guys and we had a similar makeup of it. We had been weeded down to 500. But the thing is, in order to take Commando training, you had to accept British command and British training. The Commandos took their orders from Lord Mountbatten and the King of England directly. You swear allegiance. I was supposed to swear allegiance to the King of England; one of the Scotsmen told me, 'Swear allegiance to the Crown.' You can do that as an American soldier, you can swear allegiance to the Crown of England, not the king. But it's the same thing anyway.

---

established in World War II... Soldiers and marines of the British forces trained there, but also those from the USA, France, Holland, Belgium, Poland, Norway, and surprisingly, some Germans, 'free' Germans and included Jews who had escaped the tyranny in their own country.' Source: Commando Veterans Archive, www.commandoveterans.org.

Our training was different. They would first run a background check to see whether you had any warrior-grade people in your family, a whole bunch of things like that. We didn't have instructors; instead we had a cadre from the 1st, 2nd, and 3rd Commandos, all combat veterans. What they wanted to know was how well we would respond in combat. The biggest thing was what we called 'adrenaline reflex.' In other words, if you get into a situation where you're shocked, you might freeze; the shock of battle will do that to the guys. They wanted to know how long it would take before you respond, get out of it. And one way they did it was to put a machine gunner up in front of you as you're going up a hill, and one behind you. And all of a sudden, they'll fire those machine guns closer and closer, meaning 'get over!' They don't order you to do it, you respond to a combat condition. You see? The training was so brutal that the United States Army wouldn't stand for it—[the British] would fire live ammunition within six inches of your body!⁶ It was so that when we got to our first mission, we would be automatically ready to go into combat. They tell you, 'If we need you, you're going to go tomorrow.' That's all there is to it. What they do is they try to give you a training that orients you to combat, rather than to the ['big picture'] of the battlefield. Understand? We were trained to respond to combat, not to 'authorizations' or 'regimentation' or anything else. They want to make damn sure that they no longer follow the orders of officers or anybody that was beat in Dunkirk. See, you have to train these men to understand, respond to the combat conditions, whatever the battlefield dictates, whatever weapon or tactics come up. You're no longer obligated to carry orders, and your officers in the Rangers and Commandos, they were the same. They had to demonstrate their leadership.

'Rangers Lead The Way'

I was in Scotland two months altogether, one month in training and one month resting up after

---

⁶ Of the 600 men who volunteered to undergo the training, 500 completed it. One Ranger was killed and several others were wounded; forty recruits overall were killed there in training.

Commando training, but we had a group of 50 of our boys who went in the Dieppe Raid, and of course, they got smashed.[7] Every move should have been under Ranger or Commando operation, but they weren't. [*Laughs*] We couldn't tell them what to do, but we could show them what we could do. After that, Commando and Rangers had to be in front, because there was no other way [to do it]. You know what I mean?

*

In November 1942, Operation Torch, the Allied invasion of North Africa, began. The Central Task Force would land at three beachheads near the port city of Oran, Algeria, but first the Vichy French shore batteries had to be neutralized. Sixteen miles east of Oran was Arzew, where two forts would also have to be taken in advance of the main landing of the 1st Infantry and 1st Armored Divisions. The 1st Ranger Battalion would have to lead the way, engaging for the first time the forces of the French Foreign Legion.

---

[7] *went on the Dieppe Raid-* The first American ground troops to see active combat in the ETO of World War II against the Germans were men from the 1st Ranger Battalion here in the disastrous August 1942 Dieppe Raid. Three Rangers were killed and several were captured.

Then we went to North Africa. That's when we got on the boats and headed for Oran; we made the first landing over there. Our first target area was the French Foreign Legion fort at Arzew, that's what we attacked at night. See, we did everything at night; we didn't fight in the daytime if we could help it—at nighttime you go and within the first three hours, between 11:00 p.m. and 2:00 in the morning, you've got to accomplish your mission, still under darkness, or get the hell out of there, understand?

[The fort at Arzew] was on a cape-bound peninsula, around 15 miles away from Oran. In other words, this French Foreign Legion fort controlled [the port of] Oran. They didn't have a fort in Oran, they didn't need it; they had these outposts spotted all over North Africa, and this was one of their main forts, Fort du Nord, as they called it.

We had six [companies] of 50 men each. Three of them went into the actual seaport itself, and we came in on the road, so we had a pincer movement. [The goal was to] split up the garrison from the guns, to silence those damn guns so our naval support could come right in and blow the hell out of them if they had to.

We landed at night, I think it was a mile and a half away at a very small [landing site]. We got into there and made the fast move up to the barbed wire and minefield there—we had to get through, and that was my job; I was a night minefield expert. You have to get in there and crawl on your hands and knees and start feeling around for their anti-personnel mines, and you had to be kind of lucky, too. The anti- personnel mines stick up, like three fingers.

We got to the point, and then we [brought up] the 60mm mortars, the object being to throw the mortar shell in there and slam our way into it. The French had some 12-inch cannons up there that guarded that particular area, and also guarded Oran. The point we took was their artillery position, which commanded everything. Down below us about another half-mile was [the actual] Fort du Nord. We had one group going in there. See, what you do is you cut the artillery off on the ramparts from the main headquarters and the main garrison. We tried to hit all three at the same time, which we could do at night. And there's nothing they can do but surrender. What can they do, you know? We were cutting them right to pieces! And that's the way we worked all of it. All our fighting was done under similar-type conditions. We can't take prisoners; we don't have any place for them. Our colonel talked to the main headquarters of the French Foreign Legion, and they surrendered.

Darby then had rocket flares launched to alert the invasion forces offshore that the first objective for the Allies in North Africa had been taken. The regular invasion commenced.

'Black Death'

After the fall of Oran, the Rangers continued to train and practice their special skills. Orders then came to attack Italian outposts in the Tunisian mountains at Sened Pass, not only to gather intelligence about upcoming German movements, but also to terrorize the enemy by inflicting shocking blows that would not soon be forgotten.

We were in the desert in a place called Gafsa; it became our headquarters, down south about 60,

70 miles. British intelligence knew that Rommel was coming back across Libya up Tunisia. Now, there were three passes, the Faid, Maknassy, and El Guettar, like a triple deal. We could take any one of them, but in the middle of there, at a place called Sened, there was a radar station for radar and observation so that they could monitor anybody coming to these passes to get through. I was on the Sened raid.

We rested up for about two, three weeks, and then we were called in to go out to the desert, to the Thelepte airport. We got on airplanes there and took right off and went out there to support our fighting units down south, because they were beleaguered; they couldn't do anything until they had the Rangers lead the way, so to speak. Algiers is where we landed. And we flew on these damn C-47 planes; we were never more than 300 feet off the ground, because if we got any higher, the German planes could pick us up. There was even a mountain area where we had to zig-zag through. And the minute we landed they said, 'Get the hell out!' They wouldn't shut the engines off. They just zoomed right away, they just took right off. Sure as hell, right afterward the Germans came and sprayed that darn field with bombs, within ten minutes after we landed.

On the night of February 11, 1943, they set out, covering 14 miles in just two hours. As the sun rose the next morning, they spent the day observing the outpost, finalizing their plans.[13]

Now, the Sened station, like I said, is at the point of the three passes. In order to get to it, we had to go around and get behind it, sort of like a dogleg, and spend a day seven miles away from it. There was an old French fort there, and we could look down on it during the day. We gauged the way we would hit that place so that the moon would set right between two mountain peaks; we timed it so when we got there, that moon would silhouette them, but not us.

Another twelve-mile hike brought them to within 200 yards of the enemy outpost at 1:30 a.m. 'They've got to know that they've been worked over by Rangers,' a company commander said. 'Every man is to use his bayonet as much as he can. Those are our orders.'[14]

We had small mortars and a couple of bazookas. We didn't carry much weight and we didn't put helmets on because the helmet reverberates when you use your gun. And again, there was barbed wire and a minefield, and again, that was my job, to get the boys in as close as we could get. We carried out the first and only bayonet charge [of the war] by our Rangers; we didn't fire. There wasn't much command, you just had to watch the leaders, the officers. What they did, you did, you know. So that's what happened. Actually, very few people knew that we carried out an overnight bayonet attack. I'll tell you, that's something. You see that, it'll shake you up real good.

In twenty minutes, it was over. Twenty Rangers had been wounded and one was killed, but they had inflicted 75 casualties and taken eleven prisoners for interrogation and began to quick-march out of the mountains. At their return, General Fredendall presented over a dozen Silver Stars to individual Rangers, including Darby, now known in enemy circles as 'Black Death.' The astonishing success of the raid led to the recommendation that further Ranger battalions be raised. Indeed, the

Rangers had made their mark; one corporal later recalled the savagery and ruthlessness that would make the enemy tremble: 'We swarmed over the remaining centers of resistance, grenading, bayoneting, shooting, screaming, cursing, and grunting. The remaining Italians never had a chance. We worked them over furiously, giving no quarter. It was sickening, brutal, inhuman.'[15]

'No Time to Rest'

There was little time to rest or celebrate, however. Just a few days later, a major German armored counterattack unfolded at the Kasserine Pass, developing into a rout of inexperienced American troops, leaving 6,000 casualties. General Fredendall was relieved and replaced by General George S. Patton, Jr., and the Rangers were called on to lead the way for the 1st Infantry Division again. The Battle of El Guettar would see the Rangers in action, taking and holding the high ground for over ten days in March 1943, at times outnumbered 4 to 1.

After we got through, we got back to Gafsa and we were supposed to rest up there. Then we found out that Patton took charge of the whole [U.S. II

Corps] there, because he was a tank man and he was going to go through.

There was a British intelligence unit that was in the field for three, four years already; they were down there with the [British] Eighth Army. They used to watch everything, and we got in touch with them; they said, 'There's something going wrong here, you better check it out.' So, we sent men out there time and again to see these [German] tanks [on the move].

Well, this was an ideal situation for Patton. Patton took charge of this thing, and he said he wants to catch Rommel with half of his outfit in Libya, half of it in [Tunisia]. There was no defensive area for 100 miles up the Tunisian coast, so he wanted to hit them right through there. He got ahold of the 1st Armored Division, but we had to take out Sened radar station, otherwise the Germans would know which pass we were going to go through. But the Germans, not being dumb, knew that when we hit Sened station and knocked out their eyes and ears, [something was coming]. Two days later, when we got back to Gafsa, here comes the 1st Armored Division for what was [supposed to be a] duel in the desert. In other words, Patton went out from Gafsa toward El Guettar, which was the best entrance to catch the Germans, though he was warned time and again by our intelligence, British intelligence. Everybody said, 'Don't go there you, darn fool, it's a trap.'

So, here come our boys right through, they said, 'Oh, we're going to bash the hell out of them this time,' though we told them that there's something wrong here. The day before, one of our guys went out looking at the salt swamp and he saw these big tank tracks, and he put out the [warning]. Patton said nothing on earth is going to stop him. 'We're committed, we're going to get them,' that's what he said. Well, we took the worst beating in the history of the United States Army at that point, at that position. The Germans knocked out the 1st Armored Division in less than six hours. I went and saw the place afterwards—they knocked out every tank, everything we had, our artillery pieces; tanks were lying around like a junk pile. They never mention it. What you hear about was the [previous month's massacre at the Battle of] Kasserine Pass. That was 40 or 50 miles north, and the

Kasserine Pass was like a cul-de-sac, and the Germans wanted to block us from hitting their group going all the way up to northern Tunisia. For three days the Germans were marching right by, tank after tank and truck after truck.

The Battle of El Guettar raged back and forth inconclusively for ten days, with rough casualty estimates of 5,000 killed or wounded on each side.

*

After that, we had to fight a rear-guard action. In other words, we had to help our boys get the hell out of there. We let them get out, and we stayed behind at Gafsa as the last ones and started blowing up bridges, putting up roadblocks, and whatever else we could [do to obstruct the enemy]; we didn't have much. Then we gave our trucks over to the general hospital to get their people out of there, and of course they were backed up all the way to the Kasserine Pass. Eight miles south [was another] pass. We were told to take and hold that pass, as that was the only straight-line shot to Algiers.

Almost every day, the Germans would send somebody in there trying to get through. Now remember, we were coming off of the Sened raid, a two-day rear-guard action to get our troops out of there, and then we had to get into this position and hold it against the German attacks every single day. We were under fire almost constantly by the 88s. We knew where the guns were, the British had them all marked out. Every night the British would send this intelligence outfit to expose themselves two miles away from the Germans, and it would force the Germans to fire their guns, then you'd pinpoint that spot. You know they can't move those guns any more that night. You understand? We told them, time and again, and it didn't do any good. The [commanders] wouldn't listen.

And one time, we saved their lives. In the confusion, those darn fools were taking a wrong road; Eisenhower and three command cars full of generals and officers took the wrong road! Darby had to take his Jeep and run up there to stop those damn fools. They were going into a U-shaped turn, instead of heading west; the darn thing winds up east around what they call a lateral mountain range—

[Darby] went up and stopped them, saved their damn lives…

*

We had a two-month rest period coming up. It wasn't too far away from Oran, and we were there resting up at a French outpost. See, usually we're on boats—the Rangers are a seaborne outfit. We don't have them now, but you're always either on ships or on a rest camp area or something. They don't put Rangers and Commandos in barracks. That's a no-no. We're supposed to be above that.

After we rested up for pretty close to a month, Eisenhower comes to Darby and says there's an emergency situation. He said the Germans got these damn rockets, the V2 rockets at that time; we were going to take out the V1 rockets too. From right across Oran, they were shooting the rockets and these buzz bombs into Oran. We were supposed to go there, but the Commandos took them out before we got a chance, although I was notified, because I was on the Commandos list.

Sicily

By early May 1943, the crush of the combined Allied forces on the Axis was too much to bear. The war in North Africa was over, with nearly a quarter-million Axis troops captured, killed, or wounded at the cost of 75,000 Allied casualties. The next target on the Allied springboard was Sicily.

*

Now we were preparing for an invasion of Sicily. See, the Rangers have to go in combat to be training for one [specialized] combat [situation] after another. Colonel Darby and his staff selected our own men, trained them, staffed the outfit. We did this all by ourselves because he wanted to show the British Commandos that we could do something they [weren't doing].

Operation Husky kicked off on July 10, 1943, when over 100,000 men were set to be landed in the largest amphibious operation in history to that date. The Rangers were tasked with getting in early and capturing a vital airfield at Gela. A major storm with high winds severely complicated the start.

[For the invasion of Sicily], I was on Colonel Darby's special team. He would pick a certain group of men for every different type of action that he was going to fight. I was usually on his team because I [had become] the nighttime demolition expert.

We were heading for the Sicilian shore on British landing craft and British boats... And the British admiralty knew that Colonel Darby was one of the outstanding soldiers; he could call them in to do anything, and they'd respond right away. Now again, this was Patton's big operation. Well, what happened was a storm came up and the whole darn bunch got screwed up on the landing; ships were coming in one way or another, the paratroopers were supposed to land seven miles inland from Gela, Sicily, and we were supposed to go in and meet up with them, and then have an airfield for ourselves.

The wind was so high that the paratroopers [shouldn't have made] the jump. And Patton, in his usual wrong-doing way, ordered up the 82nd Airborne. He insisted they come in. And when they started to cross [the sea], they hit some high wind, and guess what? The German air force flew wingtip to wingtip with our paratroopers. When Darby looked up at the sky and saw German planes, he said shoot the buggers down. And the Navy says no, we have to get an authorization from Patton. Well, Patton is out at sea. He wouldn't make the initial landing with us; he was still out there. He didn't get there until 36 hours after the fact.

The damn thing was all screwed up, but the next thing you know, we were taking Gela. Now, I was supposed to be the demolition man [out in front], and Darby was right there alongside me. He demonstrated leadership, you understand, the very first guys to get off the boat were us. We'd got off, and I'd had to dig my way through the darn sand to make sure there were no mines, and we were rather fortunate, because the storm covered up a lot of the mines. You know, we would carry 80 rounds of ammunition, a rifle, two hand grenades, and a canteen of water. No helmet. To cross that darn minefield, I said, 'Why don't we throw these damn bags on the ground, and if it doesn't explode, we can walk it, jump on them.' Well, the other boys weren't in on that [part] unfortunately, and we lost three officers and three men on the beach. And [unfortunately], when you fall on a mine, you become a pad to jump on. They stomped the guys right into the ground; they couldn't help it, they had to. The safest thing was to just run on those guys.

We got up there, and we finally got to the barbed wire fence. There were two pillboxes that we could see, plain as hell, too, and I was supposed to carry heavy wire snippers.

Darby said, 'Where the hell is that darn wire snipper?'

I said, 'What do you want them for?'

'We have to get over the fence.'

I said, 'I'll show you how.'

I got [the guys] by the belt, picked them up, and threw them right over the damn fence! That was the simpler way of doing it…

When we got up next to the pillboxes, my job was to take that pillbox out; they had said there would be six pillboxes I'd have to take out, so I carried extra hand grenades. Well, the first two were taken out by one of our Browning automatic men;

he just stuck the machine gun in there, and you know, you fire into one of them, and those bullets circle around in there real good. The others, I'd sneak up and try to find air holes—any holes where you could throw a hand grenade in, and that was my job, besides getting us across [the minefield].

[It turned out that] there were sixteen pillboxes. They weren't [typical concrete] pillboxes, but they were [modified strongholds] on the street corners, and they made them into [gun positions] so they could crossfire on anything. I said to my guys, 'Give me the damn hand grenades, we're going to take these buggers out.' And I think I knocked out six altogether.

Colonel Darby made a mad dash for their headquarters, there was like a fortress there, we made a mad dash for that. The [men on the] right went after the garrison and blocked it off, and the other boys went and took out the gun positions protecting Gela, but in order for us to get in there, [we had to have naval gunfire support]. Now just to give you some idea what this colonel could do, he said, 'I have to have protection, we don't have artillery!' The British sent in two destroyers, and they nearly beached them to steady the darn things, [and waited for the signal to fire]. The enemy was knocking the living hell out of those two destroyers, but the ships wouldn't fire back until we fired the Very [flare] pistols up indicating that we had taken the main position. Then they just opened up and wiped out everything, they knocked the hell out of the whole darn works, but in the process, the British lost two or three boat handlers.

Now, Patton was not on the beach yet. He didn't know what the hell was going on. Right off the bat, in the morning, we looked off to the left of us and here were three German tanks coming at us. These were German-made tanks. The Italians also had tanks—later on, after this, the six Italian tanks came through the city while we got up on the second floor, and Colonel Darby himself threw a hand grenade right on the back of one of them and blew the hell out of it personally. I mean, he'd get in there and fight just like anybody else. But when he saw these three German tanks come, right away he said, 'Jesus, there isn't supposed to be a road between Gela and the center of that town!' Right away he called for naval support, our own navy. Well, the Navy says, 'We can't take instructions from a lieutenant colonel. You can't tell us what to do.' So Darby gets on the horn and he calls the British admiralty. So right away they sent up what looked like a small battleship, but it had 14-inch guns on it. They didn't hesitate—they said, 'You tell us where to fire, and we'll fire.' So on their way in, he told them to fire a shot to see what the distance was. Well, they got the first shot within a mile, but short of the tanks, so he told them, 'It's a mile short, and do something.' So they, the next thing you know, they just blanketed that whole damn area with 14-inch rounds.

The enemy then mounted a serious counterattack with heavy German armor and Italian infantry.

If that wasn't bad enough, soon after we got rid of the Italian tanks, up the right side now came [14 to 18] German [Tiger] tanks! It was early in the morning; we saw the first of the German tanks come in, snaking behind all the hills so we couldn't get a good shot. Now remember, Patton is supposed to be a tank commander, and hadn't gotten one tank or artillery gun on that beach—five miles of beach, not a single artillery gun or tank could get on there, and here were more German ones!

We called in the British [naval] support; they had a territorial line for some reason or other, and we were in the British sector. They split Gela right down the middle, and to our left, that was American territory. We had called our navy: 'You damn fools, those are German tanks!' Darby got mad as hell at them, so he called the British admiralty. Now the British admiralty had the *King George*, the best battleship in the whole fleet, 16-inch guns. He called them up and he said, 'We can only last 15 minutes. Can you do something for us?'

They replied, 'In 15 minutes our guns will be able to reach that line.'

So, they start coming in, and when the American navy saw this battleship coming at them, they told it to get the hell out of the way, because it was coming into their fire range. So the U.S. Navy finally said, 'We'll fire, we'll fire.' The first cruiser comes up in range and they ducked the guns. And when they fired, it went 15 feet over the top of the closest tank, which was only 1,000 yards away.

Right over the top of them! Well, these Navy guys got smart, because the next cruiser was coming around the bend to follow this, and when that second cruiser got there, they could cut the grass! It knocked out three tanks right off the bat, and then they both started really opening up on them! The Germans turned around and got the hell out of there—I think we knocked out about six, seven of them, I don't know what it was, and a whole bunch of men.[8] Now again, this incident never got into newsprint, there's never been anything.[9]

When we realized that the German tanks came in from the right, we knew that they had to come from someplace that was safe enough for them. We sent some of our best boys out there [to scout], and the place was called Butera, which was like a hilltop fortress. We would have had to snake back two times on the road to get up to the top, and the two switchbacks [on the road leading to the fortress] were guarded by flamethrowers. If

---

[8] *I think we knocked out about six, seven of them-* it was at least a dozen. One source puts the number of Tiger tanks deployed against the Rangers in that counterattack at 14, another 18.

[9] *there's never been anything-*Rick Atkinson's book *The Day of Battle: The War in Sicily and Italy, 1943-1944,* published six years after this interview was conducted, provides excellent bird's-eye coverage of this incident, as well as other Ranger exploits. See endnotes.

anybody'd come up anywhere near that, they would have been just blown away with the flamethrower. This captain, he was pretty damn good, he went out there and he looked around, and he says, 'I'll tell you what we're going to do. [We're going to] go straight up instead of zig-zagging all the way up. If we get there fast enough, [it will still be open for their own troops to return to]. This captain told Darby, 'When we get up there, I want you to call in some light tanks and artillery to get over the top, and we can take the other side of the hill.'

So, this captain gets up there and he says, 'You wait for my orders.' He goes back on the two switchbacks and he shoots these guys with the flamethrower packs on their backs! We saw those burned bodies lying there; we could now wiggle our way up there—and one of our companies went right through Butera to the other side.

*

We cut Sicily right in half. Again, Patton turns around and says, 'It's a remarkable job.' I couldn't believe that. And he told Darby, 'If any damn fool in the 2nd Armored Division will follow you, you can have them in the Rangers.'[10] Then he turns around and says, 'If any one of those guys ever joined the Rangers, I'm going to charge them with desertion, insubordination, and court martial them.' That was Patton. Patton was one of the most ridiculous goddamn men that you would ever see in your life. He wouldn't [listen] to logic; he wouldn't change anything. You had to follow the damn plan step by step no matter what happened. You couldn't reason with him.

After that, we had a clear shot to Palermo. We got our men into Palermo, and got into position again, and then we brought in our own regular troops. From there, we took off and went to a sort of rest camp again, and we were getting ready for the invasion of Italy.

The Invasion of Italy

On September 8, 1943, Italy capitulated to the Allies. Mussolini had been ousted and was taken into custody in late July, only to be freed in a daring glider raid by crack SS troops after Italy's formal defection. Hitler

---

[10] *2nd Armored Division*-The division's first major action in World War II was at Gela and Butera.

raged and disarmed over a half million Italian troops; many were sent to slave labor camps.

The next day, the Rangers were sent into Italy with the main Allied invasion force as part of the invasion at Salerno, led by U.S. General Mark Clark. Their initial task, along with the British Commandos, was to seize mountain heights that commanded the passes upland overlooking the road to Naples. The planning of the operation had taken place over just 45 days, instead of the months of coordinated intelligence gathering and logistical planning. The German commander, Field Marshal Albert Kesselring, prepared a hardened defense that shocked the Allies even before they arrived at the beaches, and his counteroffensive nearly drove them back into the sea a few days later. Darby's quick assault and capture of a German observation point six miles inland at Chiunzi Pass was one of the few high points that allowed overwhelming artillery and naval support to beat back the Germans and get on the road to Naples after a month of hard fighting. Peter Deeb gave his perspective on the invasion; he would be wounded eight days into it.

Whoever planned [the invasion at] Salerno had to be the stupidest guy in the world. Here was a beach about six to eight miles, the most beautiful landing position you could get into. But five miles inland was the German Army and big guns, and they had this main road behind them to supply them all the time. We took a hell of a beating because they counterattacked us six, seven times, and I mean they came right up to the point where they would send their men right around our position.

Around the second day the Germans knocked out a whole bunch of ships out at sea; they were able to hit anything within eight miles out at sea beyond the Salerno beachhead. They just knocked the living hell out of them! Then General Clark called Darby, he says, 'Come on over here and go into rear guard action, we have to pull off the beach. It's untenable.' And Darby says, 'We're going to stay here—we'll cut the German lines.' We told [General Clark], 'Give us some supplies, give us some men, and we'll go in there and cut the line right up.' Darby was quite a man, you know.

From their landing point, the Rangers trekked six miles and 4,000 feet up to the Chiunzi Pass in just five hours.[16]

We landed at a place called Maiori, which was 10 miles from Salerno. We wanted to cut the German lines immediately, their supply lines to Salerno from Naples on the Appian Way. We had to take that position to protect the flank, to keep the Germans occupied up north of Salerno. That was a diversion there. The British Commandos [also] landed five miles beyond Salerno, and the two places were where we wanted to make sure that we could hold the line. So we went up there, and I went with Darby, and we got a hold of the Commandos and said, 'Hold on for a couple more days, if you can, we'll try to get some support for our position.' We [got up at Chiunzi Pass and] were looking down on the Germans, and Darby was yelling, 'For God's sake, give us some guns, we can hit the buggers!'

German infantry counterattacked with mortar fire and tried to scale the heights around the Rangers. The Commando forces would be stretched thinly across a nine-mile line for the next three weeks, driving off the counterattacks and calling in strikes on German positions. They held the pass.

And finally, Darby wound up with over 5,000 men under him. Now remember, he had to set these guys up for night fighting, because it was all hilly. They're all under direct orders of Colonel Darby. He told them exactly what to do and what not to do. And we got these howitzers up there, they could take them apart, [pack them up], and put them together, then we had something to shoot downhill at them, and that's what saved that damn position.

Cisterna

After taking Salerno and advancing on Naples, the Allied invasion at Anzio was planned to break the stalemate at the Gustav Line and make a run for Rome. Operation Shingle nearly turned into an unmitigated disaster as General Lucas was wary of immediately engaging the Germans, preferring to consolidate his position at the harbor and beachhead. Enemy armor and reinforcements poured in just as the Rangers, with their own forces now diluted with replacements lacking advanced Commando-style training and experience, were ordered out to cut a major highway by taking the town of Cisterna four miles from the beachhead. Faulty intelligence, poor communication, and deadly German ambushes devastated the Ranger force. The fact that it was one of the few fights not led directly by Darby also helped contribute to the feeling among some that the Rangers had been expended for some nefarious means; the destruction of the force was just beyond belief. Darby blamed himself for remaining at the command post to coordinate battalion movements; he put his head down and began to sob as desperate radio transmissions made it clear that his men were being annihilated.

I was not with the Rangers at Cisterna, but of course I found out about what happened there. Again, in my viewpoint, and a lot of other Rangers' viewpoints, Uncle Sam tried to get the Rangers deliberately [out of the way]. They called the colonel down—remember now, Darby was a front-line officer. [The Rangers] would never go into combat with a battalion without him exactly in the [lead] position; he would have set the whole thing up! They called him into headquarters, near one of the landing sites that we had control of, and they sent orders under his direction. He told our boys up there, two of our battalions, 'You go in and knock the hell out of the German tank brigade and artillery unit,' which we could have done. I mean, it was natural for us to go at night and get in there silently, making sure the Germans don't fire the guns or move the tanks.

After midnight on January 30, 1944, three Ranger battalions set off across fields and into drainage ditches, advancing without mortars or heavy machine guns. Short of their objective by daybreak, Rangers encountered German heavy armor and walked into an ambuscade, and attached units on their flanks were pinned down. American tank support could not make headway.

And what was supposed to happen, they told the officers there, they said, 'You guys do that and then we'll bring in tank [support] and everything else,' because if we get our tanks close enough to theirs, you can knock the hell out of them, no matter what they got. General Truscott said [to Darby that] he had direct orders that this is the way it's going to have to be done, and that [the Rangers] were going to also have naval [gunfire support] protection. They double-crossed him. They told him to go in... so they practically wiped out a good deal of our men at that time.

Only six Rangers out of the entire 1st and 3rd Battalions were able to escape.[17] *As many as three hundred* were dead, and many others were taken prisoner, although the massacre would be hushed and kept under wraps as an investigation ensued, contributing to the confusion. In the end, the explanation was a cascading catastrophe of the horribly ordinary; one officer interviewed stated that it had been 'contributed to by so many factors that it can be ascribed only to chance.'[18] Darby estimated that only 87 of the original 500 Rangers he had assembled for training in Scotland remained.[19] The composite 6615 Ranger Force formed for the Anzio invasion was now formally disbanded by Army Chief of Staff George Marshall, and many of the surviving Ranger veterans would leave to train other assembling Ranger units, including those who would scale Point Du Hoc overlooking Omaha Beach in Normandy just a few months later.[20] Peter Deeb's war, however, was over.

Wounded

I got hurt at Maiori, just eight days in over there in Italy. I was working on [deconstructing] a new type of aerial bomb that the Germans left behind, a delayed action aerial bomb, and it was the first time [we ever saw them]. I was going to tear one apart to see what it could do. I tied a rope on it and

I was getting ready to dangle it over a cliff, and boom, the damn thing went off on me.

They ordered a PT boat to come in to pick me up and take me to a hospital ship, and away we went, back to Africa, and I went right on through [to home]; I was discharged with 100 percent disability. They said, 'You're going home and you're going to be good. You're disabled, you don't have to worry about a damn thing anymore.' I got to Camp Fannin, Texas, they said, 'Nope, you look all right to us. We'll give you 30 percent [disability].'

I said, 'Where's my records? I can prove it.'

'You have no records.'

And if you don't have any records that you're carrying [on you], they can do any damn thing they want with you. Darby told me to go to the Pentagon to get my damn records; he said that's the only place they got them. So I went to the Pentagon, I said, 'I want to get my records.'

They said, 'We can't help you, but if you get the records, we'll honor them.'

That was a catch-22. They aren't going to release the records, and I can't get them. And that's been going on for 50 years! I've done everything under the sun. I've tried every darn thing, went to [Fort] Benning twice, I went to [another] Army base there half a dozen times—they wouldn't do a damn thing for me. And they wore Ranger patches there!

I ran into the Chief of Staff of the Army at an airport. And I said, 'Why the hell can't I get them? You're a Ranger. Go get me my goddamn...'—I can talk to Rangers, you know— 'get me my damn records!'

He said, 'To tell you the truth, I can't get those records. They're under heavy guard, and they will not permit it. But if you're lucky enough to get an ombudsman to go into those [archives], you better know exactly what you're looking for, because they're not going to help you search.' How do you like that? How the hell am I going to do it?

So I'm sitting here without [my records] ... but I got it up to 60 percent, then I went to the [VA] hospital and I said, 'I want to turn myself in. I can't think right.'

The doctor checked me over, and he said, 'Look, we'll give you 80 percent and call you unwell so that you can't work, then we'll give you 100 percent right afterwards.'

That was in 1975. 1986 comes along, and they have another review, a 'means test,' the VA calls it. They went over the whole review and they said, 'You look all right to us. We'll cut you right back down to 60%.' Now I was supposed to have 100% all the way through! I mean logic would tell you, you can't get out of the battlefield without a damn good excuse unless you're really hurt! And I wouldn't have gotten past the third general in Algiers unless I was badly hurt! I wouldn't have gotten past them in Oran, either. Then I went to Casablanca. Again, they study over everything, read it over, [thought about operating], but I said, 'The hell with you, I'm supposed to go home!' They put me on a ship, I got over to the White Sulfur Spring Hospital, and they did the operation.[11]

I'll tell you another thing that stands out. If you think that a guy [coming out of] combat isn't hurt, I mean isn't set back a hell of a way, you made one bad, big mistake. That is one of the meanest things

---

[11] *White Sulfur Spring Hospital*-U.S. Army surgical hospital and rehabilitation center in West Virginia during World War II.

this nation's ever done is to ignore the fact that guys in combat are set back [by post-traumatic stress disorder], as they say, shell-shocked. But you can't tell that to the VA, you don't get anywhere— 'Where's your scar?', you know. I went before the Board of [Veterans' Appeals] a couple of times and had special [hearings]. I told them I was under duress, and they said, 'No, no such thing.'

I said, 'You can't tell me that a combat man doesn't suffer [mental] duress after being in very intense combat! I was in eleven engagements, right alongside of Colonel Darby, and I'll tell you, you should go once!'

*

'Darby's There'

Lieutenant Colonel Darby twice rejected promotions so that he could stay with his men. After the disbanding of his Rangers, he was given command of the 179th Regiment of the 45th Division, which had been decimated at Anzio.[12] Later he was given a staff assignment, but he

---

[12] *command of the 179th Regiment of the 45th Division*-Source: Hull, Michael D., *U.S. Army Rangers in World War II*. As a side note, this was the regiment of Floyd Dumas, the escaped PoW we will meet in a future chapter, though Darby was given command after Mr. Dumas was captured.

asked for transfer to combat command and became the assistant commander of the 10th Mountain Division in northern Italy. On April 10, 1945, he was struck in the heart by a shrapnel fragment from a German artillery shell and died almost immediately, two days before the war in Italy ended. His loss was universally lamented, and one of his original Rangers commented, 'Everything he did had a purpose. Bill Darby was a man of destiny, and he knew it.'21 Shortly thereafter he received a posthumous promotion to brigadier general.

Peter Deeb outlived his beloved commander for 62 years, passing in 2007. He closed the interview, making a final point that was important to him:

'If you hear a lot of noise up front, Darby's there. You go up there to where the combat is if you want to see him. It's where he wanted to be, it's where he had to be, because that's where the Rangers fight—at night.'

CHAPTER THREE

The Scout

Edwin Israel was born in 1920 in New York City. He enlisted in the Army before the war actually began; when Pearl Harbor was attacked and it was clear that he was going overseas, he married his girlfriend, and left three weeks later. He was in 'The Big Red One,' the Army's 1st Division, and remained a private by choice because he knew the enemy would 'shoot for the stripes.' He participated in the invasion of North Africa, Sicily, and Normandy on D-Day, and was the recipient of three Bronze Stars. He was among the first soldiers to come home—by plane, no less—because of all his battle 'points.' This interview took place in his daughter's home in the summer of 2003.

'I've seen a lot of guys go crazy. Imagine a guy's hair changed to white overnight. Nice curly, dark hair and he woke up in the morning with white curly hair.'

Edwin Israel

I went on maneuvers in the winter of 1940, to an island called Culebra of Puerto Rico. Up till then we never had rifles. We had no equipment and then they gave us the Garand rifle to use. We made an invasion on this island against the 1st Marine Division. They were on the island and we were against them. [Two years later], we were traveling through the Mediterranean before we made the invasion of Africa. We had passed by North Africa, where we were going to make the invasion, and as we were going further east, they got us all on deck and they said, 'Do you remember the island of Culebra in 1940? This place you are landing is exactly the same as that maneuver on Culebra, the terrain is exactly the same. We'll be landing in the morning.' They might have seen our ships go by at night, but figured we were going down the Mediterranean toward the east. We turned around in the middle of the night and came back. I sat on the back of the boat on the edge and watched the wake all night. [*Laughs*] I never slept that night.

Invasion

[Our division commander] was Terry Allen, Terry Allen and Theodore Roosevelt, Jr., and I was on the first boat that went off on to shore there.[13] No one there, no one shot at us, no one knew we were coming in.

The captain said, 'Go over to a house over there, take a bunch of fellas and make sure there are no soldiers in there.'

I went over and listened at the door and all I heard were ladies' voices, and I knocked on the

---

[13] *Theodore Roosevelt, Jr.-* Mr. Israel shared this anecdote: "Incidentally, I saw General Roosevelt many times. He was a general that came to the front line in order to check on you; he would come right up and sit down with us. As a matter of fact, he took some prisoners from me later in France. I was marching the prisoners back and he said to me, 'One minute. Where are you going, soldier?'
'The back line.'
He said, 'No, you are not.' The prisoners were telling me where to go and I was going toward the German line! [*Laughs*]
He said, 'You are going the wrong way. I will take them.' He had his adjutant with him and they took them to the rear." The general later suffered a heart attack and died on July 12, 1944, a little over a month after having landed at Utah Beach in Normandy.

door and they were calling the police, that there was someone outside bothering them. [*Laughs*]

Nothing happened until the second wave came in, and someone leaned on their machine gun while going in and started shooting. That woke them up. But over there we fought against the Italian and the French, French Foreign Legion, who were loyal to the Vichy government.

We were fighting them house-to-house, room-to-room, over the roofs and chasing them. Then all of a sudden, they saw the American flag. They said, 'Oh, we're not fighting the Americans,' and they all gave up. They didn't know who they were fighting. [*Shrugs shoulders*] 'Invaders.'

We were told to take a hill and two groups spread out. They told me to stay on the left side and keep an eye on the side of the hill and make sure no one comes up. I was on the left side; a whole bunch had gone right, going up [firing at] the woods. I was going left and someone was shooting at me with a machine gun, so I opened fire on them and three people got up and walked toward me. [During the war] I don't remember much about being scared or afraid. The only time

I remember being afraid was when they were firing that machine gun at me and I was crying. I yelled to my guys but there was no one there, they all went the other way. [When I realized that], I got so goddamn mad and I picked up my rifle and I started shooting at them! There were three of them, and then they came walking down with their hands up. They were French, a lieutenant and two men. One was shot in the shoulder, and the other one was shot on the ear. I was so mad I grabbed that big machine gun of theirs and I threw it over the hill and I said, 'C'mon!' I marched them down.

When I got back to the rear, my sergeant said, 'Check your rifle.' I went to check it and I found I had no ammunition. I had used up all my ammunition shooting at them and they never knew it! He said, 'Gee, you ought to get a Congressional Medal of Honor for this!' I never got that, but they gave me the Bronze Star.

Then we went forward after that and then we got bogged down. We were in foxholes and they shelled us every night, and every night that they shelled us, we dug deeper. It was tough, waiting and getting shelled and everything. We had a shell fall on our foxhole. We were sitting in there, and the shell fell on top of the foxhole, and it never went off. We were afraid to move for a long time, then we started just digging deeper until we were about ten feet down. I said, 'How are we getting out?' The other guy said, 'We'll make steps! We'll dig out holes for our feet and hands to go into.' We were digging, digging, digging. We finally got out of the hole. [*Laughs*]

The captain came along and said, 'I'm looking for some men to go out. You're a first scout; you go out ahead and go reconnoiter the land out front up until the mountain up there.'

So we walked out and went through this big field. I heard Germans in the farmhouse on the side, so I said for my guys to move over to the right. I said, 'We're not going over that way, but remember that they are there.' We went as far as the hill; we heard Italian voices on the hill so we came back that night. I said, 'Germans are in the farmhouse, Italians are on the hill.'

We left the next morning to make the attack. They bombed the Germans and then went across that field that we went across the night before. It turned out to be full of mines! We never touched a mine the whole time even though we walked through it [twice]. We were so lucky. There were ten of us, too.

The next morning they sent out people and got rid of all the mines before we went out. We got to the hill and there was a whole regiment of Italian soldiers there. The captain says, 'For that you're going to march them back to the rear.' [*Laughs*] So I marched the whole regiment back. I walked in front of them and all they kept saying was, 'Mangia, mangia!' They want their food. The Germans were treating them bad; the Germans left them with just rifles and they didn't want to fight. Italians never want to fight. They were lovers, not fighters. [*Laughs*]

The German Soldier

There were a lot of hills in North Africa. One time, the captain says, 'There is a machine gun up there. You're going to go up and see if you can [find] where it is.'

They always picked me—actually, I volunteered for everything, because it was very boring otherwise, sitting in the foxhole....so I said, 'Yes,' and took two fellas with me. We went up the hill and soon the guns were shooting down at us.

I said, 'We better get back, we can't take this, they're going to shell our hill.'

So I sent one fella back and the captain says, 'No, you stay there.'

I said, 'We're not staying here, we're going back.' We ran across the field, and they were shooting at our feet. We were doing open field running, running across the field, they were shooting at our feet.

We attacked another hill, and I shot a German soldier. And then the Germans counterattacked on the hill, and I could not escape, so I decided to just lay down on top of that soldier and make believe I'm dead. They passed me by, and then they captured one of our squads. And then they came back and passed us by again. I got up and [this German I shot] starts talking to me in English, he says he's from Coney Island, in Brooklyn; he went to visit his mother in Germany and they put him in the army. And he was dying, and he says to me, 'You can take my cigarettes; you can take my schnapps.' Then he died right underneath me. And I imagine he knew I had shot him...

*

I used to go scouting at night by the stars—I used to look up and see where certain stars were, so that I could find my way back. That was how I found my way back when the fellas and I went to the mountain—by stars—through the minefield. We were so lucky. But you know, I never worried about getting wounded; it never bothered me. I was only worried about getting captured, never worried about getting shot. I said, 'They're not going to shoot me.' That was my attitude. I volunteered for everything. I only worried that I was going to get captured. With my name, I figured, oh, they're going to kill me. That's the only thing I worried about.

Interviewer: Did you ever encounter any anti-Semitism in the military?

No, not really... [*Pause*] Once one of the fellas said to me... we had a lot of Southern fellas there, from Georgia. [*Imitates Southern accent*] 'You can't be Jewish. Youse have no horns!' [*Pause*] That was their perception, that Jewish people have horns! What do these hillbillies know? There were a lot of hillbillies in my outfit. It was a New York outfit, but it had a lot of hillbillies...

A couple days later we got our men back; we overran their prison and got them back. And from there we made the first invasion of Sicily. The Sicilians were very nice to us, they gave us food, they were glad we were taking [the island]. They didn't care for the Italians, they hated the Italians, and the Germans went right from Sicily fast.

*

D-Day

After the Sicilian campaign, the 1st Infantry Division went to England in November 1943 to prepare for the invasion of Normandy. Edwin Israel remembered:

[I was in the second wave] that landed at Omaha Beach on D-Day. We did a lot of maneuvers getting ready for it; it was all very 'hush-hush' and a couple days before, they issued us invasion currency and we weren't allowed out of camp. The night before, we went down and boarded the ships. Going over, the sea was rough, and the cooks all got sick, and because I was a cook at one time in the beginning, they asked me to go in and do the cooking that night, the pots and pans were going back and forth along that stove. When we got toward land to make the invasion, I heard planes overhead; I was down below, and I heard planes overhead, so I walked from the back of the ship to the front, climbed the ladder, walked on deck to see what was going on, and I saw it was our planes, and at that time the back of our ship blew up, hit something; we lost a lot of men. They ran a rope to shore, and we had to pull ourselves to shore, what was left of us.

We had been shooting craps [before the landing] and I was running the crap game. I had all the money at the end. I said, 'I'll get out of this game', and I loaned this money out to maybe a dozen fellas. Not one of them survived, at least half of the company was knocked out; I lost all the fellas who

I had loaned money to. They were in the back of the ship; I had moved to the front.

Everything was very lucky for me. I just happened to do this, or happened to do that. When they counterattacked that time on the hill in North Africa, I just figured I'll just lay down on top of that soldier and make believe I'm dead.

Responsibility

Now by this time I was up for corporal, sergeant. They even wanted to me to go off to [OCS] school, but I refused it. I never wanted to be an officer. In the Army you have to put your insignia on your helmet, and the Germans shot you, figuring if they got rid of the leaders, the men wouldn't know what to do, but they were very much surprised. But now we had [officers] from back in the States, they came over, but what did they know? The captain says to me before we went on to shore, 'Watch out, be careful not to step on a mine.' The first thing he did was step on a mine and he got killed. He was a school teacher from Massachusetts.

The fellas all laid down on the shore, a lot of them were new guys. So I said to one, 'Come over here, follow me,' and [finally we got off the beach and] back to the hedgerows. I said, 'Do you see this hedgerow here? You go back and get the rest and bring them back up to the hedgerows, I'll wait here.' So he went back, and meanwhile I heard voices on the other side of the hedgerow, American voices. I said, 'I'm an American, the password is', 'Lou Gehrig' or 'Babe Ruth' or whatever it was.

The guys looked over the hedgerow and they said, 'What outfit are you from?'

I said, '18th Infantry.'

They said, 'Stay here, we'll get you with the outfit.' So I waited until the other guy brought up the whole bunch of fellas, the fellas that didn't know what they were doing. I got a Bronze Star for that; I got three Bronze Stars all together.

*

I think we had gone as far as the Siegfried Line and I got pneumonia in the winter of 1944. So they sent me back. They were going to send me back to the beach, to the hospital on the beach. I said 'No, you're not sending me to the beach, I've had enough, three invasions are enough. Send me back to England,' and that's what they did, they put me in a hospital in England, and the nurses and doctors there said to me, 'You don't have to go back, we're going to keep you here. The war's almost over.' They made me a clerk typist; I didn't even know how to type. [It would have been around the time of] the Battle of the Bulge, because I remember they were all coming over to the hospital in England with frozen feet. Then they asked me to do a little guard duty with German prisoners. A lot of them spoke perfect English, as a matter of fact, I had a prisoner, when I was at the hospital; I use to take him to get food supplies. He used to sing to me 'Lili Marleen', singing German songs to me, but he spoke perfect English. I had no feelings against Germans. As I said, I was only worried about getting captured, never worried about getting shot. I said, 'They're not going to shoot me.' That was my attitude, I volunteered for everything.

*

I was in the first group to be discharged; I got discharged exactly to five years to the day that I went in. When the point system came out, I think we had to have 75 points to get sent home. I had about 175 points with all my battle stars and my three Bronze Star medals, so I went in the first group. They flew me back with a bunch of fellas to Washington, and they made a big fuss over it. The Red Cross came out and gave us milk, and they took our temperature, you know, they made a big fuss about it.

Now when I got back to the States, because I had never registered, I had to get registered for the draft, and they gave me a number. And I said to this fella, 'What is this number for?'

He said, '[They'll call you] after the women and children.' [*Laughs*]

*

I'm reading a good book [on the war] right now, I've just gotten started; my doctor at the VA recommended it. It should be interesting. I have never read any books about the war. To me, none of it was interesting afterwards. [I wanted to move on]; it was over. Gone, though it was a real big experience in my life. It made a man out of me. I was not a man before I went into the Army; I was a 20-year-old kid. It taught me about life and responsibility; as much as I did not want to take any responsibility, I took it over a lot of other fellas. I did not want to be responsible for anyone. I said I only wanted to be responsible for myself and my buddy who was next to me, whoever he may be.

*

Edwin Israel passed in November 2003, just four months after this interview took place.

CHAPTER FOUR

The Artillery Man

Thomas Collins was born November 30, 1920, in Glens Falls, and was a graduate of St. Mary's Academy, Class of 1938. Sixty-five years later, he's sitting comfortably in his favorite chair wearing his button-down cardigan sweater in front of the Christmas tree. Long retired, he carries that 'I've seen it all, so nothing you can tell me is going to impress me much' look; but this day, in the weeks before his 83rd Christmas, he is suddenly alive, animated, a younger man telegraphing the emotions and feelings long buried about some of the most formative years of his life—conveying them to a young person who is genuinely interested, someone who has sought out his story.

Thus it was with Mr. Tom Collins, an artillery sergeant in a field artillery battalion of the 88th Division, responsible for a 105 mm gun crew in Italy. On this day he was interviewed by one of my students, who happened to be his granddaughter.

Thomas Collins

I was drafted on July 2, 1942. I went to Camp Upton on Long Island, where they processed me. I was there about a week, if I remember right. From there we were shipped on a train to Oklahoma, Camp Gruber, where we were the first contingent of draftees to arrive there. The camp was brand new. The 88th Division was just forming; I was with the first group that went there and I was picked to go into the artillery. I spent a year there and they trained us. The whole division was trained from scratch; we were the first all-draftee division in World War II.

In the summer of 1943 it was time to go to maneuvers in Louisiana; that took a little more than a month. From there we went to San Antonio, I can't think of the name of the camp now. There we were processed again—we got our teeth fixed and everything, if anything was wrong with us. [*Laughs*] We got issued everything that would bring us up to par on clothing and equipment and so on. From there we took another train ride to Norfolk, Virginia, and from there we shipped out and had a very unpleasant ride over the ocean. It was twenty-three days from there to Oran, North Africa. We arrived there in, I believe, October of 1943. In North Africa we trained, we got used to the terrain, and they brought up our equipment again; our guns were howitzers. They were shipped to us; some of them were in the same convoy we were in and some of them later. We finally got all of our equipment together and we had to make sure everything was in tip-top shape.

In Africa the war had already progressed through Sicily, and [the Americans and British] were just getting into Italy. They had just taken Naples and were just a short distance above Naples. We left there about a month later. It was November or early December, and it took us seven days to cross the Mediterranean Sea, and we landed in Naples. I remember that in Naples it was quite fascinating, terrifying in a way, because when we went into the harbor there were sunken ships all over the place—in fact, we pulled up alongside a capsized ship [lying on its side]. I don't know if it was American or not, but they had taken the superstructure right off so that we could come right up to the ship. We disembarked down the gang plank onto the side of the ship and down another gang plank onto the shore—that was our pier.

On the Line

A few weeks later, we were on the line. Now I was in the artillery; we were as close as a mile to the front lines behind the infantry or as much as eight miles behind them. Our guns would fire a maximum of 14 miles; we had the artillery pieces set up so we knew where we were firing and what targets we were hitting. Then, when we got to where we knew we were stretching our range, we moved. And we had to coordinate it with the infantry. Sometimes we were in an area for two hours and then we'd move again, but we could move on a minute's notice and find a place to put our guns into position.

[When we were in combat], there was fear, lots of it. I was in charge of the howitzer and the gun crew. We might be getting shelled ourselves and our infantry getting pounded. We sometimes found ourselves in fluid situations. The Germans might be attacking, or we might be attacking, and it was very fluid—we might be moving forward or pulling back. We never knew what was happening, whether we had them on the run or whether they were counterattacking—so we had to think in terms of getting things ready to move, because we might have to get the hell out of wherever we were. We had the fear, but we were so busy and had so much to do that just had to get done that it sort of beat the fear. In other words, you were scared to death, but you were busy and did the best you possibly could.

We put our guns most of the time in positions near a farmyard or a settlement where we could use a building as camouflage—we'd set our gun up alongside a building, then put our camouflage net from the barn over the gun to some outlying posts, trying to make our position look like an extension of the barn. Sometimes it worked and sometimes it didn't.

The civilians weren't afraid of us. We saw them all of the time, but they got used to being quite upset with us. We'd pull into their farmyard, and the cannoneers [artillery gunners] would be on the back of my truck. Chickens would run in the yard and the cannoneers would go 'pop-pop-pop' with their rifles, and the [Italians] would go crazy because we were killing their chickens! Then we would set up position and they would take the chickens, pluck them and gut them and cook them up in the mess kit. They were good, too. [*Laughs*]

The Guns

Our guns were the 105mm howitzers. They weighed a little better than two tons, I used to know right down to the pound. They had a long piston-type recoil mechanism, a tube on top of the gun filled with oil, and the other end of it was full of gas, so that when the gun fired, it was like a cylinder, the gun coming back like this [motions], pulling that oil down and compressing it against the gas, and the gas forced it back into battery. And that's the way that gun worked. The shell weighed

53 pounds, and when you opened the breech, the command would usually be 'Shell H.E.'—that would be 'high explosive'—and sometimes it would be a timed shell. There were 10 powder bags, little bags like bean bags tied together with string. If you were close up [to the front], they'd say, 'Charge 3,' or 'Charge 2'; you knew you were right up close when you were firing things like that. If it was a charge 8 or 9 or something, well good, the front was far out of the way, we were firing a long way away. We'd break the string that held the other bags of powder and throw the discarded [bags of] powder off to the side. In the wintertime we used that wasted powder in our four-man foxhole. We'd build a place where we could all get together, and we had a little stove made from a five-gallon oil can. And that's what we would burn in it, the gun powder. We'd throw in just a fistful of powder at a time, with a couple sticks of wood, if we could get it. If we'd cut it off the trees and it was green, we'd split it up real fine and stack it up on top of the stove and let it dry. Then we'd take the wood when it was dry and put it into the fire pit and keep

feeding the gunpowder, and it'd get hot enough to where it would burn the wood.

The book said you could fire two shells a minute, or four shells a minute for a short period of time. At one time we fired five or six shells in 18 seconds! That was a trick, it was hard to do, but we did it. We had the ammunition ready; we would fire the gun and you'd pull the rope, a lanyard, and there was a trigger arm, and when you fired it the trigger arm was pulled toward you. We had a block of wood and would stick that right behind the trigger arm so that when it went back into position we'd have to load the gun awful fast, and we had to have a good man to do it. While it was in recoil, you would load the gun as it went back into battery; when it got about three-quarters of the way into battery, it would fire again. We tore the gun apart doing it, too. I know one time we ruined the recoil mechanism; all the oil came out of it like soap suds. We had to take it back to the armament outfit and get a different gun.

We had a forward observer; one of our men would be with the ground troops as they would move. They would observe where our shells landed, and the infantry officers on the telephone would say something like, 'We need fire on Geer Street, we've got a group pinned down on Geer Street, these are the coordinates, you fire here.' And the way it would work, say it was this house we are in now, you'd fire one round that would land up in my backyard where the stone wall is. You'd get the first shell over, then you'd purposely fire one short, one right, and one left. My gun, the number 2 gun, would fire at the target until we got it pinpointed. And then they'd say, 'Fire for effect.' When they said, 'Fire for effect,' all six guns, which were making their same moves as when my gun was positioning, ended up on the same target. They would say, 'Two rounds per minute,' or 'Fire three rounds in five minutes,' depending on what kind of coverage they needed. If it was really bad, 'Just fire for effect' meant just fire them as quickly as we could load them.

We used two and a half ton trucks to tow the guns. When the truck would deposit the gun and move forward unhitched, the trails behind the gun would split like this [*splits his pointer and middle finger apart*]. The two trails would open up and they'd go down on the ground, like two leg supports. When you fired the gun the first time, they'd dig into the ground, and that kept the gun stable. If the ground wasn't stable we had logs that we'd carry with us—we'd put them behind the rails so they'd come against that log to hold it in place. When we went to move we'd pull the rails up and close them and lock them, and you had a pin that hooked into the trailer hitch on the truck, and then the truck took us wherever we had to go. Cannoneers would get on the truck; me and the driver were in the cab.

The sergeant of each gun crew would go on ahead with the staff sergeant, who was the number two gunner normally; he was number one in our outfit. They and the lieutenant in charge of the howitzers would go forward, and as they got near the place they'd say, 'All right, Collins, you go there, Smith, you go there, Jones, go there,' and so on. As the head of the gun crew, I had to remember where I was at as we moved. I had to make mental notes of the countryside, and [it was all mountains], you know. You'd pull into this place and it was like looking at the side of West Mountain here, only bigger.[14] And I had to remember that's where [the lieutenant] pointed when he said, 'That's where I want your gun.' I had to pick out a tree or a rock or some goddamn thing to let me know where I had to go when I got to where he pointed, because when we approached that spot we would be turning off the road to go off to it. We were on our own then to get it in there and get set up as quickly as possible. You pulled in there with your gun, and the truck would turn around so the gun was heading back. I would walk out where I wanted my gun to be. And I'd stand there and the driver would back the gun up—it was not an easy trick, especially in the rough going—until he would nearly hit me right in the face with the muzzle of the gun. I'd direct him, of course, we had the hand signals, this way or that way, whatever; he'd get as close as he could, then it was up to us—we'd finish it by hand. A lot of times we moved them a long way, like a place like my backyard or worse with all those trees and rocks and everything there! We were pulling or pushing a 2-ton gun through [rough terrain] with eight men—it

---

[14] West Mountain-skiing area outside of Glens Falls, New York.

was goddamn hard work, but we did it; very seldom would we hit a spot where we couldn't get the gun where [the lieutenant] wanted it. If we needed to fire right away, we just picked the quickest, easiest spot and set up to fire right away. Later, if we were still there, we'd move the gun to a better spot. So that's the way we got the guns moved and positioned.

[When we had some free time] we'd talk about home, or about the Italian girls. We played a lot of cards and shot a lot of craps. I didn't play any cards, the crew did, but once in a while I'd shoot craps. I didn't ever really understand the craps game very well, but I would sit alongside and when the man was rolling the dice, I'd bet that he would make it or he would miss; I always bet for the guy or for the dice. I never lost any money because we didn't have a hell of a lot to begin with.

I used to write the family whenever I had an opportunity. I used to write to them and tell them what a beautiful part of the country I was in, or what I had just seen, like Florence or Naples, Rome, or any of the fabulous things that I had seen, and describe them as best as I could to them, and when the weather was nice I told them. From October until April, it just seemed like rain almost every day. I believe that the war had a lot to do with that. It affected the weather. I think that the constant amount of firing and smoke going into the atmosphere kind of changed things and made it rainier. But they get a lot of rain in Italy just the same. But I think it was a little worse during the war years. Or I'd say, 'We're advancing on the Germans' and 'This looks good,' but I didn't talk about the battles, I tried to convince them that I wasn't in any serious danger. [But there were days when] I didn't want to go on, I was scared to death but I had to [keep going], because the guy next to me had to—so we had to keep going, together. I guess that's the easiest way to explain it. [We got so] we didn't want any part of it, we'd had enough. But we were there and we were stuck with it, tough shit. You live for today and you didn't know whether you were going to be alive tomorrow or not, but you did the best you could.

At one point my brother and I were together over there. My brother Jack enlisted about a year after me, maybe six months. But he went overseas with a replacement depot group. They would receive them in Naples at the docks and take them to wherever they were set up and process them. As the need came, they'd say, 'These five guys right here, they're going to the infantry, these guys are going to the artillery,' or what have you. And he wrote to me and he said, 'It looks like they're going to ship me into the infantry.' So we got together and I said, 'Why don't we try to get you shipped into my company? It's better than the infantry by any means.' So that's what we did. We went to my colonel; I was able to do that. He was a great guy, Colonel Ivery, and he gave me a pass to go to Rome and see my brother and try to get him switched into my company. Between my colonel and his commanding officer, whoever he was, they finagled something. In his case, they just turned him loose and said, 'You're in the 88th Division, 338th Field Artillery Battalion, they're up north, go find them.' He thumbed a ride and joined me, and he got into my outfit the day before the war [in Europe] ended!

Surrender

I was way north, north of the Po River, when the war ended. But we had a ball together, especially because the war was over. And we were great together. Those guys were like, 'Wow, [look at] these two lucky bastards.' But it was me and Jack. They didn't have anybody like I did. We were lucky, very lucky.

I didn't actually see any German soldiers until the war was almost over, and by that time, they were surrendering all the time. We'd pull into a field to set up our guns, and all of a sudden there'd be two or three of them standing there saying 'Komrade, komrade.' They were more or less waiting for us. They wanted to make sure the infantry got by us, because we weren't as mean as they were. Understandably so, because the infantry had it tough, and they had grudges, which we didn't have so much.

A million Wehrmacht soldiers surrendered on May 2 alone.[22]

After the war, we saw thousands of Germans because they were in the POW cages. They were there for like the last six months. The whole half of that last winter and right into the spring of 1945, they were quitting whenever they had the opportunity. So we saw a lot of them and we'd take the gun away from them and say, 'Go on down there,' and we'd throw the gun off to the side of the road.

I think being on the prisoner of war cages took 90 percent of the bitterness out of the way I felt towards the Germans, especially just north of Naples. I don't know if that happened for everybody. But there we got to meet the Germans who were just [ordinary] carpenters or cooks or people like that. We'd go into the prisoners' kitchen and have coffee and a roll or whatever happened to be available. And we got talking to them, cooks and carpenters and just people like that, you know, and they explained their predicament. They were just regular guys, and it was a case of 'go in the army or be shot.' And they didn't agree with [Hitler], especially when the war became such a mess, you know.[15] Most of those guys were like regular fellas, like the [German] colonel who gave me this knife. You couldn't ask for a nicer man; a very intelligent, well-educated, good man.

Home

When we got home, the sudden change [to civilian life] seemed difficult for me. I felt more and more that I had changed, so I would stay home. I didn't go anywhere. It took me a couple of weeks before I would go out, you know, go downtown. I remember the first few times I went uptown from there—I wouldn't go unless my sister was with me, I wouldn't go alone. I can't really put it into words, but I really felt strange; I felt unusual. I thought, 'Will I speak right, will I act right?', because when we were in the Army, foul language was commonplace, and we were using crazy phrases like the Southerners used, things like that; it became the way I was speaking and living. But [after a while] I warmed up and I was fine.

---

[15] *they didn't agree with [Hitler]*-GIs after the war were indeed hard-pressed to find Germans who admitted they agreed with Hitler (unless of course they were SS).

Thoughts

I think the war today in Iraq [2003] is the biggest mistake the country has ever made. We went there basically to get one man and to protect our oil interest. Our 'looking for the weapons of mass destruction' is a bunch of bullshit. I think the president used it as an excuse to get there; I don't think we should be there, there's no reason. However, we're there and we'll do the job and we'll back them up as best we can. I'm hoping we can get out of there quick.

Thank you for talking to me, sweetheart. It was a pleasure.

Thomas Collins passed away in 2011.

CHAPTER FIVE

The Captain and the Nurse

In the summer of 2003, I sat down at a camp kitchen table with a couple of World War II veterans of the Italian Campaign. Elizabeth and Jim Brady were married in 1946 after a romance that began in the combat zones of Italy; she was a nurse and he was an army captain. They settled in Long Island, New York, but summered in the foothills of the Adirondacks, where we had the interview. As I explained my project to them, Elizabeth insisted I eat her cake; Jim puffed on his pipe and gestured expressively throughout our conversation.

Jim was born in 1919 and had decided to join the Army without his parents' knowledge. Elizabeth was also born in 1919, the oldest of three children.

Jim and Elizabeth Brady

Jim Brady: I went overseas in a C2 cargo ship, you probably heard about them. They were very slow, but by then they were making almost a ship a week in the shipyards—they'd turn them out to carry cargo, to carry personnel. I ended up on one of them, and we're in the middle of this big convoy. It took us 28 days to go from Virginia to Africa, because you're only going as fast as the slowest ship. They had Navy boats patrolling the outside and all that. So we were finally about to go through the Strait of Gibraltar, and I said, 'Oh, gee, the Strait of Gibraltar!' But it was all blackouts, I couldn't see the strait! [*Chuckles*] It was early in the evening, it was dark. Right in the middle of that, down the middle of the convoy comes this pleasure cruiser, and I'm looking at it, and I'm standing with a Navy officer, and I said, 'Christ, there's nobody on that ship!'

He said, 'The Germans are on there; they're taking pictures of the convoy. We'll probably get bombed tomorrow.'

[*Leans in, incredulous expression, looks up at ceiling*] 'Bombed tomorrow?'

The next night, just when the sun was setting, six German planes came over [*gestures with a downward swoop of his hand*] and they started dropping bombs, and I was scared! I'm in the middle of the Mediterranean, and they hit some ships near me, and they hit the water near where we were, and I'm looking for the [African coastline], wondering if I could swim that far! [*Points far away with finger, shaking his head*] It was about five or six miles—I couldn't swim that far, for crying out loud—but that's what I was thinking. So, all of a sudden, two British Spitfires came out [*motions overhead with hand again*]. They shot down two or three of the planes, and the rest of them took off. I have to give those guys credit, man, they dove right in the middle of these planes! Those pilots knew what the hell they were doing, there's no question about it.

Axis Sally came on the air—we used to listen to her on the ship. She was saying how they sunk a lot of ships and killed a lot of our guys. They sunk one ship, but no one got hurt that way.

So, we're wondering where the hell we are going, [we figured] we're probably going to land in Sicily. We used to get regular reports, what Patton was doing, on Sicily. We were all convinced we were going to Sicily. But we passed it, and all of a sudden, the ship made a U-turn and came back and we landed in Bizerte on the coast of North Africa, and it was all bombed out! Bob Hope had been there the day before but at the airport; they were filling in the holes on the airfield because the Germans had bombed it.

They put us on trucks, and we rode out in the country for a couple of miles, and we bivouacked in an olive grove. And that's when I first came into contact with Arabs. I was there for a while. Then we got orders; we still thought we were going to Sicily but we ended up in Naples, and that was an education. Walking down [the street], these little kids came up to me [*makes tugging motion at sleeve*] and said, 'Hey, Joe, my sister!'

'How much?'

'A Hershey bar!' [*Shakes head, puts hand up as if to swear an oath, with wife present*] I didn't, believe me, I didn't accept any offers.

Elizabeth: It was very sad.

Jim: But it was really something. So we ended up in a race track, which was Mussolini's favorite race track.¹⁶ It had become a replacement depot; I was there for a couple of weeks. Then I was assigned to the 36th Division up at Monte Cassino.

The Rapido River

The soldiers of the 36th Division, a National Guard division from Texas, had been in combat since the landing at Salerno. Exhausted, General Clark now told them to do the impossible: cross the dammed icy river as a diversionary force to pull German troops back away from the main attack at Anzio. It was the beginning of a two-day slaughter of over 1,300 killed or wounded that one survivor recalled turned him 'into an old man overnight'; German losses were negligible. ²³

If you look at a map of Italy, around Monte Cassino there is a little stream called the Rapido River. 'Rapido' means rapid. Here I was in February, and this river is really flowing. It wasn't frozen, but there was snow on the ground. I had an order to go across that river in a rubber boat, with a detail of six GIs, and another officer, and see what the Germans were doing, but not to make any contact

---

¹⁶ *Mussolini's favorite race track*-Track outside of Naples turned into a camp for replacement soldiers, which also featured a hospital.

with them. [*Shrugs shoulders*] These were the orders you get. So they cleared the minefield, from about here to there [*points across the kitchen*]. They put white tape down, so naturally the Germans [across the river] would go, 'Oh, let's bomb between the tapes!' So we get in the river raft, and just when we were ready to push off, they open up fire from the other shore, which wasn't far, with machine pistols. And they sunk the boat right away, we lost our guns, and we're in the river. This was February 1, middle of winter, and I'm in the water! So, I drifted downstream, not far; it wasn't far. I figured, 'Well, I got to get out of the water.' I get out, and I look at this big field; there's no white tape there. I was scared to death, there's no question about it. So I started crawling to a spot from here to the next house [*points*], across that field, and it took me over two hours to go that far! So, I go like this [*makes slow crawling motion, putting one arm in front of the other*]. Nothing happened. Then a little bit more. So, I finally got back to battalion headquarters. I went up to report, told them what had happened. The C.O. says, 'Ehhh, don't worry about it, Lieutenant, probably just a couple of

Germans out to take a leak. Do it again tomorrow night.'

Then I heard all this ruckus outside of headquarters, and I go out and there's my sergeant, who had come in at Anzio, hell of a guy. And he goes, 'I'll kill that son of a bitch, what does he mean they're out to take a leak? What the hell, he's sitting there smoking a cigar!' It took three or four guys to hold him back! Finally, I calmed him down.

We were going to go back the next night, but they called it off. Instead of going that way [*points forward*], we went around this way [*makes half circle motion with hand*], where there were more mountains. And my last day up there, the Germans were shooting at us from the abbey, [*points upward*] with machine guns and rifles, that's how close we were! They said there were no Germans up there, but somebody was shooting at us, I know that.

They began throwing artillery shells in, and all of a sudden, my arm was bleeding. I didn't know what the hell happened; I was scared to death, no question about it. So, I get down, and I go to the aide station to get it treated. So, I'm standing there talking to the officer, and I said, 'Do you remember Sergeant Woods coming through here?'

He says, 'Oh, yes, yes, he was here yesterday.'

I said, 'Well, how is he?'

He said, 'Oh, he's had it.'

I said, 'What do you mean, was he hit?'

He says, 'No, no [*points to head*]; he's out of his mind.' All that combat, you know?

We had been on this patrol, and I had looked at Woods and said, 'You know, Sergeant, you've got your safety on.'

He says, 'I don't take it off until I see a German—I haven't taken the safety off since Anzio.' That's a long way.

Monte Cassino

The Allies waged a months-long struggle in the first half of 1944 to dislodge Germans entrenched at a centuries-old monastery in the mountains on their way to Rome. At the time it was considered a paramount objective; eighty miles to the south of Rome, the struggle for Monte Cassino was a 123-day epic battle waged on the belief that the Germans were using the 800-year-old Benedictine monastery as an observation post to sight in the roads leading out of the valleys to the north. On

February 15, 1944, American bombers flying from England dropped 1,400 tons of high explosives.

'I was lying in the hospital, and I heard this awful roar—what the hell is that? I look up, out the tent flaps; I never saw so many planes in my life! There were probably more at Tarawa, but I'd never seen so many planes; they bombed the abbey! All you could see was this big smoke, and dust; they just wiped out the abbey.

The Benedictine abbey was reduced to rubble—which, ironically, gave German paratroopers greater flexibility and cover in its defense.

When the doctor was examining me, he said, 'You have trouble breathing, huh?'

I said, 'Yes, I've had a lot of trouble lately.'

He said, 'I think you have bronchial asthma.'

I remember I used to play basketball, and if the gym was hot, I could run like hell, but if the gym was a little cold, I would have trouble breathing. You don't give it a thought when you are in your early twenties, you know? So they listed me, they said I was 'limited service.' I couldn't go back to my company, because nobody in the infantry who can't breathe right belongs up in the infantry. Well, he saved my life. He really did.

Jim's claim that the doctor's diagnosis saved his life is more than idle speculation; despite further heavy bombings, the Allied troops made four head-on assaults in the coming months against superior German defensive positions amidst the rubble at a cost of 55,000 casualties. Monte Cassino finally fell on May 19, 1944, with 20,000 Germans killed or wounded.

There were many, many casualties at Monte Cassino… because the Germans were so good, and also with the onset of trench foot. With trench foot, you'd get an infection, and gangrene set in; the only way to cure it was to cut off your foot! I had two or three friends—I saw them down in Naples later on, after I got off the line—and they were all smiling. 'I'm going home; I lost my leg, but I'm going home!'—and they were happy as hell! 'I've got one foot left, but I'm going home!' That's the way they felt about it, you know?

With the Gustav Line finally broken, the road to Rome was now open; the abbey was rebuilt after the war.

*

The Hospital

Elizabeth: I was 22 years old and working in Glens Falls Hospital as an RN. My girlfriends were going in the Navy, and they kept asking me to go. I didn't realize you didn't go where you wanted to go, so I went down to Albany and I enlisted for the Navy. They told me they don't need me in the Navy, so they sent my name down to the Army and of course they accepted me.

That was in 1943. I came down to New York City—I had great-aunts there, and they never thought I grew up at all! You know my Aunt Cattie would not let me go down to Camp Kilmer [in New Jersey] by myself, so we got on this train and she took me to Kilmer. When Aunt Cattie went down there, the officers had a fit… 'Miss Rozell, why is your aunt with you?' She left as soon as she deposited me there, but you know, they were always so protective; I guess they thought I would get into trouble or something.

I was there [in New Jersey] a year, which is what they call a 'station compliment.' I had a friend who wanted to go overseas, so she talked me into going overseas. I didn't have to go, they needed us there... but we went. They sent us to Virginia to Newport News, and then we got on this ship. We were traveling alone and we had to travel at night in total blackout. When we got to Gibraltar, we had two destroyers that took us in to Oran.

I was in Oran for about six or seven weeks because I came over as a replacement, and of course my girlfriend, who had talked me into going, was assigned to a general hospital in Italy, but I went to a station hospital in Oran. I lived in a hotel, and I was so amazed when I was there because where we went to Mass, you know, you had to use the sidewalk, and all the Arabs were having 'siesta' and you had to walk around them on the sidewalk!

I guess we were like detached service; I was there for about a month, then we got orders to go to Italy. They put us on a hospital ship and we went from Oran to Naples. They sent a lot of people ahead of us to set up a station hospital in Leghorn, so the nurses and the doctors I was with were still on detached service, so they sent me to the 12th General Hospital in Mussolini's Fairgrounds because they had made it into a hospital complex. And that's where I met my friend again, that's where she was assigned!

When I was there I had a very sad ward, because most of the boys were paralyzed and had wounds, you know, spinal injuries; it was sad. We had to do everything for them, write letters and things, and really it was a big awakening for me of what I was getting into, when I saw that. It was still 1943, 'See the world with Uncle Sam,' you know, but by that time I had also met Jim in Naples.

The Fight

Jim: [Gestures with pipe towards his wife] I got in trouble meeting her....

My C.O., the colonel, showed up with this girl at the [officers'] club—you know, in Italy in those days, with the war on and everything, all you had to drink was cognac. There wasn't whiskey over there yet, there was no beer there yet—we're all drinking cognac—and so this colonel has her [*points to Elizabeth*] with him. So he gets up to go to the bathroom, and I said, 'What's a nice-looking girl like you doing out with a jerk like him?'

She says, 'Oh, I don't know, he told me he could get you to work nights so he could take me out!'

So he comes back to the table and I said something about 'trying to beat my time.' I know I was out of order, because he was a 'chicken colonel,' and I was only a 1st lieutenant. He called me in the orderly room next morning and said, 'I'll give you a chance to apologize.'

I said, 'For what? You had it coming, I'm not apologizing.' I had a chip on my shoulder.

Then the phone rang. He said, 'Yes, I got somebody.' So he says, 'I don't have to worry about you anymore. You're being transferred to an Italian outfit, second in command of an Italian truck battalion.' So I reported. In those days with the Italians, when the Germans were there, if somebody refused to do something [*pulls imaginary pistol out of imaginary holster*], bang, you're dead. So I always packed a .45 with me and I got along pretty good with them: [*speaks Italian*] 'A lot of work and nothing to eat,' that's all I used to hear.

I used to go down on the docks, at Naples, and steal food for them. And then they got a little upset because I didn't steal the K-rations, which had cigarettes in them—they complained about that, and I'm stealing stuff for them, to feed them! So finally we got orders to go up to Piombino, Leghorn, Italy. We had about 90 trucks; it took two days. We left Naples, we went right up on the coast road Route 6, and we go through Leghorn and I set up a bivouac area—we didn't have a building yet. I passed the station hospital. So I walk into a tent and ask, 'Is Betty Rozell here?'

They said, 'Yes, she's in the next tent!' I walked in the tent; I'll never forget the look on her face when I walked in that tent. We were doing pretty good then, so we spent a year up there together like that. That fight [with the colonel] was the biggest break I ever got overseas, as far as that goes. I ended up with her [*points to Elizabeth*]. And I didn't get hurt!

*

Elizabeth: We had a ward, you know, that had German prisoners. I felt so sorry for them, because they had some men, old men, who really weren't able to fight. They had ulcers; they had a great many physical deformities. But they put them in the German army anyway. They were scared to death, because on the same ward we had two SS men. We knew who they were. They scared the other ones so bad! In fact, one time one of the German prisoners knifed one of the SS men in the lavatory. But I really did feel sorry for some of these German people, because they just were putting anyone in the army, you know?

Jim: We were pushing through Italy, and Genoa was liberated. So, I got a hold of her [*points to Elizabeth*]; we were going up to see Genoa. It wasn't all that long of a trip. So we got up there, and I had a camera and I needed some film, and I saw a Kodak sign. It was all in Italian, but said, 'Kodak.' So, I go in there to get a roll of film, and this British soldier walks in and he says, 'Well, mate, it's all over, huh?'

I say, 'What are you talking about, it's all over?'

He says, 'Hitler's dead, Germany surrendered.' This is how I found out the war was over, you know? So, I go back to tell her—I go back to the Jeep and there's people crowding around the Jeep. I thought something was wrong.

Elizabeth: I don't think they had seen a woman.

Jim: These Italians hadn't seen an American nurse; they wanted to look at an American nurse! That's why there were all the people.

Interviewer: That was probably early May. Mussolini was dead by then.

Jim: Oh, I was in there when they strung him up! I just happened to be there, in Milan. I mean, I wasn't looking for Mussolini, but I saw this big crowd, and they had him strung up in a gas station, hanging by his ankles, with his girlfriend there. They would come up, and spit on him. His eye was hanging out, and they are kicking him…he's dead!

Elizabeth: I thought that was so cruel.

Jim: And then with his girlfriend, they tied her dress around her knees, and she's hanging upside down, and they tied her dress around her knees. Weird, the Italians did some weird things, I'll tell you that.

Elizabeth: And of course, a lot of them hated Mussolini. They just had to go along with him.

*

Jim passed away at the age of 89 in 2008; Elizabeth passed at 90 in 2010. They rest side by side in the veterans' cemetery at Calverton National Cemetery in Long Island, New York.

CHAPTER SIX

The Mortar Man

Harold D. Erdrich is a native New Yorker. In high school he had been a champion runner, and this came to the attention of the Army, so he served as a liaison between four companies of mortars of the 2nd Chemical Mortar Battalion, frequently on the front lines spotting targets and relaying information.

He was involved in 'four invasions, five invasions. The first invasion was a practice invasion near Casablanca in North Africa, after we had left Newport News with a tremendous fleet of boats. Then we got back on the boats. We headed towards Greece and Crete. Middle of the night, they turned around and headed back and we invaded Sicily. After Sicily, we had two invasions in Italy, and then we invaded on the Riviera in southern France. We went up France about the middle, made a right turn, crossed the Rhine River, and headed south.'

He would also be one of the first soldiers to encounter a place called Dachau.

He was 81 at the time of this interview in 2001. 'I went through plenty. 'Lucky' wouldn't be the exact word, but I am appreciative that I survived World War II. We were able to help the infantry; we were successful in doing that. We fellas felt we played a good part in helping defeat the enemy.'

Harold D. Erdrich

I was born in the Bronx, New York, August 7, 1919. I graduated high school in Brooklyn. I started to go to Brooklyn College at night. I was working in the grocery store and I drove a taxi on the weekend; I did that for a year or two. I had to stop college because I couldn't keep my eyes open, I was sleeping in the class every single night. The teachers and professors said, 'Harold Erdrich, you may as well quit it. You're not getting nothing out of this. You're not going to pass the test.' I stopped.

I first heard about Pearl Harbor at my future wife's house when I was going to eat there; I ended up going home later and I said to my mother and father, 'I'm going to go down tomorrow morning and enlist.' They tried to talk me out of it, but I said, 'I'm going to do it. I'm going.'

I went down and took the physical. I passed everything, 20/20 vision. I took the colorblind test and I flunked. I didn't believe it. I said, 'Doctor, let me take the test again.' You know the test, little colors, you see a letter and a number. I called them all wrong, so I didn't become a flier. Two months later, February 10, I was drafted. When I got to Fort Bragg, I took the whole test again, flunked again.

I couldn't be a pilot. I was on the list to go to Officer Candidate School when we got the alert that we couldn't because our outfit was frozen. We were due to go overseas. My girlfriend and I are talking over the phone and in letters, and we decided to get married. I asked the captain. He says, 'Okay. Go home next weekend, because the weekend after we have to go on mountain maneuvers in Virginia.' That's just what happened. I called up, and her folks and my folks, they made wedding [arrangements].

We went on mountain maneuvers, and then to Newport News. I got on the boats, and we went to

Northern Africa for a practice invasion. That was October, and we got married on October 25, 1942. I was discharged September '45, so I was in the service a little over three years.

*

I was attached to the headquarters company with the 2nd Chemical Mortar Battalion. When we were put into that battalion, we fellas said, 'Chemical? They're never going to use gas. We're not going to go anywhere. We'll probably be in the United States for the whole war.' Then we found out that it wasn't such a thing at all, that those mortar shells held high explosive or smoke. Big mortar. 4.2 [inch diameter] mortar, 26-pound shell. There were four companies of mortars, A, B, C, and D; I was in the headquarters company. We were the liaison between the mortar companies and the divisions [we were attached to]. We supported many divisions: 36th Division, 45th Division, Airborne. We were in the 3rd Army, 7th Army. I saw General Patton a number of times. He didn't know my name, but he would come traveling around and shake hands.

I was given the job [of target spotter] because the Army had found out that I had won medals for running in public school and high school. When they saw this in my record, they teamed me up with an officer and we were target spotters. We were always with the infantry, right behind the infantry. If they saw a target ahead, they'd send somebody back to tell us—we had a telephone, no radios. The telephone had a spool of wire, which I carried on my back. I had my helmet, my rifle, two pistols, hand grenades, extra ammunition in my pack, and the telephone. At the other end of the wire was the gun position.

I would do this target spotting with an officer; we would climb trees, bombed-out churches and buildings, hills, wherever we could get and not get shot by a sniper or something like that. We would relay the information back to the gun position and were very successful with the targets and the damage that we did to the German Army. We'd see a target, and of course I had a map, a chart. We'd give them code numbers that had been arranged before, what coordinates we were at, and where the target may be. Then we'd say, 'G,' just in case somebody was tapping the line. 'G' was 'go.' They would fire one shell. The shell had powder rings on the back and a shotgun cartridge in the back so that when it comes down, the firing pin hits the shotgun shell and it explodes, and off goes the shell. The powder rings give the distance that the shell will go. That's basically the raw explanation for that. Of course, the tip of the shell is primed. When the tip hits, boom. We had a fabulous weapon, and nobody even knew it until we started to use it. We used it in Sicily.

*

We were the first wave in all the invasions. They made an attempt to fire a mortar from a boat, but it really didn't work. The movement of the ocean could have caused the shell to go up instead of the direction of the target and we'd be in our own danger. Overall, when we landed in Sicily, we didn't have much of a problem. The infantry, and of course, all of our planes and all the shelling, had chased the enemy north.

We had a chaplain, Francis O'Brien, who was assigned to our battalion. He was from the Bronx; he and I were good friends. After the second day, he said to me, 'Can you get two of the fellas? I'll get a Jeep. The colonel gave me permission to ask you. I have to go investigate something ahead of us here. Not far, as far as we know.' The night before, there had been an awful lot of aircraft activity over us. The LSTs and the whole fleet of boats that had anti-aircraft guns were shooting. We didn't see anything, we were huddled down in our foxholes trying to stay alive.

The chaplain told me, 'Get one of the Italian fellas.' The guy, Lou Demasi, was also from the Bronx, and he spoke very good Italian. We went up this road and that road. We see a farmhouse. We pull over; there's two women with a few small children. They heard the Jeep coming out, so Lou questioned them. The chaplain had him ask, 'Did you see any airplanes here last night? Anything crash?'

'Yes.' She pointed. We went and we found it.

It was an open field plus an olive grove. There was an American paratrooper plane, all burnt. Everyone was killed. I'm not sure of the figure, but this information is probably available. I'm taking a guess, but I thought it was about 47 men and 3 of the crew—the pilot, an assistant pilot, and maybe a navigator.

We see this and Father O'Brien says to us, 'Fellas, we all have to get all the dog tags off the bodies and bring them back.'

I said, 'What's going to happen with our outfit? They're going to be going forward.'

'We'll catch up with them.'

We started collecting the dog tags; that took us the better part of that day. Then I had to ask the question, 'Father, do we have to bury them?'

'Yes, we have to bury them. Tell everybody to bring their shovels.'

We dug 50 graves in sandy, hard ground. We were just [covered with] blood and sweat, but we finally got the job done. It took us three days. Got back in the Jeep, we went back to the farmhouse. We had had our own rations, so we had something to eat. We used their well and we cleaned up as good as we could, then we went all the way to Palermo, Sicily.

By the time I got there, I had a high fever and I was shaking. I had malaria. The other fellas didn't get it. There was a big hospital ship in the port, anchored out in Palermo. They took me out to it. Father O'Brien and the rest of the fellas went to where the outfit was; I didn't know where they were. I was there four days, then I was fine. They let me off the boat, took me ashore. There was a little building to go to for information. I found out where the outfit was, and a truck took me and other fellas to Messina, at the other end of Sicily. I found my outfit down near the water somewhere, and the boys said, 'Wow, you're here. You came back just in time, Harold.'

'Yeah, why?'

'We're invading Italy tomorrow.' What I'm telling you is 100 percent absolutely the truth. We invaded Salerno. The second invasion was Anzio.

*

Salerno was terrible, we could hardly get ashore. The infantry was pinned down a mile up the beach by the Germans, the Italian soldiers were very few. After Salerno, the Italian army surrendered.[17] They were out of it. It was strictly the Germans we were against. They maybe thought it was going to

---

[17] *the Italian army surrendered*-The Italian armistice was announced the night before the invasion of Salerno, on Sept. 8, 1943.

be an easy invasion, but it wasn't. The aircraft and the warships, they shelled like the devil, and strafed and bombed; then we were able to get ashore and put the mortars into operation.

We got the mortar companies ashore with all the mortars and all the ammunition and dug in. The mortars, the base plate of the mortar with the barrel, was on a two-wheel carrier. You put that on. Of course, trucks were used to bring the shells because there were two shells to a wooden box. That was 52 pounds, 53 pounds to lift up. Then, the mortars went into action. I think we were with the 36th Division.

Monte Cassino

We went, then we invaded Anzio. We were at the Rapido River for quite a tussle. We were at the Abbey of Monte Cassino; we were at the bottom of the mountain. There's the abbey up on top. Germans had gone into it. Of course, they had dug in in front of the abbey as you come down the mountain. It wasn't really a high, high mountain, but it was high enough. The infantry, the airplanes, strafing and bombing, and our mortars, four companies of mortars shooting shells. At one point we heard there was going to be a big aircraft group coming over. They bombed the monastery; it was unbelievable. We could see the bombs coming down. The monastery was a tremendous structure. As the bombs hit, big, tremendous chunks of the monastery came down the hill. Whatever Germans were there, they skedaddled, otherwise they would have been crushed or something, you know? They were gone. The monastery was pretty much destroyed. We were able to advance then; we went up the hill with all the outfits that were around there. There was nothing in the monastery that was worth waiting for or fussing about. We just kept going. We did not have any reservations about the bombing of the monastery, because by that time, we were resigned to the fact that we're going to be in this until the end. I certainly understood that this mortar was an unbelievable weapon and they're not going to stop using it.

We went to Rome, and the advance on Rome, the Germans just retreated. We were there a few days; we were all allowed to visit St. Peter's and the Vatican. The Pope had come out, I remember.

Then, we went past Rome towards Florence, Italy. We were moving fast too. Sometimes we supported tank outfits; they were advancing and they used the mortars to shell ahead of the tanks.

France and Germany

We got through Florence, and we were in a rest area. We were advised that we're going to the coast, and we were going to prepare to invade, another invasion. They didn't say southern France. We said, 'Well, where are we going to go? To Corsica? Or Sardinia?' Those are those two big islands, but we bypassed that and we went to southern France.

The invasion was not troublesome at all. As we got ashore on the beach, we started moving inward, and there were some German and American boys who had been killed; I remember seeing them.

There was a lot of resistance near Metz. We did a lot of target spotting there. Then, the Germans headed towards the Rhine River, so we did the same in pursuit. We crossed in pontoon boats. They put up a pontoon bridge after that to get vehicles across. We got across on foot. Then, we headed south. Doing the same thing. Same target spotting through different towns. Our mortars, of course, also contributed to the destroying of some parts of towns, churches, other industrial buildings possibly as we went. We never questioned what it was. We reached a city called Türkheim; the German soldiers themselves had left the area.

*

Dachau

Colonel David Meyerson was the head of the 2nd Chemical Mortar Battalion; he was a native of Texas and a West Point graduate. He had been in some very secret action that we never knew about, but he had been in something. We didn't know what it was.

He was a very brave man. I used to go with him in Italy, and France, and Germany, just me and him. I drove the Jeep, and two fellas had a .50 caliber machine gun mounted there. We'd go down roads, and twice we came on German patrols that were on the road, also with a vehicle. They quickly jumped out of the vehicle and ran like hell. We didn't even go up to their vehicles because we didn't know what they had around, you know? We'd just race back, report it, and send some mortars over in that direction.

The colonel was sitting next to me one day and he wanted to go investigate something. I was a staff sergeant at that point. He says, 'Harold, go up that road.'

I said, 'I know where we are, Colonel.' I knew what was ahead of us.

He said, 'Take two of the boys.'

The road was a dirt road. I said, 'I know what we have to do.' We took out our bayonets, and we crawled on our stomachs, probing the ground for mines. There were no mines. The German soldiers had gone, they were gone already.

We got up to the gate, and we probed the gate for booby traps. We watched the trees for snipers; nothing there. We opened the gate and went in. We saw a lone figure standing way across a big open field. Coming out of the woods was a train, which was not moving; open box cars. We looked, and we didn't see that figure anymore. He must have seen us and then he left.

I said, 'Let's go over to the train, fellas.'

We went over to the train. As we approached the train, there were dead bodies on the ground.

I said, 'Let's climb up and see.'

We had seen this before in Türkheim, Germany, while going south chasing the Nazis who were trying to escape into the Alps. We were given that job because the shelling of targets was over by then. We climbed up, and the box cars were loaded to the top with dead bodies. Children, women, men, all ages.

Then, one of the fellas went back and waved to the colonel. They came in with all the vehicles and everything and followed us. They saw all this. Then we went into the concentration camp. There weren't too many people there, a couple hundred. They were in pretty bad shape.

There were no Germans at all. On the other side of the field where we saw that lone figure standing, there were three houses, nice houses, like a football field away. When our outfit came in, we saw three people start to walk towards us dressed in civilian clothes, two men and a woman. I had taken German in high school. I took a refresher course at Fort Bragg, where I was put into this outfit from basic training in Fort McClellan, Alabama. I could get along in German. I wasn't fluent, but I could question prisoners of war, and I did that many times.

I questioned these people. They had nothing to say. The colonel said to me in English, that maybe these people understood English. He said, 'They may be understanding everything we say.'

I said, 'That's very possible.'

But he wanted me to ask them if they worked at the concentration camp. 'Oh no, no, no, no.'

Behind us the grave registration outfit would be coming up. On one side of the camp we were searching and looking. There was a big trench dug out, 40 feet wide, a couple hundred feet along, loaded with dead bodies. They had poured some chemical on them. We didn't stay long. When the other outfit came in, we packed up and we continued our trip back to the boat. We got on the boat, in Le Havre, France, just us. One single boat of soldiers, 3,000 approximately.

*

That was the gist of my adventure in World War II. I was awarded the Bronze Star medal. After I was awarded the Bronze Star, Colonel Meyerson said to me, 'I've also recommended you for the Silver Star.' We had helped a mortar position bring them ammunition while we were under fire; thank God we all didn't get hurt. I said, 'Colonel, all the fellas were with me there. I didn't do all of that myself.' I never got [really] wounded in the Army, in the war, [though] I got hit by shrapnel once in a while from shelling or bombings. Once we were in a railroad station in Germany, and we were bombed by a German plane. I didn't get hurt badly, just like a scrape, like a band-aid. I never applied for a Purple Heart.

The Clothing Store

That is about my story. [Another time near the end in Germany], there was a labor camp and we were directed to it. It was a barbed wire prison camp and we found a few hundred young Polish fellas and girls from Poland in there; they had been taken from Poland to that place. They were used in the village and the town as domestics, doing work for the people and whatever businesses they had, cleaning and all that. The United States Army and other outfits that had entered after us, all these people were set free, but not to just go wherever they wanted. They had to stay there. With a lot of these young people, some of them could speak a little English.

A young fella came to me when we were eating one day. This fella says to me, 'Oh hello.' Then he says, 'New York.'

I said, 'Do you have family in New York?'

'Yes.' He gives me a piece of paper. It was an uncle of his who had a little clothing store on 6th Avenue between 43rd Street and 46th Street on the south side of the street. I said to him as well as I could, because I spoke a little German, so maybe he understood a little German, that I would try to get this paper to his family there. I was shipped home about a week or two after.

I said to my father, 'You want to go with me there? We'll go there.'

'Sure.'

We went, got off the 6th Avenue subway right there. Walked along and there's a clothing store. We went in. A man comes over. Middle-aged man, maybe, no more than 50. I give him the paper. I don't have my Army uniform on. He looks at it, then he looks at me.

I said, 'This is your nephew?'

'Yes.'

I said, 'I can't tell you anything about him, [but I was] going to try to help him.' I said, 'If you are able to bring him here ...'

He said that was what he was going to try to do. I did give him the name of something in the government to contact.

Oh, it must have been two years later. He finally calls: 'My nephew is here. He's working in the store.'

I went with my wife. Walked in, and there he is. Speaking a little English already. That happened, absolutely. Unbelievable. All we did was cry.

Harold D. Erdrich passed away at the age of 86 in 2006, five years after this interview took place.

*

CHAPTER SEVEN

The Dog Man

Following the attack on Pearl Harbor, many civilian clubs and organizations approached the United States government with suggestions to help in the war effort. A coalition known as 'Dogs for Defense' organized and encouraged owners to donate their dogs initially for training as sentry dogs, but by the end of 1942, the army had created four facilities for the specialized training of dogs and their human handlers for tasks such as mine detection, scouting, messengering service, and attack.[24]

Fred Crockett was one of these dog handlers, and his bond with his dog was apparent decades after the war. He was also a recipient of the Bronze Star. In 2007, he gave this interview in the comfort of his own home in Cazenovia, New York.

Fred Crockett

I don't know where the years have gone now. This August I'll be 83. And all your World War II veterans are that old…

I was born in Syracuse, New York, on August 7, 1924. I went into the service right out of high school; I left when the war was right in full swing. I left in the 12th grade, but then after I came home, I did go back and get my high school diploma. And I wanted to go to college, but I was shaking so bad I couldn't even write, so I never did go off to college.

I volunteered at the last minute, because I knew that I was going to have to go anyway. I had heard about war dogs and I wanted to get in with dogs.

In March 1943, I left Syracuse and went to Fort Niagara near Niagara Falls, then I went down to Camp Lee, Virginia, for five weeks of basic training. It was hard training. You know, you went through a lot and they made a soldier out of you. I asked for war dogs and, of course, they wouldn't [let me do it]. Anyone who knows the service knows they'll never give you what you want. If you were a cook in civilian life, you drive a truck in the

Army, because there's the right way, the wrong way, and the Army way, and they wanted you to do it their way. Well, they wouldn't give me the war dogs.

After I left Camp Lee, they put me in ordnance, way out in Jackson, Mississippi. I went through the entire training and became an ignition specialist with a sergeant's rating. Then, at the last minute, they discovered that the ordnance battalion was overstrength, and they had to get rid of two or three men. They had seen where I had kept asking for a transfer to the K-9 Corps, so they called me in the office and asked me, 'What is this K-9 Corps?'

I told them, 'It's war dogs.'

They said, 'Well, are you still interested in that?'

I said, 'Yes, I am.'

They said, 'Well, where would we send you? Where's their camp?'

Of course, I had done a lot of checking and I knew that it was at Front Royal, Virginia, in the Blue Ridge Mountains. By God, they gave me the transfer; took me into town, put me on a train, meal tickets and the whole business, and I went to

Front Royal, Virginia. When I got into town, I called up to the camp and they sent a truck down and picked me up and that was that. That was my beginning of being with the war dogs.

Front Royal still exists today. When I was there, we had 8,000 horses and mules in Front Royal. They built the dog camp up at the top of one of the mountains, and all the barracks and everything were just made out of wood; you could tell it was more or less a temporary camp. We had our barracks buildings and our mess hall, and we had the headquarters where the officers were, and a veterinary hospital to take care of the dogs. We had 1,300 war dogs in Front Royal.

The Army at that time didn't have any special breed specifications for dogs. They had to be within one to five years old, and they had to be a certain height and weight. There were some breeds that were worthless, like certain hunting dogs weren't any good, and big dogs like Great Danes and Mastiffs and those large breed dogs, they weren't any good. The best dogs were usually German Shepherds and Doberman Pinschers and other cross-bred dogs, like my dog Duke. Now, I wouldn't have traded Duke for any other dog, but it was all based on their training and their personality and aggression and so forth. The dogs were all donated by people; they were loaned to the federal government for service.[18]

The first thing we did was test them for gun shyness. If they were gun shy, we immediately sent them back where they came from; they weren't any good to us. The dogs couldn't be gun shy in any way. Then we would put them through a basic training, just like we had to go through, and teach them how to come, sit, down, stay, and so forth, you know. After the obedience training, they went on to special work, like scouting and attack dogs, guard dogs, messenger dogs, and things like that. I worked with scout dogs and then my dog was also part of a team of two dogs trained for carrying messages.

---

[18] *special breed specifications for dogs-*The Army would finally settle on seven breeds. 'At the outset of the program...[they] accepted many different breeds of dogs as long as the dogs were healthy and showed the proper disposition. It was soon discovered, however, that certain breeds were superior to others in performing the types of duties the Army desired, and by 1944, the list of acceptable breeds had shrunk to just seven: German shepherd, Doberman pinscher, Belgian sheepdog, collie, Siberian husky, malamute, and Eskimo dog.' Source: Paltzer, Seth. *The Dogs of War: The U.S. Army's Use of Canines in WWII.* https://armyhistory.org.

Scout dogs were always on a lead, and they were 'debarked,' so they never whimpered or barked or made any sound. They were taught that they couldn't make any noise, and by God, they never did. Whenever they whimpered or growled or barked, we would have to punish them and let them know that they couldn't do that, see? It was all through training, but when you worked with a dog day after day after day, all day, and got to know that dog and his personality and everything, it was amazing. You had to get to know your dog. They would detect wherever there was any [presence of the] enemy, and they would never respond unless we commanded them to attack.

When we trained them in Front Royal, we had a group of men who were called 'teasers.' They wore very heavy, padded suits, and the dog could grab them without hurting them, and that's the way we trained them to attack. It was amazing, just on our command, what they would do, then they would shut it off just as quick. When you work with a dog for that long, day in and day out, all day, and that was our only work, working those dogs, it's amazing what they can do.

Before we got orders for overseas, I was working twelve dogs. When it came time to go overseas, we were told to pick the one dog that we wanted to take with us. And that's when I picked the dog that I worked with for two years. His name was Duke. He was just a big, black dog. One little white spot on his chest, but it was solid black, and he was listed as a Dalmatian, but he didn't have the spots or anything of the Dalmatian, short-haired and good, large dog.

Like I said, I lived with that dog for two years. My dog went from a scout dog also to a messenger dog. I had a partner who came from Columbus, Georgia; he had a big German Shepherd by the name of Thor, and we worked as a team—two men and two dogs. They were trained to carry messages, and by God, they were good. We had a special collar with a pouch in it that you could put the message in, and we trained them down there in the Blue Ridge Mountains of Virginia, where nearby our camp we'd hike off into the mountain and then we would separate and run the dogs maybe a mile between the two of us, back and forth, see. Once they knew the trail, they could run on instinct, but otherwise they would use their nose and smell. The dogs knew both of us, and [with] just one word, [they would do their job]—we'd look them right in the face and tell them, 'Report!' They knew what to do then. My dog Duke would even respond on sign, just by me moving my hand—I didn't even have to talk to him and he'd respond. They were amazing, those dogs. They would play with you like a kitten, until you put your lead on them and gave them a jerk on their collar and told them to 'heel.' Then they knew they were working—they were a whole different dog. They were ready to kill.

*

When it came time to go over, our outfit consisted of 20 men and 25 dogs. We had five extra dogs that we took with us, a veterinarian, and a captain in charge. It was known as the 34th Infantry War Dog Platoon. Before we went over, they gave us special infantry training so that we knew how to react as an infantry soldier as well as a dog man. When we went over, we went over in a convoy, but they wouldn't put us on a regular troop ship because of our dogs, so we were on a Liberty ship. We went across and went through the Mediterranean, and we landed in Algiers, Africa. Our officers had to get orders of where we were going to go or what we were going to do, so we didn't have any action in Africa. We went across the Mediterranean to Sicily, and we stopped at Sicily for a little while, and then we continued on to Italy; we landed at Naples.

At that point, we were assigned to the 34th Infantry Division, which I understand was really the first division to get in conflict with the Germans in World War II in Europe.[19] We were attached to them to do patrol and scouting work. I understand that the 34th Division was over 200 percent replaced [due to those] killed and injured; they were the old 'G.I. Joes,' and we were scouting and patrolling with them for quite a period of time. At first, the riflemen refused to have anything to do with us and a dog leading a patrol, because they were afraid the dogs were going to bark or

---

[19] *first division to get in conflict with the Germans in World War II in Europe-* After combat in North Africa, the 34th Infantry Division came ashore in Italy during the invasion of Salerno on Sept. 9, 1943.

whimper and give the position away, and then they'd all be sitting ducks to be killed. We guaranteed them, 'No, our dogs won't make any noise.' They set up one patrol just to experiment, and the patrol headed into enemy territory and they ran into a little problem, and the dog man himself got hurt. But after that, all the riflemen said that, by God, they wanted a dog [with them].

We stayed with the 34th for a period of time and then we were attached to the 92nd Division; it was the only division in World War II that was 100 percent Negro. They were all Negro, and I did a lot of patrolling for them; we just referred to them as the 'Buffalo Soldiers.'[20] [Being that we were viewed as 'outsiders' by the regular division soldiers], they resented us, and of course, to a certain point, we resented them, you know? If it wasn't for our dog, there was no way to get along with them, but they were afraid of the dogs—they knew that on the slightest command, our dogs would attack them. We let our dogs bite a couple of them just to

---

[20] *we just referred to them as the 'Buffalo Soldiers'*- Native American nickname for members of the African American units of the U.S. Army serving on the western frontier after the American Civil War, colloquially adopted in World War II for segregated units, especially the 92nd Division.

let them know that, you know, and that was the only way. If we didn't have the dogs, we wouldn't have been able to live with them. We would go out on patrols into enemy territory, and we would patrol between machine gun nests on the front line to prevent the enemy from sneaking through. I remember one night I was out there patrolling, and it was Christmas Eve; all I could do was think of home.

The Messenger Dogs

The division would set up headquarters behind the front line, and HQ would then send out what we called 'spurs,' or platoons of men—one to the east, one to the west, and one straight ahead. They would go out maybe a mile or so until they could locate the enemy, so that they then could direct artillery. As they were going out, they would drop a communication line so that they could talk on a telephone back to headquarters. It was a common thing for the enemy, if they knew anything about a patrol being out there, to sneak behind us and cut the communication line. Our guys would have no contact with headquarters, and they would be sitting ducks. Well, that was when they needed our messenger dogs. My partner and I were chosen to carry messages from the outpost and back, and we would flip a coin, because one of us would stay at HQ, and the other one would have to go out to the outpost.

I remember one time I lost the flip and I had to go out. One of the riflemen had come back into headquarters, and he took me out to the outpost. When we finally got out there, the officer gave me a message and I put it in the pouch on my dog's collar and told Duke, 'Report!' Of course, he had come out with me, so he left his own scent and knew his way back. But then the other dog would have to smell all the way out there, and we waited, and by God, the other dog got out there to me all right, and we ran the dogs until about two o'clock in the morning—after they had made one trip, it was easy, because they knew their way, see? Finally, the lieutenant in charge of the outpost told me to lie down and get some sleep and that would be all the messages for that night. When I woke up in the morning, it was starting to get daylight, so I got up and noticed that the man that I was lying next to didn't get up. I asked one of the other fellas, 'Why doesn't that guy get up?'

He said, 'Oh, he's dead.' I had lain next to him all night. Anyway, after that experience, why, that gets you to the point where you don't care anymore.

*

I was hit many times from artillery shells or whatever, you know; when they hit the ground and blew, why, everything flew. Once I got hit in my right eye. We used to get [small fragments] in our hands and we'd just take our knife and dig it out, we wouldn't even report it. You didn't really know what it was, and it didn't matter. The medics would be quite a distance back from us, so you wouldn't go back to them unless a man was really hurt bad.

I received the Bronze Star [for evacuating wounded under fire with a Jeep]. We were going up this road to the front lines, and other troops were coming back out. After a month or so on the front, you would lose your mind, with the constant fear and the explosions and all the noise and everything, you would just go out of your head, so they would only keep you up there in the front for a certain amount of time. Anyway, we were going up to the front, these other fellas were coming back, and all of a sudden, the Germans started to throw in all kinds of artillery! The shells were blasting all over the place, and naturally, you'd head for a hole in the ground or any place you could get cover. But these poor fellas were so much out of their mind that they didn't even run for cover when the shells started bursting!

I saw these men get hit and fall to the ground. I don't know why, I just jumped out of my hole and grabbed a Jeep and drove over [to where they were] and loaded three wounded men and took them back to the medics. It was just an impulse. They weren't buddies, I didn't even know who they were. After I took them back to the medics, I came right back up and joined my unit and continued what I was doing. General Truscott [personally] decorated me in Viareggio, Italy.

A Sunday Evening in the Po Valley

Most of that action was in the Apennine Mountains. I have the medal for the Apennine Campaign and the Po Valley Campaign. We were beyond the Po Valley when we lost five men and six dogs all in one night.

After we had gone across the Po Valley and the Po River, we got into the city of Bologna on a Sunday night; we had gone for nine days without taking off our boots. All the way up through, we found abandoned and deserted vehicles because they were out of gas and we knew that the Germans didn't have much food. When we got into Bologna, we were told that the Germans were pretty well defeated, that they didn't have anything left, so we figured we could kind of relax, you know? Rest up.

It was a full moon night and it got to be about nine o'clock, and all of a sudden two German airplanes came in. They were open cockpit with machine guns on the front; they started to strafe us, and you could see the bullets coming. They were using what they call tracers, and we had no holes or any place to go, except jumping into a little water drain ditch. So that's what a lot of us did. We jumped into a drain ditch, and my God, you would just lie there, and you could feel the bullets hitting the ground! Finally, when it stopped, we went to get up and I noticed that my buddy ahead of me was hit, and a buddy behind me was hit. I didn't get hit, but like I said, I could feel the bullets hitting the ground. I picked up my buddy ahead of me, and blood was coming out of his mouth, so I knew he was hurt kind of bad.

Anyway, we thought the Germans were through; but instead, before we could do much, they came back again. Instead of machine gunning us, they threw anti-personnel bombs off the side of the plane. Now when those hit the ground, they [throw shrapnel above] the ground; they don't even make a hole in the ground. Now all of our vehicles had flat tires.

This went on for quite a while. It was about 3:00 in the morning before we figured it was over with and we finally got the word that some place down the line behind us, they had some artillery guns and they managed to get the planes shot down.

There wasn't any artillery up where we were, because we'd gone so fast.

That night we lost five men and six dogs. My partner's dog, Thor, was dead. We had a truck with our dog kennels on it, and so as long as we were resting, we put our dogs in their kennels, and so the kennels were just sitting on the ground and that's how they got hit, probably mostly with the anti-personnel bombs.

The End of the War

Mussolini had a big estate home up on one end of Lake Garda, up in north Italy, at the foothills of the Alps Mountains. That was the last place he was known to be, and from there he had to flee over into another country, see? There were a lot of nights when we could see partisan patrols going out into enemy territory; they were helping us fight the Germans. Anyway, they went after him and caught him and killed him and his mistress and seven henchmen. There were nine of them altogether, and they brought them back into Milan and hung them up on display in front of the gas station there in Milan.

Of course, at that point, the war was pretty well over, so we were just more or less waiting for orders up there at Lake Garda and Milan. We went into the castle that Mussolini owned and went all through the place, even before we knew that he was caught, looking for him and couldn't find him. Like typical GIs, full of hell, you know, and we found his bedroom and he had a big canopy-covered bed in there and we all took turns lying in Mussolini's bed. [*Laughs*] But that was where I saw them, and like I said, the war was over then and we stayed up there at Lake Garda, just occupying any empty buildings until we got orders to go back down, and we went to Leghorn, where we stayed until we were finally able to be put onto a ship and brought back home.

*

Ernie Pyle was right with us all the while there in Italy, and we used to always keep remarking to him, 'Ernie, why don't you go home? You don't have to be here.' We didn't see him every day because he did wander around some. But he was there, and as soon as our war in Europe ended, he went to the Pacific, because that went on after our war in Europe ended. He was only over there about a week and he got killed. He was an awful nice little fella.

*

We got off the ship in New York City, we landed in New York; coming into the harbor, a boat came out to meet us, with a band and girls in their bathing suits! My God, what a thrill that was! We came down the gangplank at the harbor, and of course, the Red Cross was right there to meet us. They took us to Camp Kilmer, New Jersey, and that was where we got our home-cooked dinner. A day or two later, they took us into New York City, and right in Times Square they had a big stage set up; they had the square all blocked off. One at a time, they would read our name and the name of our dog, and we would walk up on the stage, and they put a medal around our dog's neck. They decorated all our dogs.

After we were told that we could go home for furlough, all our dogs were loaded and taken to a dog camp in Nebraska. On board ship coming back home, I had been told by our officer in charge that if I wanted Duke, I could take him home and he would turn in a report stating that the dog had died on board ship coming home. I said, 'No. Let him go back.' And that was the last I saw of him. I regretted many times that I didn't bring him home. [*Pauses; gets emotional*]

I got the names of the people in New York City who owned him and wrote to them. I asked them if I could have him, and they didn't want to give him to me. They wanted him back. [*Cries softly*]

The dogs went back to this camp in Nebraska and we all laughed about it, because supposedly, they had a program set up for detraining the dogs. [*Emphatically*] There's no way in a million years that they could de-train those dogs, because we more or less whipped them every day, to keep them fierce, on command! There was no way that they were ever going to take that out of them. If they *ever* saw a person with a stick in their hand, or who raised their arm [*suddenly*], that dog would be ready to attack. I've seen men killed by them, and I know what they can do. We had an officer down in Front Royal who was killed by a

Doberman one day. The handler thought he had control of the dog, and he was working him off leash, and another officer was coming down the street and the dog just went after him. Leaped up and got him right in the neck and killed him. So you know, they can do a job on you.

We never did hear [what ultimately happened to the dogs], but I would assume they were put to sleep. They wouldn't have been any good for anything else, and they couldn't take that fierceness out of them, and they were used to working with a particular man. But a dog gets used to a man and I don't think you can just swap it off to different people, you know? I think we always figured that they put them to sleep.[21]

*

After I was discharged, I wanted to go to college. I wanted to be a veterinarian, or something in that order, and I just... [*Pauses*] See, I had been in the hospital for shell-shock way back in Rome, Italy,

---

[21] *we always figured that they put them to sleep*-Further investigation indicates that the Army did invest heavily in retraining programs and that they were generally successful; out of 3,000 returning dogs only four were unable to successfully transfer to civilian life. Source: Paltzer, Seth. *The Dogs of War: The U.S. Army's Use of Canines in WWII*. https://armyhistory.org.

and I couldn't even eat, I shook so bad. I was there for four days and I was sent back out. I went into a hospital there and a nurse had to feed me, but we were too short of men and equipment at that point, just before the big drive that ended the war in Italy. That's all the rest I got, four days! Anyway, [at college] I shook so bad that I got too embarrassed and I just got up and walked out of class. I never did anything [about it] until 1983, when I [had another condition and] applied at the VA Hospital, and they've been taking care of me ever since.

I stayed in contact with some of the guys, mostly Christmas cards and things like that. I work all day, every day; I work here at home now. But they're all gone.

Fred Crockett helped to pioneer the first use of war dogs in combat, a legacy that continues today in the military and government agencies. He passed away in 2011.

Floyd Dumas (L) and two other escapees, Bill Robb of Scotland and a South African, pose for a portrait while behind enemy lines in Rome, 1944.
Courtesy Floyd Dumas.

CHAPTER EIGHT

The Escapee

Floyd Dumas was a soldier in the 45th Infantry Division. The author had heard about Floyd's story and called him up to invite him in for a World War II prisoner of war symposium at his high school. Mr. Dumas was gracious and thankful on the phone, but initially declined. Then he had a change of heart. He had something to say.

Floyd J. Dumas

I was born in Malone, New York, on January 26, 1920. I will be 88 years old next month. I had two years in high school; I could never finish high school because it was a depression time. My father had worked for the railroad, New York Central Railroad in Malone, and lost his job, and I was the oldest boy in the family so I had to quit high school and go and join the CCC camp, this side of Saranac Lake.[22] Well, it was a good thing, because the camp got me ready to be in the Army. We had regular uniforms from World War I. It was in the wintertime and we would dig up big pine trees and transplant them to a different area. In the spring we went into a side camp in tents, and we had regular Army-style barracks that we lived in. We also built a dam on a brook; I think it's Route 30 going into Malone. Did that all one summer. You could have like six months at a time and then you could quit if you wanted to, so I stayed in about one year. It was a good education. It was started by President Roosevelt in 1938 and the pay was 30 dollars a month. Twenty-five dollars a month went to our parents. We had five dollars to spend for the month. I guess the only entertainment we had was we used to shoot craps for cigarettes. [*Laughs*]

When I heard about Pearl Harbor, I was up in Alexandria Bay in the Thousand Islands, the other side of Watertown, New York. I was cooking steaks in this bar and restaurant at the time. It was

---

[22] *the CCC camp*-Civilian Conservation Corps; New Deal work relief program employing young men on environmental projects during the Great Depression.

the slow season; they wanted me to stay on [after the summer season], so I did bartending and cooking in the kitchen. It was right around Christmas time, I think, when I got the notification that I was drafted into the service; I think I went into the Army in February of '42.

We went from Malone to Camp Upton, Long Island. Had a physical, and they gave us a uniform to put on, and by train we went to Camp Cross in South Carolina, I think for 18 weeks of basic training, infantry training. A lot of us took training on a 37-millimeter gun, which was useless when we got in any combat action on it. [*Chuckles*] We shot it at a couple of German tanks; it just bounced off, so they got rid of those. We took all that training on it for nothing. In the summer we took amphibious landings in Cape Cod, Massachusetts. Got in the regular big trench forts, made regular invasions of land, and I think we were there about a month. After that, we went to Pine Camp, New York, near Watertown. I don't know why they sent us there because it was 40 degrees below zero. A lot of times we couldn't even have any training. The training was done inside the barracks, you know? But we didn't stay there too long. We went to a couple of other camps. One in Massachusetts, at Fort Devens—I can't tell you how long we were there, but we had training there. And eventually we were shipped out for overseas from Hampton Roads, Virginia.

Replacement

I was sent over as a replacement. And they put us in the 45th Infantry Division. Company F, 179th Regiment, Second Battalion, the Thunderbird Division. Most of the guys were from the southwest, I think a [federalized] National Guard unit. We were fill-ins, anyway, a bunch of Yankees who got filled into the division.

We got along with the Southerners. [*Chuckles*] There was just one sergeant, the Southern sergeant in South Carolina, that was a little tough. But on the whole, we had Indians and cowboys in our division, you know, from Oklahoma and Texas, and they were a good bunch of guys. Real tough. We joined them in Fort Devens, Massachusetts.

[We joined a convoy] out of Hampton Roads and zig-zagged a couple of weeks and went into the Mediterranean. We pulled into Oran, North Africa, and made a mock landing when we landed there. We took training there, a dry run for the invasion of Sicily.

We were in the first wave. I would say over half of us were sick to begin with from the boats we were on, the landing craft infantry. [*Chuckles*] And the water's wake—they almost cancelled the invasion of Sicily because the weather was so bad and everybody got sick on the big boat coming down the ladders and getting into the landing craft [for the] infantry. A lot of us were sick, but they didn't call it off. We invaded it anyway.

We landed at Gela in Sicily. We went from Gela, Sicily, in the southern part, right up through to the most northern part of the capital of Palermo. We were with Patton then. We saw him; he was pretty rough and ready, yes. He was an excellent general, but he was a little bit too wild, you know, by slapping that kid in the hospital… after hitting Sicily.[23]

---

[23] *slapping that kid in the hospital*-On two occasions during the campaign in Sicily, General Patton slapped hospitalized soldiers he described as cowards—'Your nerves, hell—you are just a goddamned coward!' Overcome with rage, in the second incident he even reached for his sidearm. He was told to apologize to his men and Eisenhower removed him to England, where he would play a role in the invasion of France after D-Day.

He was a little bit too rough on soldiers, you know. He was a good general, otherwise I guess they wouldn't have him there.

[My impression now of the battle of Sicily was of] a lot of snipers, and constantly moving from here to there. Of course, we were walking all the time—we never rode when we were in the infantry—and the civilians were real good to us. We got a three-day pass at Palermo; we all got drunk and sick, that didn't help us out any. [*Chuckles*] Then from there we went into bivouac someplace a while, and a little more training.

Then we invaded Salerno, Italy. When we invaded Salerno, we got the notice over the speaker that Mussolini had [been removed], so we didn't have the Italians to fight, we had just the Germans to contend with. I can't remember quite how long we fought there in Salerno, but I guess it was long enough. [*Long pause*]

*

From Salerno, of course, we went to Anzio, which was terrible, terrible, terrible. Our division suffered terribly at Anzio; my regiment lost 55 percent. That's all I can say. We got hit hard, a lot of us got killed, and a lot of the soldiers just couldn't stand it, they went right out of their minds—they couldn't take it. It was so, so bad, the worst that I've ever seen. Very, very bad. I think I'm pretty lucky to be sitting here talking about it; I was wounded in the left leg right here. [*Points to leg*] Shrapnel wound, nothing serious; I think it was a grenade.

Taken Prisoner

As General Lucas set out to consolidate his lines and build up strength for the push to Rome, the Germans launched a fierce counteroffensive.

[In the beginning] we were going good, we were headed right for Rome. We weren't too far from Rome and all the divisions were pushing forward. General Lucas put a stop to us. I don't know why. I guess there's a lot of talk about it, but I don't know. But we had to [pull back and] dig in, slit trenches and foxholes; at least three weeks we were dug in. It rained and sometimes it even snowed, and I remember we were just stalemated right there. Well, that gave the Germans time to draw some of their troops out of Russia and here and there and stop us at Anzio, which they did—they almost pushed us in the ocean! All the rear echelon was issued rifles and hand grenades and there was no more cooking; [even the cooks were fighting]. We had to stop the Germans, and that's the time when I was captured.

We were dug into the Mussolini Canal. The only good thing that Mussolini ever did for the Italian people was to dig that canal for irrigation purposes for Italian crops, you know? That's what they say; anyway, he didn't do any other good. And early in the morning, the Germans came at us, I'm telling you, with tanks and hundreds and hundreds of infantrymen. The canal is like this [*motioning canal position and military positions*], the Germans were here, we were dug into this part here in a slit trench, and those 88s were firing right [at us from] the opposite bank of the canal. They were shooting everything at us! Well, anyway, it's a good thing our engineers knew what they were doing, because they blew up all the bridges over the canal [to the American lines] the night before. They must've known what was going to happen, and that stopped the Germans from getting their tanks over the canal, but their infantry just ran right on through us, and they grabbed a whole bunch of us. The big 88s were just pointing right at us and we were in the canal. We smashed our rifles and threw our ammunition in the water in the bottom of the canal, and we surrendered to them—I don't know how many of us, but quite a group of us, all in one catch there.

They marched us to their lines. The worst part about being captured was that we were now in the German lines and we're getting hit by our own artillery! The Germans were rushing us to get us into their lines, you know? And I remember a German officer running out of one of the buildings and wanting us to run, run, run. We'd run a while, then a shell would come in and we'd hit the ground—we're trained to do that. Well, that was the end of him! One of those shells landed right at his feet and he never gave another command. [*Laughs*]

*

It was quite a few miles to the prison camp, as I remember, two or three days. Well, that first night, we got into this small town. Must've been Anzio, the town of Anzio, and they put us way down underneath the ground in tunnels, way down underneath homes. When we got up in the morning, the American bombers had leveled the town. Every house in Anzio was bombed completely out. That's why they put us down there, for protection; I could never understand why [they did that]. When we got out of there, we started the walk, fifteen or twenty miles to the prison camp.

It was February, I guess, but we didn't have any winter gear at all. Anyway, the Germans marched us and they made us bury their dead. They had hundreds of dead soldiers lying along the side of a dirt road; in one area, [one of our planes] had come down and had strafed and killed twenty or thirty of them. They made us dig trenches, and we threw all those German soldiers in there, all the way to the prison camp; they didn't give us any water, no food at all.

Cinecittà

They got us to the prison camp, it was named Cinecittà. You know the story of Cinecittà? [24] In Italian, it means 'City of Movies.' It's still in Italy there, about 30 miles from Rome. [After the Italians surrendered], the Germans took over Cinecittà and made a transit camp out of it, with barbed wire and the whole bit. They marched us to this Cinecittà and locked up the gates with the wire and everything all around it—we were only supposed to be there twelve days; they said they're going to ship us to the Black Forest in Germany by boxcars. Well, that was embedded in my mind, you know, 'twelve days.'

In the yard that we were in, they only had one latrine, a big, long place where you went to the bathroom, and it only had one faucet. We didn't have any bathing or any showers or anything like that, you know. In the morning they gave us German green tea, but they didn't even have cups or anything. You'd take the liner out of the helmet,

---

[24] *Cinecittà*- ('Cinema City') Large film studio near Rome, still the largest film studio in Europe, built originally by Mussolini to bolster the Italian film industry at the outset of the Depression era.

and pour the green tea into the helmet! And at noontime, they gave us some [soup] concoction of Italian greens; one day they had a horse in there, which they cooked up. At night they lined us up to have a prison count into columns of five, and they would hand the fifth guy a small black loaf of German bread to be cut up between the five of us. That went on every day I was in the prison camp. We might have had pork there one day, I don't remember, but I think that's the time we all got diarrhea, when we ate the pork. We all got diarrhea, but the German doctor took care of us all, he gave us something to take care of it. The food was terrible! In fact, the local newspaper asked me why I wanted to escape—I told them I didn't like the food. [*Laughs*] Didn't ever see a Red Cross package, not one package. Of course, I wasn't there that long. I was only there ten days.

Escape

[The day I escaped], it was in the afternoon and we were in the big building where they'd lock us in at night, after they gave us the loaf of bread. During the day they kept it unlocked, so you could be in the building or out in the yard. There were a bunch of us playing cards in the big building when an air raid sounded. All the guards were looking up at the sky and watching our Air Force bombing near the prison camp. One of the men who was in the yard came in while we were playing cards and said two men ripped the fence and escaped. He asked if anyone else wanted to try and get out. I said, 'I'll go,' and a British guy said, 'I'll go,' but no one else would try.

We went out in the yard. The fence was ripped open and a large group stood around to block the guards' view, and the Englishman and I went through, but we were still inside the prison camp! We scouted around and found a small room with fake scenery in it, I suppose as a part of the movie industry. We hid in this room until dark, [and miraculously] a storm came up and it started to rain hard, with thunder and lightning, which was good for us—I don't know how we got that lucky. Now I don't care if you're an American soldier, a British soldier, or a Japanese soldier, but when you're on guard duty and it's raining, you're going to look for a spot where you're not going to get too wet, and that's what the Germans did—they never saw us going through the yard even with the lights on.

The Germans must've been doing some work next to the [outside] wall, and they had thrown dirt up against it just high enough so we could get up to the top of the wall and throw ourselves over. They had barbed wire and broken glass on top of the wall, but the two of us got over and fell down on the other side.

We ran across the countryside, and on the way we were so hungry, we're pulling up carrots and stuff and eating the dirt and all. We came upon a farmhouse and knocked on the door, and an old Italian couple was sleeping next to a fireplace on the floor, an old man and the old lady. We knocked on the door, they came, and we had little [Army] booklets with Italian language phrases, you know, so we said, 'Americano soldato' and 'Inglese soldato.' They said, 'Sì,' and let us in. We were wringing wet, but we were able to dry out our clothes; they had us sit by the fireplace and dry off and gave us some bread and ricotta, which the woman warmed up. The old man spoke a little

English, he said, 'You no can stay here tomorrow, the Germans catch you here, they kill us.'

We said, 'Well, what are we going to do? Where are we going to go?'

He said, 'Half a mile away down the road there's a bombed-out house. You can go down in there and hide for a while.'

At daybreak, the Englishman and I left and found it, but then he wanted to try to get back to our lines. Can you imagine that? [*Laughs*] Here we are, way behind the German lines, and he wants to get back to our lines.

I said, 'What are you, crazy? You can't get through all those German soldiers!'

He said, 'Well, I think we should try.'

I said, 'You want to try, you go ahead.'

He tried, he got challenged by a German outpost, and they shot him right there. I heard the shot.

I stayed at that bombed house for three or four days, and I still had an American uniform on. I said to myself, 'I've got to do something pretty soon.' There was a small town not too far away. I said, 'I got to take a chance and when there's no Germans around, I'm going to have to walk into the [town] and tell them I'm an American soldier.' The people all hated the Germans anyway, so they greeted me, and I was all right.

They got me into civilian clothes. I traded my combat jacket to a sheep herder for his long black coat, [and the family I stayed with gave me] a silk shirt and an old pair of shoes with holes in the toes; I wish I had a picture of that. I held on to my dog tags and put them in my shoe, to prove I was an American GI, and I stayed there quite a few days. I heard there was another soldier nearby—an Indian soldier who spoke English, so they got me in touch with him. I don't know if he was [an escaped] prisoner of war, I don't know what he was. He was staying with an Italian family and had learned a lot of the language, and we got to talking.

Each morning, the Indian and I would go to a neighbor with a bucket to get some ricotta cheese. There were a lot of Germans manning anti-aircraft guns in the area. One morning, one of the Germans asked the Indian, 'Why doesn't your friend with you ever talk?'

The Indian responded, 'He was in the Italian Army and a bomb fell near him, and he became deaf and dumb.'[25]

The German said, 'That's too bad.' So this is what I did. After living in this little village for about a month, more and more German soldiers arrived in and around the village. I started to get a bit scared that I would get caught; maybe one of the villagers would squeal on me. I said to the Indian, 'I don't like staying in the country here like this.'

He said, 'Well, I've been here quite a while, and they haven't been bothering me at all.'

I said, 'Well, you've got to notice that the Vatican was taking in escaped prisoners of war, so you suppose you could get me into Rome and over to the Vatican and I could try to get in there?'

He said, 'Yes, in a couple of days.' So we headed for Rome.

---

[25] *He was in the Italian Army* –Mr. Dumas noted, 'At this time, the Italian Army had surrendered to the Allies. All the Italian youth who were in the Army were home.'

Rome

Getting to Rome was not a picnic. We had to go through a number of German roadblocks [to get to the train station], but they did not bother us as hundreds of people went into Rome each day to bring their produce to the open market. Some walked the eighteen miles; some took buses, drove horses and carts in, or took a train. We walked to the train station and got on the train. The train was always packed with people bringing in pigs, hens, and vegetables for the market. When the train stopped in Rome, we took a bus to Vatican City. We went up and the Indian talked to one of the Swiss guards at the Vatican.

He said, 'No, they've not allowed any more prisoners in the Vatican. We're neutral and we're not allowed to do it.'

I said, 'Well, we've heard that there were escaped prisoners in here.'

He said, 'There are, but they've put a stop to it.' They wouldn't let us in.

He said, 'But you've got to go back to the country where you were, and after three days, you come back here, and right over to the left here, there's an alleyway. When that clock strikes twelve there, you look across the street. There'll be a man standing there with a black overcoat on, and in his right-hand pocket he'll have a newspaper. When he takes the newspaper down from his face and puts it in his pocket, you go across the street and say, 'Americano soldato,' and that's all you've got to say.'

We went back to the country, and then three days later we went back there, and that's exactly how it happened. The man I met with the newspaper was a priest; he worked with the Italian underground. The priest went ahead and I followed him onto a bus. He paid the tokens and we got on the bus, rode for a while, and then transferred to another very crowded bus. Finally, after about an hour of busing, we got off and walked two blocks and came to a big building surrounded by a high wall, with a huge iron gate and a bell on the side.

The priest rang the doorbell, and soon a nun came to the gate and let us in. We walked in a side entrance and opened a door that led to a small room. A small table for two was set with a loaf of bread and a bottle of red wine. The priest closed the door and put out his hand and said, 'You did fine, and we got here okay.'

He said, 'Tomorrow you will be introduced to a Scotsman who is here, and you will be together until Rome falls to the Allies.'

The Scotsman's name was Bill Robb, from Aberdeen, Scotland. He was taken prisoner at Tobruk in the desert of North Africa by the Germans. [In Italy], the Germans piled him and a large group of prisoners into a train to send them to Germany. He tore the bars off the boxcars and jumped off the train. He broke his left leg in the jump, but the Italians hid him and nursed him back to health. He had been behind the lines a long time and learned the Italian language fluently. So, we met in that convent and would stay together until the war in Italy was over.

*

Bill and I were to stay in the nuns' convent until the priests and the underground found a safe place for us in Rome. Two weeks later, they found a place in Rome on Via Vetulonia, where a woman was to hide us in her apartment on the fifth floor. Her name was Signora Capisoni. She was about forty years old and alone; her husband was an Italian Army officer but was missing in action. She taught me Italian, and how to play Italian card games. She fed us, but the only time [she would want us] to go out in the streets was to get water from a well three blocks away, or to buy eggs on the street. At this time, eggs were $12.00 a dozen! Cigarettes were also very hard to come by—and this woman had to be paid somehow.

Signora Capisoni was now hiding three of us there; she didn't know what to do, and as escaped prisoners of war, we didn't have any money. She called up her friend in Rome and she told her the story. Her friend said, 'You send the American and the Scotsman to the Swiss Legation in Rome.'

We got on the little trolleys and we went to that address and walked in there. The guy had a sign on his desk, 'I speak seven languages, take your pick,' so we told him the story in English.

He said, 'Oh, so you want to borrow money?'

'Yes, we want to borrow money. This woman doesn't have any money and she's feeding three of us.'

He said, 'You can borrow money, just sign your name, rank, and serial number, and when the war is over, the American and [British] governments will repay Switzerland.'

So for the five months I was behind enemy lines, I borrowed Italian lira from them four times, a total of $108.12.[26]

*

After a couple of weeks, two more escaped PoWs were brought in our house—another young

---

[26] *I borrowed Italian lira from them-* On May 1, 1947, Mr. Dumas received a letter from the U.S. Army Finance Office. The letter stated:
'Dear Mr. Dumas: This office has been advised by the Office of the Chief of Finance, Washington, D.C., that on 8 March 1944, while a member of the U.S. Armed Forces in Italy, you received a payment of Emergency Relief, subject to payment at a later date of 2,000 Italian Lire ($108.12 American dollars - converted at the rate of .05405) from the Swiss Legation in Rome, Italy, through Captain Leonardo Trippi, Inspector of War Prisoner Camps, which obligation has now been transferred to the War Department for collection. While it is not the intention of this office to disturb you with collection letters, this indebtedness not withstanding your faithful service to your country during the time of War, it nevertheless represents a legitimate obligation due the United States and should be repaid with the least practicable delay. Remittance should be drawn in favor of the Treasurer of the United States and forwarded to this office.
Very truly yours,
C.F. Hathaway, Jr.
Captain, F.D.
Assistant Finance Officer'
Mr. Dumas contacted his congressman, who contacted the Washington press corps. The headline in the *Washington Evening Star* on May 20, 1947 read: *Army apologizes for 'Dunning' GI on Escape Cash.* The article continued: *'The War Department, in a hasty review, revealed the demand for repayment was a 'mistake,' and it was unfortunate and regretted.'*

American named Bob Schultz from Pennsylvania, and a guy from South Africa. Bill and I got bored staying in the house all the time, so finally we told Signora Capisoni that we were going out to look about the city of Rome. She protested and said, 'You will be caught in a round-up!'

As I said before, the Italians were out of the war, and there were a lot of young ex-soldiers roaming around Rome. The Germans would block off a square of streets with machine guns and tanks and gather up all the youths in this area and put them into trucks and drive them to the German front lines and make them dig trenches and bury their dead for a few days, then they would drive them back to Rome and let them go. Bob Schultz was [eventually] caught in one of these round-ups.

Bill knew some elderly farming families who grew all kinds of fruits and vegetables in a small town outside Rome. Bill and I would leave Rome about once a week in the morning, walking and taking a bus to this town of Tor Sapienza. They would give us fresh vegetables and chicken to bring back to our apartment in Rome. This helped

Signora Capisoni a lot, because we would not have to pay for it.

We got to know Rome pretty well; we knew what trolley or bus to take. We went into the wine shops and ordered bottles of vino and sat and listened to the old Italian men talking about the American and British bombing their homes. We went to the library and got books in English and then returned them ten days later. We even went to a carnival in Rome one weekend and watched these six-foot German soldiers riding the merry-go-round and eating ice cream cones.

We were stopped by two Germans one day. Their truck broke down, and one asked, in Italian, if we would know how to start it. Bill took a look at it and told them they were out of gas. They laughed and laughed and thanked us.

We had a close call traveling on a trolley on our way out to the countryside. The trolley was halted and German SS troops and Italian fascists, the 'Camicia Nera' or Black Shirts, climbed aboard. One of the Italian fascists said, 'Everyone show their identification cards as we approach you.' Bill had a false one made up by a priest who did this; I had had my photo taken for one but did not have my card yet because the priest had been caught and shot.

I whispered to Bill, 'You have a card. There is no sense in both of us getting arrested. Get away from me.'

He didn't move. There were steel bars on the windows of the trolley and both exits were covered. I was doomed.

Thankfully, the trolley was packed with people sitting and standing, like pickles in a jar. They started checking, got discouraged, and said, 'Everyone hold up your card and photo over your heads.' I took my wallet out and just stuck it up eye level. They looked and said, 'It is well, go on.' Now, you realize I was an American soldier in civilian clothes, behind enemy lines—[I would have been taken out and] shot as a spy. I was saved, thank the Lord!

*

We lived on the fifth floor, and on the bottom floor was a wine shop; Italians drink wine like we drink water. One night things went bad in the street and someone shot and killed a German soldier as he went by on a motorcycle. The German High Command said if this ever happened again, they would line up twenty-five civilians and shoot them. This incident got us scared. Bill and I decided to leave Via Vetulonia and move out to the countryside to Tor Sapienza. We stayed in Bill's friend's farmhouse—'Old Pietro,' his wife, a 14-year-old boy, and one little girl about 5 years old. They were all beautiful Italian people and so happy to hide us on their property. We ate in the farmhouse, but slept in a smaller building away from the house, with hay on the floor and a few blankets. German soldiers were always coming to the farm and asking for eggs or wine; Pietro would give them eggs, but would always say he did not have any wine; the Italians would dig holes and put the wine in the ground.

When 'Old Pietro' went to Rome for provisions, he would load a small two-wheel cart with hay, and Bill and I would get under the hay to hide, as we had to go through German roadblocks. A little old donkey pulled the cart. When we went through a roadblock, they would just ask him where he was going, and he had to be back through the roadblock before dark, as no civilian was allowed out after dark.

One day we went into Rome, as I had to get a shave and haircut. Bill was still doing all the talking in Italian, as he was excellent at it. But this day, he did not go, and rehearsed with me how to ask for a haircut. I went in and said what Bill told me, but the barber was very talkative, and I could not answer him. I stared at him in the mirror and gave him a big wink; he shut up immediately. [*Laughs*] The haircut and shave, as I remember, came to forty cents. I gave him $1.00 in Italian lira, and he thanked me three times.[27] I guess he thought it was a great tip.

As I said earlier, the Italians were out of the war, and a lot of the Italian youth were like us, hiding from the Germans. The Italians hated the Germans. The Germans would come upon a farmer who had cows and help themselves to the cattle, bringing the cattle to a slaughterhouse in Rome,

---

[27] *The haircut and shave*-Mr. Dumas continued: 'After Rome fell to the Allies, Bill and I returned to this barbershop. I said to the barber, 'Do you remember me?' He said, 'Oh, yes. But I thought you were a German. I see now you are American.' The five barbers got out the wine and cognac and we had a party.'

and then they would return to sell the beef back to the Italian people! The Germans also killed a few Catholic priests.

Harassing the Germans

Bill and I got together with six [of these Italians] and harassed the Germans every chance we could. These young men had dug a huge cave in the side of a hill about the size of a dining room. They had even planted berry bushes over the mouth of the cave, so no one else could find it; years ago, you see, the Italians had prepared for the invasion of their country. We lived in this cave for weeks [with plenty of] water, bread, and wine, [coming out at night to hit the Germans].

One night there was a group of German soldiers in an open field with a bonfire, playing music and singing 'Lili Marleen'—a favorite song with all the troops. [*Begins to sing a refrain*] Six of us crept up and opened fire on them and killed most of them; we also blew up some of their trucks. All of our attacks were done [under cover of] darkness, and we never got caught.

When the Italian farmers cut their hay, they would stack huge piles of it throughout the fields. We were always looking for a place to hide, so at night, we would hollow out the haystacks, pulling out the hay from the front and middle and throwing it on the top of the stack. We would leave a small entrance so we could crawl in. It made a nice cool place to hide when there were Germans around, and also a place to escape the hot sun in May and June. We used these haystacks for some time until one day some Spitfire airplanes started strafing the haystacks and the haystacks blew up! We didn't know the Germans used to stack hay on top of ammunition to hide it!

Another incident while we were in the country was this Italian woman spying on us; she was a fascist working for the Germans, and a neighbor told us this. Bill and I and three Italians went to her house and burned it down! She had a bicycle built for two, so Bill and I took that. We would ride all over Rome on it; one day we even rode it to see the Colosseum! [*Laughs*]

Bill and I went back near Rome to look for another house to hide in, and the underground found us one north of Rome. A single girl lived there with her father; he was a conductor on one of Rome's trolleys. The girl was going out with a German SS trooper, just to get money out of him to buy food for us. They would be in one room and there would be four of us escaped prisoners in the next! We had to be real quiet, and we did not stay there very long, as it just became too dangerous.

We went to another house in Rome, where a couple with two daughters lived. The daughters' names were Guiseppina and Teresa, both very nice Italian girls. The father said to us one night, 'You can stay here, but please do not get too friendly with my daughters. If you want to meet girls, I work at a Rome theatre where there are plenty of showgirls. If you want to come to the theatre tomorrow, I will have a table on the sidewalk cafe for you. I will have two girls come out and sit, talk, and have a bottle of wine on me.' So, that is just what we did. They were just friendly girls who were wild about meeting an American and Scotsman. It was lots of fun.

Bill knew a very rich Italian man who ran a huge biscuit factory in Rome. On two different Sundays, they invited us to dinner at their lovely home. He opened up a closet door one day and said to 'help yourself' to any suit of clothes we wanted; I picked out a gray pinstriped single-breasted suit. He also gave me a beautiful white silk shirt. Bill also picked out a navy-blue suit and a shirt of some kind. He also wanted to give us money, but we refused.

Liberation

From that house, we went back up to [that cave near] Tor Sapienza. We had the young Italian kids on guard while we slept at night. Finally, one morning at 5:30, two of the young guards came in the cave and hollered, 'The Americans are here, in the town next to us. There are dead German soldiers all over the place!'

We said, 'Ahh, you're crazy, they're not here yet. They aren't going to take Rome yet.'

'Come here, come here!' They showed us a package of Camel cigarettes, and Holy Jesus, right away I knew it was true! I'll never forget it. Sure enough, the 88th Infantry Division was coming through, so we walked right in with them. We talked to an

American officer and told him who we were; I showed him my dog tags and we followed them into the city of Rome. There were German tanks burning in the streets and snipers shooting all over the place in the city, but in six hours, Rome was completely taken.

We were interrogated by American officers and told them our story. They turned us over to a British outfit; I guess they were going to stay in Rome to keep things under control. The British said we had to get out of the civilian clothes. So, they gave us British uniforms, shorts, knee socks, heavy shoes, a shirt, and a beret.

They gave me the name of a captain who was in Naples and said I was to report to him as soon as possible.

I said, 'How do I get to Naples?'

They gave me a map and said, 'Hitchhike. We have no transportation for you.'

So, with my nice new British uniform on, I did just that. I found the address I had been given but it took some time, as Naples is a large city. The captain I was to see ran a PoW camp with hundreds of German prisoners. He asked me a lot of questions about what we did behind the lines and what we saw, then told me to get out of the British uniform and he would supply me with one of ours.

I was in Naples about a week before he could get me a plane to Oran on July 21, 1944, a mail plane with bucket seats and everything. From North Africa I was put on a ship for Hampton Roads, Virginia, for about ten days. Eventually I was flown with three other soldiers from Camp Pickett, Virginia, to Washington, D.C. The Army put us up in a beautiful hotel and gave us money from the American Red Cross. For two hours each morning, we had to answer questions from high officials at a building in Washington. After that, we were on our own to do whatever we wanted; we had a great time, drank a lot of beer, and ate in nice restaurants—but the next morning we had to go back to interrogation.

I was given a ten-day furlough from Washington to Malone, New York, where my family and girlfriend lived, then I reported back to duty to train new men for overseas infantry fighting.

After that, I was shipped to a camp in South Carolina for two months, training men for the infantry overseas. Then in March 1945, I was shipped to Camp Gordon, Georgia. I got a furlough to go home to marry my sweetheart on April 3, 1945; after our honeymoon, we went by train to Augusta, Georgia, where I was allowed to leave Camp Gordon each night to stay with my wife. We lived there until June 1945. My wife had to take a train home as she was about to have our first child. On October 10, 1945, I was discharged as a staff sergeant.

*

Home

I was out of the Army in 1945 and was working for a milk company, and there was an ad in the paper for a men's clothing store. I went and applied for the job; I had to learn tailoring, store management, window trimming, and all that. I got the job and I picked up the tailoring really quickly. I learned it in six months; they couldn't understand [how I picked up the trade so fast]. I'm telling my sister this, and she said, 'Well, your Uncle Eli was the top tailor in Malone here years ago, maybe he's brushing off on you.' After my training was done in the Malone store, they gave me a store to run in Danbury, Connecticut. Then they transferred me to Glens Falls, Steins' Men's Clothing Store, and I have been here ever since; now I do tailoring out of my [basement shop]. Do you know that I have had three millionaires as my clients? That's right, Charley Wood used to come over to my house to get measured up.[28] Then I started going to his place...

*

Bill Robb went back to Aberdeen, Scotland, and we kept in touch over the years. He had got married and had a child, but couldn't find work in Aberdeen. [Unbeknownst to me], he moved to Montreal, Quebec, just an hour and a half from my hometown, Malone, New York! He was in a pub drinking beer in Montreal and these old guys were talking about Malone.

---

[28] *Charley Wood*- Charles R. 'Charley' Wood (1914-2004) was a pioneer in the American amusement park business and later a philanthropist; he famously teamed up with actor and philanthropist Paul Newman to create the Double H Ranch to provide camp experiences for children with life-threatening illnesses.

'Jesus,' he said, 'that guy Giovanni behind the lines with me in Italy said he was from Malone!' [*Laughs*] In Italy, my [alias] was Giovanni Ganzi; there's no Floyd Dumas in Italy. [*Laughs*] So he said to his wife, 'I've got to go see him,' and jumped in his car and went to Malone. He found my parents on Brown Street, and my parents said, 'No, he now lives in Danbury, Connecticut!' They told him how to get there.

He came and stayed two weeks with us; can you imagine that? [*Laughs*] Everything panned out good. And I used to hear from him here and there. In the last Christmas card I got from him quite a few years ago, he was a steel worker in Chicago working on bridges, but that was the end. I haven't heard from him since; [he probably] died like a lot of them. I don't know of one other person who is still alive in the company that I was in; I don't even run into anybody in my division.

*

The war affected my life, sure, but I would say that I got over it good. Yes, I've thought a lot about it. I used to have wicked dreams, but I wouldn't talk about it for a long, long time. Finally, I sat there with my wife and I said, 'What's the matter with me? They're not teaching this in school. I better start opening my mouth.' So, I went to Hudson Falls High School and I gave [several] talks over the years, and Mr. Rozell tells my story.

Mr. Dumas continued to come to my classroom for years after our first meeting. He passed away in May 2020, at the age of 100.

CHAPTER NINE

The Battery Commander

Abbott Lansing Wiley was born in 1916 and raised on a farm outside a small village on the Hoosic River in Rensselaer County, New York. In 1942 he was commissioned as a 2nd lieutenant and sent to North Africa, and from there to Italy, landing south of Naples as part of the Fifth Army. He was promoted to captain and made a battery commander in the 347th Field Artillery Battalion of the 91st Infantry Division, seeing action in Anzio, Civitavecchia, Grosseto, Pisa, Florence, Bologna, Treviso, Udine, and Trieste. Some of his stories from the war are harrowing, others hilarious—[The wartime experience] sure changes your life. It's funny seeing the guys from Iraq come back and they have stress, but I never had stress. I always wondered about this... [but]

my wife has never seen me laugh and never heard me cry. That's kind of a funny thing, how do you figure that out? It's a mystery. So [the war] changed me.' He was honorably discharged at the end of the war as a major, and as a recipient of the Bronze Star. This interview took place at his home in Valley Falls, New York, in 2013.

Abbott L. Wiley

I attended a district school, which had about twelve, thirteen, or fourteen kids. Then later I went to Lansingburg High School, which involved a trip four miles to the railroad, and then thirteen miles on the railroad to high school. I graduated in 1934. [Instead of college], I worked on a farm; we lived on a dairy farm from age 17, when I got out of high school, to 24. I intended to be a farmer, but in 1940 Congress passed the draft. We had just built a new cow barn on the side of the milking herd, but I decided I wanted to get the year training over with. So on April 3, 1941, I joined up; that year lasted until February 6, 1946. [*Laughs*]

'You're all goddamn Yankees'

I enlisted in the Army—I'd always done rifle shooting, hunting and trapping and all that, so I think it was natural for the Army. For basic training I went to Camp Wheeler, Georgia. They were just building the camp. Our company, half Tennesseans and half New Yorkers, was the first company there. I remember that because a whole bunch of us got sick and we had to go to the hospital, and the hospital was just being built. We were in a big room on cots. I was really sick.

I said to one of the orderlies—it was about 2:00 a.m.—'Boy I don't think I can make it till morning, is there a doctor here?'

He said no.

'Is there a nurse here?'

He said, 'No, I'm the only one.' He'd probably been in the Army a couple of weeks too; he was a medic.

I said, 'I'm in tough shape,' but he said, 'I'll tell you, I shouldn't do this, but when I left home, my grandmother gave me a bottle of medicine'—she was in the mountains of Tennessee— 'and she told me if I ever got sick, to take a couple of teaspoons of this.'

He went and got the medicine and gave me a couple of teaspoons. I don't know what it was, but I went to sleep and didn't wake up till the next morning. So that ended that deal; the next day I went home.

We got along good with those boys from Tennessee. I remember one Sunday, one of the guys said, 'All you guys really ain't that bad, the only trouble is you're all goddamn Yankees.' [*Laughs*] The training was normal, all the rifle training, you know. I always remember—and they talk about women getting into combat today—but when we were at bayonet training, [they taught us that] if you stick a guy with a bayonet, you'd turn it 90 degrees and pull it out. Did you know that?

We were training with the old World War I Springfields back then.[29] We shot with a Springfield, and of course we had a lot of map reading, a

---

[29] *old World War I Springfields*-Model 1903 Springfield Rifle, clip-loaded, 5-shot, bolt-action. It 'kicks like a mule' because the 30.06 cartridge is very powerful. Used in WWI and WWII, one WWI veteran recalled that U.S. troops in France could operate the '03 so rapidly and accurately that the Germans thought Americans had machine guns. Army Times, www.armytimes.com/legacy/rar/1-292308-269297.php.

lot of night marching, compass reading, and so forth.

Next, they sent me to the 113th Infantry [Regiment] at Fort Dix, New Jersey. The commander was Colonel Schwarzkopf, the father of General [Norman] Schwarzkopf, from the 1991 [Gulf] War. While there, they made me a radio operator, which I didn't really know much about. Then after there, we went to the Carolinas for maneuvers. We were there for quite a while; I think that was in the summer. So on the way home from maneuvers, we stopped, I think, in West Virginia overnight. Me being on the radio, I got the message that the Japs had bombed Pearl Harbor. Of course, you write out a notice and give it to the commanding officer. But while we were eating, I couldn't keep it to myself, so the guys got mad at me for starting a rumor. But then we were called out after eating chow on the side of a hill, and a major explained to us what happened, that the Japs had bombed Pearl Harbor, and we probably wouldn't be going home—which we didn't.

'I don't want to be an officer'

Then we went fast back up to New Jersey, walking guard [duty] on the Jersey coast. This is the funny thing about walking guard. See, in January, Hitler's submarines were working off the coast. We were walking guard without any guns, and I wanted to bring my deer rifle from home so we'd have a gun; that's how well-off we were. [*Laughs*] But I remember walking guard one night and seeing five fires out to sea. The Coast Guard tried to get their boats through a six and seven-foot surf, to go out and pick up what I presumed would be people.

Well, then, this was the headquarters battery that we were in. My job was just the radio. They were lousy radios compared to today. I was a corporal; our first sergeant was Sergeant Monaghan. He'd been in the Army six years—a short Irishman with black hair. He wanted me to be a corporal. To do that I had to take a test—a written test. Then I had to go before a board of officers. I took the written test, and then I went before four officers. There was a captain, and the rest were field officers. So because they were all from the city, they found out I was from the farm, and they were kidding me about making hay and milking cows and that kind of stuff.

Finally they said, 'What do you think of the outfit?' I said, 'Do you want me to really tell you what I think of the outfit?' They were all for that. I said, 'The first thing, we're walking guard and it's so cold, [but] we don't have any clothes. I wear everything that's issued to me, and half of some other guys' [clothes when I'm] on guard. The eats are leftovers from World War I, and they're also small. And another thing—I have an engineer in our company, and if we're going to win the war he should be in the engineers. There's also a telephone man, and he should be in the Signal Corps.'

Then, I shouldn't have said this, because these guys were all field officers so they were a little out of shape—

I said, 'We're really not in shape for an infantry outfit, we should be doing more calisthenics and walking.'

So I was dismissed.

When I went back, First Sergeant Monaghan said, 'How'd you make out?'

I said the written test wasn't too bad, but then they asked me what I thought of the outfit.

He said, 'Well, what'd you tell them?'

When I finished, I thought he was going to have a stroke. He sat down in a chair and for two minutes he couldn't stop laughing.

He said, 'In all my life, that's the funniest thing I've ever heard, you telling them what you thought of the outfit.' He said, 'You know what you've done? You made'—you know what it is—'the shit list. I've got to get you out of here.'

I said, 'Well, get me in the Marines.'

He said, 'No, I ain't going to get you in the Marines. I'm going to put you in for Officer School.'

I said, 'I don't want to be an officer!' He said, 'You let me handle it.'

Well, I had learned enough from being a private in the Army that if a captain or a lieutenant tells you to do something, you could always get out of it by telling them you didn't understand it. But if the first sergeant tells you to do something, you better do it, because he could make life so miserable for you the next two days you'd wish you'd never been born.

A couple of days later somebody said, 'The first sergeant wants to see you.'

I went up and he said, 'I got some papers here for you to sign. You better read them over.' It was for me to go to school at Fort Knox for Armored School. I signed the papers and that went along for two or three days. Then he wanted to see me again.

He said, 'Now this afternoon, you've got to be down to 113th headquarters. You've got to meet Colonel Schwarzkopf. And for gosh sake, get the mud off your shoes, and if you have a clean pair of pants put them on, and be shaved, and you'd better brush up on your 'Yes sirs' and 'No sirs'.'

At two o'clock I was down at headquarters. There was a corporal there and he said, 'What do you want?'

I said, 'I was told to report here.' He stuck his head in the door and said, 'Go on in.' I went in, and standing behind the desk was this rather medium-sized man, and he had a mustache under his nose just like Adolf Hitler's.

I said, 'Private reporting as ordered, sir.'

He said, 'Sit down.'

I sat down, and he stood up and said, 'The other day you took a test for corporal. You took a written test'—I found out the written test was what he used to give the New Jersey State Police when they were trying to get in—'You passed the written test, very highly. But on the oral test before the officers you didn't do so good. Tell me about it.'

So I told him exactly what happened, and he probably already knew it. But after, he said, 'Well, you're dismissed,' so that was it. I was glad to get rid of that. But then three days later, the first sergeant wanted to see me again.

He said, 'Here, I have a pass for you. You can go home for three days, and when you come back you're going to Fort Knox.'

So it took a day to get home, and I was home a day, and then I went back. When I reported back, he said everything changed. The Army said I was too high in math! [The first sergeant] said, 'You're going to Fort Sill. I've got your train tickets here, I've got your meal tickets here, pack your stuff and we'll take you up to the railroad and you'll be off.'

That was the last I was on the East Coast. I don't know how long I was on the train, but it probably took a day or more to get to Officer School at Fort Sill. I remember when we got there, the officer said, 'We've got a year's worth [of work] to do in three months. The day starts at five, and ends at eleven. You never walk; if you're going anywhere, you will run!'

That was it. So three months later I got out of there, as a second lieutenant. Then I came home and I had orders to go to Oregon. They were activating the 91st Infantry Division, and all the new guys were going in there. They had jobs for second lieutenants and captains and everything else. I went there and this is a funny thing. They took me out of the infantry and put me in the artillery because of my math [score]! But when I got to the artillery, because I was from the infantry, they put me in service battery, which I was upset about. But later in combat, I realized that I had the best deal; I was on the go, by my own self, and not staying in one place.

Overseas

[They sent me overseas] in the first part of '44. I know [in] the 346th and 347th Battalions, we had all the guns and equipment on one train. It came straight through to Newport News, [Virginia]; it never stopped. There, a couple of days later, they brought all the troops in and they had to check all the equipment on the boat. Then in 21 days the whole division landed in Oran. [We went over in a convoy]; it was a lot of ships. The captain would let us go up in the lookout, and as far as you could see to the front, right, left, and rear, there were ships. I think they went down to the West Indies, and across to Africa, up along the coast of Africa, through the Strait of Gibraltar, to Oran. What we were supposed to do there was train for landing operations, and of course the rumor was that we were going to land in southern France. We were there a month or so. Oran had been taken, between the British and Americans.

One little incident happened there. Our army had to capture Oran from the French. I know when the guys were unloading our guns they dropped one, so it bounced. The colonel was looking overboard and yelled about it. Well, they dropped the next one so it bounced a little bit more, and I remember the colonel grabbed a carbine and shot four or five times over their heads; that ended the dropping.

From there, the Navy took us across the Mediterranean to Italy. We thought we were going to southern France, but in the middle of the Mediterranean, they opened the orders, and we were to go to Italy. Another little incident I remember was the captain of the boat said the officers could eat in the officers' mess—I was a captain. He said when we did, we needed ties. Our Colonel Lynn said to him, 'Just where in the hell do you think we got ties? Everything we have is on our backs.'

I remember climbing down that big rope ladder—it was a hundred feet wide—down to the landing craft. This was near Naples; the British army had taken Naples. So we got in the landing craft and I always thought the guy was afraid of getting mud on his boat, because he let us out in about four feet of water. When we got to shore we were all pretty wet.

Nothing really happened until we got north of Rome; the [Allies] had taken Rome [on June 4]. I remember north of Rome we got news that the landing on June 6 from England to northern France had started.

Then we were really on the Italian Campaign. The war in Italy was mainly artillery and sniper fire; there was a lot of artillery. The British had the line, and it takes a little while to prepare for battle—you've got to get a lot of ammunition up and that stuff, you know. The British Eighth Army had a lot of different nationalities; there were Canadians, Gurkhas, Sikhs. The Gurkhas were from northern India, and the Sikhs were big, tall guys with beards. There were Hindus. The Gurkhas, their religion said nothing would happen to them until the time came. I remember one instance, I was going across this bridge, and the Germans were shelling it, so we stopped and didn't get through. But the Gurkhas came up and walked right through it! They didn't believe anything would happen because everything was predetermined. The Sikhs had their own live goats with them and they didn't have utensils, just a big bowl where everything was cooked; you used your fingers. They asked me to have something to eat with them one night—you just reach in the bowl and pick something out, and that did away with all the extra utensils!

Three Strikes

I don't know how much time elapsed there, but we were to take over for another division that had been on the line. I'll tell you this, this is a funny story. [For] a new outfit going on the line, the custom was for the new officers to go up for a day with the other guys, the old outfit. I think it was the 34th Division we were replacing. An officer from the 34th took us out, and we were driving through the countryside—no noise, no nothing. Finally he stops. He said, 'This is as far as I'm going, but that ridge over there'—about half a mile away—'that's German territory. If I were you, I would sit around here and listen to see what's going on.' There was no battle noise. It's different than on TV when they've got guns and racket, bombs bursting—there was no sound, no nothing. I was with another captain, Captain Ben, from our headquarters battery.

So we sat there probably for an hour and there was nothing there. Between us and that ridge, there was a house. We thought we'd go over. So we went over to the house and were there maybe a half hour—again, no noise, nothing. This house was dug into the side of a hill and it slanted out, so I thought I would go around the back of the house and climb up on the roof to see what was going on. There was a red chimney there, I remember. I just scrambled up the house on my belly and got up next to the chimney; my ear was up against the chimney, looking around, still no noise, nothing. All of a sudden near me on the chimney there was a little ping, and little bits of mortar hit my cheek! Then I heard a sound—I didn't need an education to tell me that was a bullet! So I scrambled back down the roof and went inside and told Ben what happened. We stayed there for a while. Then there was a little window in this house that had little panes, about four or five inches square. So after a while I thought I had to see out of them, so I got along the right side of the window to look out.

That went on for four or five minutes. All of a sudden, the next pane over from me disappeared! So I got out of there.

Captain Ben said, 'Did you ever play baseball?'

I said yes, I'd played a lot of baseball. He said, 'If I were you, I'd watch for the third strike.' So anyway, we didn't do much else; that was the first time I was under fire.

That afternoon we wandered around a little and ran into a squad of Japanese out of Hawaii, the 442nd Regiment.[30] They had been on patrol that night, I think, and were all sleeping in a ditch—they had their blankets over them, and had one guard. This guy was sitting on the chest of a big, dead German, eating his K-rations. The German had been hit with a shell, and the little [guy] said to me, 'Boy, this guy really got hit, didn't he?' I thought to myself he must be pretty hungry to be sitting there [on top of the dead body], eating that K-ration.

Afterwards we went on back to our Jeep, and that night, we were going to sleep in a ditch by the

---

[30] *the 442nd Regiment-* A highly decorated unit made up of mostly Japanese Americans, some of whose families were in internment camps.

Jeep. I was pretty near sleep and I looked up, and silhouetted by the sky is somebody who says something. I look up and I can see he's got an M1 rifle, so I knew I was okay.

He said, 'Look, guys, you'd better get out of here. Intelligence tells us the Germans are supposed to attack here today, we've got it covered with artillery and mortar fire. We're pulling out and leaving it to them.' So we pulled back and then the next day we went to our outfits.

Strafed

Maybe I should tell you about Sergeant Riley and the German Messerschmitt. One day—Sergeant Riley was one of my better men—one day I remember asking him to do some detail. I said, 'Take your friend Rayban to do this.'

He said, 'Oh no, I can't take Rayban, he's reading the Bible.'

I said, 'Reading the Bible?'

He said, 'Yes, last night while he was sleeping a shell hit terribly close to him, so ever since daylight he's been reading the Bible. I can't use him.'

I said, 'Okay, get somebody else, I'm glad somebody's reading the Bible.'

Then one day I was talking to Sergeant Riley out along the road. He's got his back up the road. About half a mile up the road, around a bend, comes a German fighter. They had two machine guns in each wing and [the pilot] had the tracers lined up on the road, so there's just a sheet of flame coming down the road. I jumped in the ditch and Riley jumped on top of me. It was only seconds when bullets were hitting around us and digging up the dirt. This is the funny thing about the mind: while I lay in the ditch, my mind returned to when I was nine or ten years old, and we had a terrible hailstorm at home. The wind was blowing at about the same angle as these bullets were coming. Every time a hailstone would hit the ground, it would splash water; the only difference was these bullets were splashing dirt. Anyway, after probably forty seconds, I said to Riley, 'Get off of me.' So he stood up. Knowing that he had his back to the plane, he couldn't see it; and since it was traveling the speed of sound, he probably couldn't hear it. I said, 'What the hell did you jump in there for?' He said, 'I jumped because you jumped.' That's a trained soldier.

Shelled

Another time, my battery was in this area about two or three acres. Between Florence and Bologna was all mountains, and there was one road—Route 65, it was a good road—and going up it were three infantry divisions: the 85th, 88th, and 91st. When we moved into this area, the firing batteries were off to the right, in front of us was a big hill, and to the left of the hill was what used to be a path—probably for cattle, but the infantry used it for their Jeeps—then off to the left there was a river. Across the river on the other side were other divisions. When we moved in there, I got a message at ten o'clock at night that nobody's on your left, and Route 65 was behind us. So I got up and looked out, and boy, it was terribly dark. You couldn't see anything. So I thought, 'I don't think the Germans can see anything more than I can.' I knew my sentries would be holed up in the cab of a truck, and they didn't like guys running around who weren't supposed to be there. So I thought we could wait till morning, so I went to sleep.

Everything went along, but one thing I did after being there for a few days: I looked in some of the foxholes and they had snow and mud in them, so I gave the first sergeant orders that I would be around before dark, and every man should have a full foxhole. That was one of the best orders I ever gave. I had a tent, probably six feet wide and eight feet long. There were two lieutenants and I, and we were playing some kind of foolish game with matches. We had a candle. We had about probably six or seven months of good artillery fire, so we were pretty well-tuned to artillery. While we were playing there, we heard a heavy gun sound, and then we heard the shell. I'll never forget, all three of us froze, because there was no use in running. It seemed like it almost skidded against the tent and went into the ground; it was a dud. I always said if I ever ran into the slave-laborer that made that fuse, I would kiss his rear end in St. Peter's Square. [*Laughs*]

Then they started shelling us, and that went on for six minutes; boy, that was heavy stuff. After a little while there was a pause, and then I thought I'd better see what's happening. But then they started shelling us again, another six or seven minutes. After that, there was a stop, and I thought, I'd better get out of this hole, you're a damn coward, you've got to get out and see where your men are. I started out on the right side of my area and I passed a couple [of men] who were in foxholes. You know when you're being shelled in a foxhole, you only take up about six inches of the bottom. So as I went on, a shell landed in front of me—now this is big stuff—and dirt went all over me, shrapnel went past my ear, and I don't really know what happened.

The next thing I know, there was a light shining in my eye and I came to after a while. It seemed like dawn was breaking in the east. I realized I was in a hole with another man. He was a Montana sheep herder. He was snoring, and I couldn't believe that; how could he be snoring with all the shelling going on? Finally, I came to a little bit more, and I went out across the battery area and I ran into one of my sergeants. He tried to tell me something; his lips moved but I remember no noise. So I went on and ran into more people and had the same problem: they tried to tell me things but there was no noise. I thought, 'Boy, these guys are really shook up.' Finally I found a guy that could talk, and he said—one of the sergeants had dragged me back into the hole with the other guy who must've been knocked out—they shelled us two more times for six or seven minutes, and only one guy was wounded and we got him to the hospital. I thought, boy, somebody knew we were behind that hill.

Finally I got my Jeep driver and I went up and told Colonel Lynn I had to move, so he said find a better place if you can. So I looked around but couldn't find a better place, so I sent a truck back to pick up sandbags. I told the guys we were going to stay here, but we're going to sandbag ourselves in. After a while, probably ten o'clock, the truck came back with sandbags. We started sandbagging where we slept. Some of them we dug into the hill. I said I wanted three feet of sandbags around the sleeping tents. I got right in and helped them. I probably didn't let anybody sit around because I thought work would be the thing to do. I remember it was noon, or afternoon, and this Corporal

Slater was holding a sandbag and I had a shovel pouring in the sand. He looks up at me and says, 'Now we know why you've been such a son of a bitch all morning. We feel better already.'

After that we did pretty well, but a day or so later, down the corner of this hill comes an infantry Jeep and they've got a German officer as a prisoner. I couldn't believe my eyes—here's a German officer in full dress, with a hat on, full uniform, everything, a monocle in his right eye, his boots are as black and polished as could be. I looked at my boots, they were mud and snow, I'd probably had my trousers on for three weeks, but anyway, I thought I must be in the wrong army. [*Laughs*] They went on with him, but a day or so later a platoon of infantry had been brought back to go get some new clothes. The quartermaster had an exchange back there, where you'd get a gallon of water and you could shower and change your clothes with some other outfit that'd had it done before. Anyway, when they came back through, the platoon was all jumbled up, and I ran out and told the lieutenant to spread his men out, because when they turn that corner they may get a shell from

German artillery. He came back with the dumbest answer I'd ever heard—he said, 'We're not afraid.' Twenty minutes later, the medics brought four guys out of there on litters. Whether they were killed or just wounded I never knew, but that lieutenant was really nuts not to spread those guys out. You should never take a chance if you're an officer; if you have any little bit of information, use it. I had told him what might happen, but now there were four guys gone.

Money

Two-thirds of the way through the Italian Campaign, our battalion had fired a million shells. I know the Germans fired half that many back at us. Another time, in December [1944], the Army set up the payroll, which was real silly, because there was nothing to buy. It would be Italian lira they would pay us with. I went around and paid all the guys, because you couldn't call them together—you kept them separated as much as possible. The guys were dug in the side of the hill with their tents, so I went down to them. When I got near the next-to-the last tent—you've got to always play your hunches—I was in the tent and got those guys paid, and said to them, 'Now you scram out of here and tell those guys in the last tent to come on over here.' So they came over and I paid them. One guy was missing, and it happened to be Corporal Slater. He'd been on guard that night and he was sleeping in the tent. So I sent his sergeant over to get him. So he goes in the tent, wakes him up, brings him outside the tent, and they're about eight feet outside the tent when a shell hit directly inside that tent. Because the guys were protected by those three feet of sandbags outside the tent, they didn't get hit with any shrapnel. So Slater came over to me and said, 'Captain, you keep the money.'

I said, 'No, I want to tell you something—this is the luckiest money you will ever have. Please don't spend it, just keep it.'

[This brings me to] the value of money and another story. When I played baseball [before the war], there were six of us, and we had an old car [to get around in], and we had an accident. The guy [we collided with] wanted some money because we had bent his fender. Between six guys, we had six quarters and one fifty-cent piece which we gave him to fix up his car. The opposite of that was when we got to the Po River to try to cross it. The engineers had been trying to work to build a pontoon bridge. The Germans had three fighters and they kept strafing them, so they had to quit during the daytime and wait until night; we were all waiting to cross for a mile around there. The Germans had [left] a lot of equipment there, but they'd gotten their troops across [before the bridge was destroyed]. So each one of my men either had a German horse or German car that they were monkeying around with. But there was one big covered truck there, and the doors were closed. I remember one of the guys started opening it, and I yelled, 'Don't touch it! It may be booby trapped.'

We hooked a rope on it, tied it to my Jeep, got a hundred feet away, and opened it. It was full of money, Italian lira—the same money Uncle Sam was paying us! The guys had piles of it three feet high, burning it to warm their hands! There were Italian citizens there going crazy, like 'here's these crazy Americans burning money to warm their hands!' This I learned: money, if you can't use it for something, it's not worth any more than the *Troy Record*.[31] We better leave it at that.

Peach Pie

I'll tell you a funny story. Going up Route 65, through the Apennine Mountains, there was no motorized stuff, just infantry and artillery. Of the three divisions, there would be two on the line; the artillery would stay in line, but they would change the infantry. This one time, for one reason or another, in the 91st, the artillery came back, and the next morning one of my lieutenants—we must've been five or six miles behind the line—said, 'There are orchards here, and they've got peaches.'

So I beat it over to the mess sergeant and said, 'Suppose I got some peaches, could you make peach pie?'

He said, 'I think I could. I might have to substitute something but I'll try it.'

So I said to Nick Marcella, who spoke Italian, 'Take some trading stuff and go get some peaches.'

He came back with about a bushel and a half of peaches. The kitchen help went over to start

---

[31] *Troy Record*-local newspaper

peeling them, and I went over and sat down with my jack knife and was helping them peel peaches. It didn't take as long as I thought, because everyone would come over and say, 'What are you guys doing?' and I'd say, 'Can't you see we're peeling peaches? Don't you have a knife?' So they'd help us. It wasn't long before we had all the peaches peeled. Sergeant Hall, the mess sergeant, had them all in the square pans, ready to put in the ovens.

So probably twenty minutes later he came to me and said, 'I can't bake the pies, because I got orders that the general is going to inspect the kitchens.' We were in the back. He said, 'What'll I do?' I figured we might have a few hours, so I said bake the pies. So he started baking the pies. Then probably twenty or thirty minutes later, who comes driving in the yard but the general, my Colonel Lynn, and of course one of the general's staff and the driver. The general drives up to my kitchen, hops out, walks up to the kitchen, and is met by Sergeant Hall, the mess sergeant, an old army man. The general says, 'Sergeant, I've come to inspect your kitchen.' Sergeant Hall says, 'But I'm baking pies.' The general says, 'Baking pies?' He turns to

Colonel Lynn, and by that time I'd appeared on the scene, and he said [to Colonel Lynn], 'Didn't you tell this man I was coming to inspect the kitchen?' He said yes, there was no argument. Then he turned to me and wanted an explanation. I told him just what happened. He seemed a little bit perturbed. Now this general was a full-blooded Iroquois Indian, and I don't think he was known for his humor. I think he was really perturbed. I would say on a number one to ten, he was perturbed about a ten.

Anyway, he went back to his Jeep and got in. Colonel Lynn got in and he wasn't smiling either. Then when they drove out, even the driver spun the wheels. I always think the reason the general was so perturbed, that morning he probably got up and went to get a cup of coffee, and a new man on the job gave him lukewarm coffee and the dried eggs weren't up to swath; he couldn't find his kitchen inspecting gloves; his staff told him he had to inspect the kitchens; he gets out and there's dust on the star; and he's driving over three miles to the 347th Battalion over roads that Julius Caesar had built and no one had done anything with them since. He picks up the colonel and probably thinks, 'Of the 300 or 400 kitchens in the Fifth Army, I had to pick this dummy who's baking pies.' Well, the next day Colonel Lynn says, 'Well, you came the nearest to getting court-martialed of anyone I ever knew.' I know the general was after the colonel three different times—I learned through the grapevine—to relieve me of command. I always wondered why the general didn't relieve me. But you know around a general's headquarters, there's usually a *Stars and Stripes* reporter, or one from the Fifth Army. I can see the front page of *Stars and Stripes*— 'Captain gets relieved of command for giving his men peach pies.' [*Laughs*] Well, I never heard more about the peach pies till Colonel Lynn—he and I had always exchanged Christmas cards—said coming back on the boat—he came from the upper crust of the Army—that the funniest thing that happened during the whole Italian Campaign was the peach pies [incident]! It must've been a tale the colonel told, because on the Christmas cards, his wife would write out, 'Merry Christmas to the man who thought enough of his men to give them peach pies.'

On the Road

I'll tell you a little story about my Jeep driver. He was about 18 or 19 years old, and I think the reason First Sergeant Weiss talked me into using him was because he could never find him to do any work. But anyway, we got along well. When we moved, my job was to get everybody organized—the kitchen, the latrine—and see that was done and that they were spread out, and he would find a place for our Jeep. Anyway, this little town where Highway 65 went through, on the outside of it, [the road] went around a hill. Out at about eleven o'clock across the way, about three quarters of a mile, the Germans had an 88mm gun dug into the middle of the mountain. The 88 was probably the best gun of any army in all of WWII. It was a 3-inch gun, and they used it for anti-aircraft, they used it against tanks, and they would shoot at a man with it, because they figured if there was one man there was usually another. Well, they had an area outside this town that was under observation and had a man on this gun. Whenever a truck would go across this 200 to 250-yard area, he would shoot at them. After a while, we knew what that area was. So when we got up there we would stop, look for shell holes, and then go as fast as we could over that area. But this morning, for some reason or another—I must've been asleep—the sun was out bright and early, and we were about a quarter of a mile across there when I woke up. My driver was only about a quarter of the way across, and I said, 'Get this damn Jeep moving.' Just then, about thirty or forty feet ahead of us, a shell landed in the road. Edge [the driver] says, 'Look, if we'd been going faster, we'd have caught that one.' So we got to the other end and we had a one-way discussion that never again would a shell land in front of us while we were going over there.

I got even with him a few days later. Now down below us was a house. Edge and I had taken it over—it was right near the shelling but it was near the front. The Italian houses were built in the side of a hill. There would be an entryway and a middle room, then another room, I guess a bedroom. The Germans did a lot of stuff that seemed to be by clockwork. One day, below this house at about four o'clock, they dropped in one shell. Then they moved up to the road with the whole battery shelling. So this one shell would give them an idea of where they were hitting, and of course the other guns would move their sights with that gun. The second day the same thing happened at about four o'clock—why I happen to remember that, I don't know. But then another day, later, for some reason or another, I was either reading or doing some paperwork in this house, in the room to the front—it was the most open. I looked at my watch and it was about four o'clock. I thought, maybe the German data is a bit better today; they'd been eighty yards below the house, then they were forty. So I moved out of that room and Edge was in the middle room, and I said, 'Edge, come on out of this room, maybe this guy's data is a little better today.' But he didn't move. So I got to the entrance room, which was right off the ground. I got there, and who runs by me but Edge, and he's covered in mortar. He said, 'You can't believe it, that room you just left ain't there anymore.' That was pretty lucky. Just playing hunches, I guess.

When we were attacking or something there would be more artillery from the Germans. During one period, I think the maintenance unit of our battalion changed 155 tires in eight days, from Monday to Monday. See, a shell could come and hit near a truck and not do too much damage, but it would blow the tires from the shrapnel. One little thing I probably should've had, but this Sergeant Riley—the one that was with me with the strafing incident—I remember him this one day, too. Our trucks used to go down through Florence, then on to Leghorn, the depot, to pick up ammunition for the artillery. They would have four or five tons on the trucks. Coming back through, the first one got hit with a shell—it blew his tire and the driver jumped out and left the truck there. So the guys behind him were all stacked up, although they'd been spaced. They were all there and the Germans had been doing quite a bit of shelling in that area, right at the spot where the trucks were. So I looked and I thought when it got dark we'd get the trucks out of there—the other drivers had to go out too because they couldn't move. After a while, I got a note from headquarters to move the trucks. Well, I took a look again, and the shells were coming in pretty heavy. I thought, 'If headquarters wants the trucks moved, they can come right out and move them themselves.'

So that didn't last very long—half an hour later they said I had to move the trucks because they wanted to get tanks through. Not thinking—Sergeant Riley happened to be there—I said, 'Sergeant, we've got to move the trucks.'

And he said, 'Captain, I don't have the guts to send a man in there.'

I said, 'Sergeant, if I go, suppose you can find a couple of men?'

He said yes. So, he came back with a couple of men—they weren't too enthused about it.

But I said, 'We'll go over as near as we can, because you know with shelling in an area, there's dispersion.'

So we got as near as we could, and I picked out what trucks we were going to take. Now these Germans do everything by clock; we had to check them. So I took my watch out, and for two minutes, the shells would be coming in real fast, and for two minutes, they'd be slack. Then two more minutes there'd be shells coming in fast, and two minutes they'd be slack.

So I said, 'The next time after shelling, I'm going to yell 'Go!' We've got two minutes to get the trucks.' And we got the trucks. I should've written up a citation for those guys, but we were so happy to get out of there we didn't bother with any citations.

*

New Officers

At the end of the war we were crossing the Po [River]. The 10th Mountain [Division] was on the other side, along with the 92nd, which was Eleanor Roosevelt's division, the all-colored troops. Most of the officers were white, but it was a colored division. The 10th Mountain was over on our left. At the end of the war, we were combat teams, and I remember we had a regiment of infantry and a battalion of artillery. The orders were to go up this road and go as fast and far as you can. Pay no attention to anybody on the right or left and just get through the German army; if you can get behind them, the war will be over. Well, in front of us it seemed like there was a bigger unit of Germans retreating, and they would leave out units of rear guards once in a while. They would stop us with firefights. This one time, they stopped for a little firefight. Of course, the artillery is in a line, one behind the other. I remember talking with the guys, bullshitting with them, you know. I had new lieutenants and new replacements. This new lieutenant had been in the Pentagon all during the war.

Everybody knew the ones you had the most trouble with were the ones who'd just come in. The old soldiers knew to stay right on that road. Out about ninety degrees to the road was this wind-break, out probably a hundred yards. Out at the end of this wind-break to the right this lieutenant called me out. He'd heard something back at the Pentagon about living off the land and thought there was a pig or a sheep or something. He had his pistol out and he calls me up, so I'm thinking that there's some animal out there. I walk right out of the hedgerow, a little unconcerned. I get to the end of the hedgerow, and off to my left, probably twenty-five or thirty yards, is a German gun emplacement manned by two German soldiers, each with a light machine now aimed at me. Now, there's 2,500 to 3,000 men within a quarter mile of me, and [these Germans] really didn't want to start a war. But the only thing I could think of, I remember sliding into second base when I played baseball and the umpire would stretch out his hands, and that's what I did. [*Gestures with arms out*] They laid the guns on the edge of the earthworks, and I waved this lieutenant back to our column. When we got back, I explained to him that if he wanted to go get himself killed that was his business, but to call me out there, that was a different thing. I said he should stay in line there or I might shoot him myself!

I hadn't gotten over that, then this other new guy was of German descent. He hands me this German Luger, and says, 'You're a captain, here's a gun for you.' It's all engraved with gold.

I said, 'Where in the devil did you get a gun like that?'

He said, 'Over here in the gully.'

He said there was a German colonel that wanted to surrender to an officer. You know there were two departments of the German army, the old German Army and the Nazis.

So I said, 'Did you bring him in?'

He said, 'No, I shot him.'

I felt bad about that. I was all ready to ball him out for shooting a guy when I realized they had sent him over from the States to shoot Germans; so that was that.

'A column of German infantry'

I no more than got over that and the firefight had stopped. Up the road, there was a town about three miles up. Colonel Lynn, the artillery commander, said, 'I think we'll be up to that town. I want you to go up there and pick out a spot for the battalion to come in.'

So I went out to the right of this main road, found a dirt road, and got to the town. There were some civilians there and they were glad to see us, but I went outside the town, found a good place for the battalion, and after looking that over, I went back to the road, and who comes by but an infantry scout. He's all alone and he's coming back—we were on kind of a ridge. He said, 'Watch it, guys, that valley there is full of Germans.' So we went back to the town.

The road I came in on and the main road come together in a Y. So I situated there because I had been told to stay there till the battalion got there. The townspeople wanted to talk, but it started getting late. I told them to get inside and stay inside, because I had a machine gunner on the Jeep, and if we saw anything move [after dark] we may shoot. I told them to stay inside and if there was any firing, to get in the cellar or something. It's pretty dusky, and who comes in to pick us up but this Captain Ben. He calls me up and says, 'Wiley, what the hell are you doing up here? Follow me.' Captain Ben was a guy who always smoked cigars, which I thought was a funny thing. Actually, most of the time he was out of cigars, but he had about a third of it in his mouth.

I said, 'What the hell are you so excited about?'

[Captain Ben] said, 'Here I was trying to get something to eat and the colonel [ordered me to head out and look for you]. I went back and found out which way you went. I got my Jeep and driver and started up the road. In front of me was a column of vehicles, so I told my driver to pass them. In the dusk, we got about halfway up the column, and I looked up and everyone had a German helmet on. I told my driver to jump this ditch and we went around and got up to you!' That was probably a [whole] column of German infantry. Can you imagine? I always wondered what happened to that cigar in his mouth. [*Laughs*] They were still moving north to the Alps. I think about three or four days later we got word that they were surrendering.

*

No Flags

At the end I was at Gorizia, which is on the Yugoslav border. There was just a little creek between us and Yugoslavia. Everything was as quiet as could be. It was a funny thing, no celebration, [no flag waving]. Everyone wonders about flags; I don't ever remember seeing an American flag in all of combat because you were just telling the Germans where you were.

I think they were planning to send us to Japan. That's what happened to me. They had an order that the captains who had so many points could go home. I had about a hundred more points, so I said to my colonel, 'Well, it looks like I'll be going home.'

He said, 'No, you won't be going home. If I have to go to Japan, you're going to go.'

But this I never understood either. I was a captain all the time. We were still in Italy, getting ready for a boat to come in and pick us up to go to Japan. I remember I'm sitting on a cot talking to Captain Ben. A German prisoner walked by. He said the war was over.

I said, 'How the hell do you know?'

He said, 'It came in on my radio.'

The boat had come in to take us to Japan, and he was two days late because he'd stayed in New York to wait for milk to arrive from Wisconsin. The next day we loaded on the boat and it turned around and brought us home. [So, in late] 1945 I was home and on furlough. Then I had to go back and help deactivate the division. I met Ruth and then thirty days later we got married. That was 67 years ago. [*Laughter in room from wife and others*] Then we went back to deactivate the division and get all the stuff that we took overseas. Somebody had to sign for it, you know; the battery commanders and so forth had to go back.

Rank

I'm getting out of the Army and on my papers they have, 'Major.' I said, 'Jesus, don't put me down as major! In New York State if I'm a captain I get $250, if I'm a field officer I don't get anything.'

He says, 'You've been a major for a long time.'

I said, 'I have?'

He said, 'I got the orders right here.'

I never got the orders. But the only thing I can figure is when my colonel said I wasn't going home, a major wouldn't get to go home. I was probably in for major then and didn't even know it! The paperwork going overseas would be separated from us and was all screwed up. Then again I owed the [government] some money because my sister was getting an allotment from home and they paid me $250 for my allotment. The finance officer down in Camp Rucker, Alabama, said, 'Here's all the papers where you owe the Army.'

I said, 'Is this all the paper?'

He said, 'Yes.' So I threw them in the wastepaper basket and never heard from them again. That must've been the orders.

*

I got discharged February 6, 1946. I came back to New York,
I stayed around the farm. It was about Thanksgiving time, I guess. Then this guy that owned this business in Valley Falls, New York, he and his partner wanted to sell the thing and came to the house two or three times to see if we wanted to be involved in buying it. Of course, there were sixteen million guys in the Army and there weren't going to be too many jobs [when they got out]. That's when we bought this business in Valley Falls. It was a feed and coal business, something new. This is a funny thing. When I got out of the Army I came to Albany, got a bus up to the end of the bus line, and walked home. Then I stopped at my brother's place at the farm in the morning for breakfast. I said to him, 'Boy, these eggs don't have any taste.' He was quite insulted. Of course, the eggs we had had in the army were probably six months old; they were dried.

*

I've been a life member of the VFW and the Legion. I had so many new things with being in business. Then I was in politics. First they wanted me to run for supervisor, so I was supervisor of the town for six years. Then we were running this business with my brother, and I was president. Then we moved over to where we are now with what was a wholesale hardware and lumber center. That was a lot of work. Then I got involved in the county legislature, I was finance chairman. Then I was a Hudson Valley [Community College] trustee. According to my wife, I spent a lot of time away from home.

[The wartime experience] sure changes your life. It's funny seeing the guys from Iraq come back and they have stress, but I never had stress. I always wondered about this. When I went to district school they used to call me the 'laughing fool.' When I went to high school, under my picture they had a bit of mirth, and in the history they said, *'Whenever there was a bunch of guys having a lot of fun and raising a deuce and laughing, Ab would be there.'* And probably two years ago, I met a girl working in the bank whose grandmother had been a friend. I said, 'Remind your grandmother you saw me.' She came back a couple of weeks later and said her grandmother was so happy, that I was always the one laughing and having a good time. Now, my wife has never seen me laugh and never heard me cry. That's kind of a funny thing, how do you figure that out? It's a mystery. So it's changed me.[32]

Mr. Wiley passed away at home at the age of 100 years and eight months in August 2017.

---

[32] *So it's changed me*-On the day that Mr. Wiley passed, his grandson wrote: 'For the rest of his life, he would see the world through the lenses of that experience of the war. He believed that every issue could be addressed through the application of some lesson he'd learned in the army or would draw parallels to an experience during the war. He treated that experience as the source of wisdom that guided him throughout his life. He was even shaped in his personality: he had had a reputation as something of a joker before the war, but afterward, although a wry comment might drop from his lips from time to time, he had taken on a much more serious, stoic demeanor.'

CHAPTER TEN

The Map Maker

He sits at home with his wife, lively and talkative on a beautiful spring day in upstate New York, bantering back and forth with his interviewers. A history buff with a specialty in the Civil War, Anthony Battillo has enjoyed composing paintings and illustrations of important moments in American history, and proudly holds up his work to be photographed before the interview begins.

Before he enlisted in the regular army, he was with the 14th New York Regiment, a Brooklyn National Guard unit with a history that went back to the Civil War. 'I was part of it; there was an awful lot of pride in that outfit, even eighty years later.' Later, he would paint the 'Red-Legged Devils' in battle scenes. 'They started off from Brooklyn in 1861 with about 900 men, and when they came back, there were fewer than 100 men marched in the parade. The rest of them were *either captured, dead, or missing.' Today, some of his paintings reside at Gettysburg, the site of the battle that became the turning point of the Civil War, and where the 14th fought tenaciously. In 2002, Mr. Battillo was in his 85th year when he gave this interview about his own wartime experiences in Italy.*

Anthony Battillo

I was in Africa and Italy. Because I had experience in drawing, they took me out of the infantry and made me a map maker, making map overlays. I was an artillery officer in Headquarters, IV Corps, 5th Army. Mark Clark. I know the importance of those overlays. It tells you things that the map doesn't. Everything changes, and you can't keep changing maps, so the overlays tell you what's going on.

Just think of this—the field commanders, they're in a strange country, in the dark. They don't know where they're going sometimes. It's not chaos, but it's a tough job. So what our job was in my section was engineering maps. We used aerial photographs, and we had patrols going out, and all the intelligence would come back to us, and we would put it right on those maps. We'd have 'bridge out,' 'road closed,' whatever it was. And we had a hand-operated machine [*makes cranking motion with hand*] to make copies of the overlays on tracing paper. Now those maps were referenced, and the coordinates were referenced, and they were copied and given to the commanders, and they put it over their map, and they knew 'don't go this way, go this way.' Somebody had to tell them where to go. And the overall head, for example, in our case, was the colonel in charge of the engineering, roads and bridges. So before anything went out he had to approve everything. And it was a responsibility that we had to take seriously. Sometimes he'd send us up closer to the line so we'd get the latest bit of intelligence to put on those overlays.

*

I was born in Brooklyn, New York, on June 7, 1917. I went to high school in Manhattan, and I attended the Art Students League in Manhattan for a couple of years, then I went to the National Tech Institute to study mechanical engineering drawing.

When I first heard about Pearl Harbor, I was out duck hunting on the north shore of Long Island with some friends, and we didn't have a radio in the car. When we got finished hunting, and were coming back, we had just been talking about the Japanese envoys in Washington, hoping that they could make some kind of a deal. And then I got home for suppertime, and my sister-in-law said to me, 'We're at war.' And I said, 'What?' That's how I found out.

I was surprised that they attacked, but I wasn't surprised that we were going to be in the war; I knew we were going to, sooner or later. But Pearl Harbor was as big a shock to my generation as 9/11, really it was very bad. When you look at the casualties, I think it was 2,400 at Pearl Harbor, and a little under 3,000 in New York and Washington, and in Pennsylvania [on 9/11]. It was a shock to us all.

I was 25 when I volunteered for the Army shortly after. Basic training started in Camp Shelby, Mississippi, in October of 1942. And after basic training I was assigned to the IV Corps Headquarters in Camp Beauregard, Louisiana. And there is where they found out that I had engineering drawing experience, and they asked me to go into the Engineering Section of the Corps to do overlays and other things too. After the European Campaigns were over, they asked me to do combat illustration. I did several publications for the Army. The main reason why they didn't send me home when the Corps went home, they wanted me to finish up a history of the Italian Campaigns, written and illustrated. They kept me there about six more months. I didn't mind. We were having a lot of fun. [*Chuckles*] I was single, you know, girls, wine, women, and song. My wife didn't know me then. It was a good experience, really good.

In basic training, in the 85th Infantry Division, it was tough going. For three months, they really told us, in plain English, 'You civilian idiots are going to be soldiers within six to eight weeks.' And they weren't kidding, they weren't kidding. They put us through all the training you could think of. Like, for example, get up at three o'clock in the morning and walk through a swamp. Very interesting, you know, things like that.

And you've heard of the machine gun courses in World War II? Well, there were two machine guns mounted on high stands across from each other. There was live ammo, and it was about twenty minutes of crawling, and I went through that thing in Mississippi. Then I was transferred to IV Corps and we went to the State of Washington, and they told us we were going to go through that thing again. So I said to the first sergeant, the morning we were supposed to go out for this machine gun class, 'You know, Sergeant, I took this already, do I have to take it again?'

He said, 'Get your butt in there!' And so I get in there, and that was the second time.

Then we went down to California, and the commanding officer said, 'Everybody goes through the machine gun course at night.' So I said to the first sergeant, 'What do you think?'

And he said, 'Yeah, you're coming with me.'

So we went through the course together. I was holding the barbed wire up so he can get through, and somebody else would hold it—you know, the buddy system—and he was cranky the whole time, squawking—I don't want to use the word 'bitching'—that's what he was doing the whole time. And I said, 'What did you think the Army was, a picnic? This is the real Army.'

And he said, 'Yeah, I guess you're right.'

Well, anyway, I went through that thing three times, and I did three twenty-five-mile hikes, three times, and every time I said, 'This is on my record already,' [they'd say], 'Good, then it'll be on there twice now.' So, three of those marches. That was fun.

After basic training, I must admit that the government did a great job of making an army fast, very fast. Within six months, we were thick into the war, and I never regretted the tough training we had because it paid off. What they were trying to teach us, more than anything, was survival. This lieutenant I had as a training officer said to me, 'You know, you've got to be skillful to survive, not just lucky. You got to use your head, otherwise you won't make it.'

One of the things he did was put us in foxholes holding up targets in the morning. It was out in the desert in California. He said, 'Don't come out of the holes until you're relieved. This is live ammunition flying around—don't put your head up, don't be nosy.' That taught us how to stay down. Then, when the firing was all over, I knew it was time to eat. We were still in the foxholes. Nobody said come out, so we didn't get out. So, four o'clock in the afternoon, we'd just had breakfast that day, the guys who were in the hole. And when the lieutenant came around and said, 'Okay, you guys can come out now.'

I said, 'You know, we're starved!'

He said, 'That's what you have to learn in combat. Staying where you are until it's safe to come out, and if you don't eat, you don't eat. You'd rather be eating and dead, or hungry and living?' That's the way they put it to us. But you see the point, what they were doing? That was tough.

*

We had gotten to North Africa just as the African Campaign was just about over, it was in the cleanup stages. [At the time], the Army did not know for sure whether we were going to go to Italy or to India. If we were set to go to India, we would go through the Suez Canal. We got to Algiers, from Morocco; from Casablanca, we went to Oran, North Africa, where the officers' command changed. We were told then—they didn't tell us where to—just to board ships, and we went on a twenty-one-ship convoy to Italy.

Breakout

At that time, the main front was at Cassino. The Anzio beachhead had already established itself, but they were stalled. So we were in the campaign. Our first campaign was to break out the Anzio beachhead. On May 23, 1944, we knew something big was happening, but we didn't know exactly what. At eleven o'clock at night a barrage started from the west, the Mediterranean side of Italy to the Adriatic side, which is about a hundred miles. British, Americans, Australians, South Africans, you name it, we were all in this together. It was a barrage of artillery that lasted for two hours, and during that time we moved in with trucks in blackout, doing about ten, fifteen miles an hour. We moved under that umbrella of [artillery] that lasted for two hours, and we didn't know where we were going, we had no idea.

Pandemonium ensued the next morning. There were troops from all nations running all over the place, and finally the beachhead broke out. Then the real campaign started for the attack on Rome. Hitler had said to his people that the Gustav Line, which was a terrific fortification south of Rome all the way across Italy, was impregnable. He said, 'They'll never get through.' Well, we got through.

Rome

The entry into Rome was something that you'll just never forget. Here was a country that was supposedly our enemy, and we got a welcome in Rome that—well, have you ever heard somebody hit a home run in Yankee Stadium? That's what it sounded like. It was just great coming in. We didn't stay long, we stayed about a few hours, and the city was declared open by the Germans, because the pressure was on them not to destroy Rome. We would have hit it with artillery, and air bombing if we had to, but we didn't want to. They gave them three days to pack and get out. They went fifty miles north of Rome, where the war resumed.

From there on in, there was another campaign called the Rome-Arno—the Arno River goes through Florence—that campaign took a couple months, then from there we went to the North Apennines Campaign. That was the winter of 1944-45. We were really bogged down. We were losing more men with sickness and car and truck accidents than we did on the line, that's how bad it was. It was stalemated. But then in the spring, April, this time of the year, of 1945, Crittenberger and Clark, they all got together there and we broke out into the Po Valley. We crossed the Po River, and it wasn't too long after that when the surrender came, and when Mussolini was captured.

General Crittenberger was our overall commander. He was a major general at the time, and he joined us in Africa and took command of the Corps in Italy. He put us through three campaigns, from Naples all the way up to the French-Swiss border, then the war ended. I admired him because he and Patton came up together in rank from West Point on. Patton was the big theatrical type, you know. Crittenberger said, 'I'm not going to lose men. I'm going to win without losing a lot of men.' And I admired him. I remember I used to do maps for him, and I used to hear him say to his staff, 'If we go this way, it's going to be bad; if we go this way, we can still get there and we're not going to lose so many men.' He was very concerned about his men. He lost two sons in the war, so he felt it, you know?

He stayed with us for the whole thing. [At the end], we were in the area where Mussolini was trying to save his tail. He was ousted, as you know, and he was heading for the Swiss border in a German convoy. He had with him his mistress and five Fascist officials, and they had fifty million dollars in gold bullion in the truck with them. They were trying to get into Switzerland, where they would have a safe haven. So Crittenberger sent his MPs out: 'Let's get this guy.'

Then all of a sudden, the German commander of the northern army of the Nazis wanted to talk surrender. So the press said to Crittenberger, 'What's more important, catching Mussolini or taking this guy's surrender?'

He said, 'Look, I'm a Corps commander, and an army wants to surrender to me,' with, I don't know, a hundred, eighty thousand men, whatever it was—I forget the number. 'I'll put the priority on the surrender. The MPs will get Mussolini.' Well, they didn't get him. The Italian partisans, the underground, stopped the convoy. There were several hundred in the whole German convoy, they outnumbered the Italian underground. But the Italian underground commander bluffed and told them he had many, many more men behind the hills: 'So you better do what I tell you.'

'What do you want to do?'

We want to search the convoy.'

They went through the trucks, and they found Mussolini sitting in the back of one of the trucks with the canvas over it, with a German corporal's overcoat over him, trying to hide himself. And they took him out, found out who he was, and they took him and his girlfriend and the five officials and they kept them in a villa overnight. The next morning, they summarily shot them, just like that. And they put the bodies in a moving van, and they brought them to Milan, and hung them up by their heels outside of a gas station under construction with a canopy over it.

A few of us in the Jeep were in Milan, and [we saw] a terrific crowd of people. [*Points out the window*] You see that house over there? That's about as close as I got to Mussolini. There was just a mass of people there, civilians. British military police were there, and they said, 'Look, Yanks, if I were you, I'd get out of here.'

We said, 'What's the matter?'

They said, 'This crowd is not too calm, we expect some kind of trouble here today.' Fortunately, the people who were on our side outnumbered the few Fascists left. They were diehards, they were almost as bad as the Nazis, you know. Nothing really happened there. What they did do is take the bodies down, in the van again, and bury them in a place unknown. They didn't want to make martyrs out of them. Especially Mussolini. So his own wife didn't know where he was buried. I don't think she cared; he was buried with his mistress. He wasn't a nice guy. [*Laughs*] Neither was Hitler.

*

[I remember one time] I was up with the 10th Mountain Division one night, and with the 34th Infantry Division for two nights in a row. The artillery was brutal, but we sat in a pyramid tent with a Coleman gasoline lantern, my friend and I, making overlays. This guy next to me, Sgt. Bond, always had a bottle of wine under the drawing board with him. [*Chuckles*] He used to say, 'Don't worry about these shells whistling overhead.'

'Why? What do you mean, don't worry?'

'Because my father was in the First World War, and he said you'll never hear the one that hits you.'

'You know,' I said, 'Ted, I feel better now that you told me that, I really feel better.' [*Laughs*] That's the kind of guy he was.

*

Colonel Gillette sent me up to the line one day to do some drawings of tramways. And the reason why was that we were still in the mountains, and the roads were winding back and forth, narrow and whatnot, and getting down into a valley and up again—you know, Italy had seven hundred miles of mountains! Anyway, they built these tramways because they could go from one mountain to another without dealing with the roads, to send supplies over, what the guys really needed. On the way back, they would send out the wounded and the dead. It was a great thing.

He sent me out there to make drawings of these things. Photographing them wouldn't be good because they were so far away; all they could photograph was the mechanism on one side. In a drawing, what I did was show this side, and you could draw the line just where you wanted to. And then I would make a drawing of the other side. Put them together, and you had the complete picture, some very rough sketches of the tramway. When I got back to my post, I would do them over again in ink. The Americans ran one tramway, and the Brazilian troops were taking care of another, so I was with them one day. While I was there, we got shelled, so I had to get into the bunker with these Brazilian soldiers, and it was around four o'clock in the afternoon. Well, anyway, while I was in there they started bringing out some Italian cheese, and bottles of wine and whatnot, garlic and you name it! When I got back to the camp it was dark, and Col. Gillette met me by the tent, and he put his arms around me and said, 'Son, are you all right?' And I said, 'Yes, I'm fine. What happened?' He said, 'We heard about the shelling up there.' And I said, 'No, I was in a bunker with the

Brazilians.' He said, 'You know what? You smell just like them!' [*Laughs*]

The 5th Army Headquarters took my original drawings. At a reunion in New York City in 1952, one officer said to me, 'Those tramway drawings are being used in Korea as the basis of how to do this from one mountain to another.'

I said, 'They're still good?'

'Oh yes, they still do them the same way.' So that made me feel good, too.

The Po Valley

The Po Valley was the last campaign. Surrender came there, and of course, the surrender of Germany came six days later. Like I said, my group stayed to do historical documentation. It wasn't just the war and the fighting itself, we also had to document what the engineers did in Italy. The number of bridges that they put up, Bailey bridges, you know—temporary bridges, the number of culverts. Everything that we did, repairs, this all had to do with accountability, and had to go back to Washington, as to what we did over there, why did we spend all this money. When soldiers broke somebody's fence, for example, we had to pay for it. All those bombings—as a matter of fact, I read recently that after we gutted Cassino, and the war was over, the United States government rebuilt their village. Those people were bombed out, so they built new houses for them. So this was the accountability we had to give to the government. This took about four or five months. The war ended in May, I got home December 1.

*

The Duffel Bag

I have [another story]. There was a fella close to me in the Army; his name was Hendrickson. His first name was Arvo. He was from an upper Michigan farm family. He and his twin brother, Arno—Arvo and Arno—were drafted on the same day, and an older brother who was thirty-five years old. When they went to the draft board they asked if they could be put together in the same unit. And the draft board said, 'No, we just had a very bad experience, the Sullivan brothers were lost on one ship, no more brothers together.'[33]

So Arvo came to my unit, and he said, 'You know, my brother'—his older brother, not the twin—'is in Italy in a different unit.' So there was a terrific fight going on in a place called Santa Maria, south of Rome. While we were going through, in transit, we stopped at a truck stop, where there was a kitchen for transients; it was a big Italian barn, or warehouse. We went in there and they had a kitchen set up, and we had our own mess kits. As we were going through the line, we saw this huge rack of shelves with American Army duffel bags packed on there. And Hendrickson said to me, 'Hey, Tony, you know what? My brother must be in the area someplace. There's his duffel bag.' The name was stenciled on.

So I said, 'That's nice.' So we went through the line and I was thinking, why is his duffel bag there?

---

[33] *the Sullivan brothers*- On November 13, 1942, during the Battle of Guadalcanal, five brothers of the Sullivan family of Waterloo, Iowa were lost when their ship, the *USS Juneau*, was sunk. The brothers had insisted on serving together, and despite Navy policy, their wish was granted. Due to this and other incidents of brothers being killed within months of each other during the war, a 1948 policy was adopted designed to provide exemptions to families if they have already lost members in military service.

Well, there was a military policeman guarding these bags. After the lunch was over, he went to wash his mess kit, and he went outside to the truck. I went back to the MP. I said to him, 'Can I ask you a question? What are these bags doing here?' And I told him about Hendrickson.

'Well,' he said, 'I don't know if you want to tell him, but these guys are all dead. They were all killed at Santa Maria.'

There must have been about a hundred bags up there. So I didn't say anything to him. I had to really do some soul searching. Why am I going to upset him? Let him hear it through family. I didn't think it was my duty to say it. So about two weeks later I saw him sitting under a tree with a handkerchief in his hand. And I said, 'What's the matter, Arvo?'

And he said, 'My brother was killed.'

I said, 'Oh, I'm sorry to hear that.' You can see my point. I just didn't want to be the guy to tell him.

Then I said to him, 'Look, Arvo, let's do something. Let's go to our captain and ask him if we can go to your brother's company commander and get more information about your brother's death.'

We did. We found out where his brother's unit was; they were in a rest area in the woods. We went there and asked for Captain So-and-so, and he was sitting on the ground playing cards. And I said, 'Sir, would you mind… This is Hendrickson here, and his brother was in your unit, he was killed.'

He never even looked up from his cards.

He said, 'Your brother didn't know what hit him. He was killed immediately, that's all I can tell you.' Just like that.

We got back in our Jeep and went back home. Of course, it didn't make Hendrickson feel too good, but this guy was shaken up, that captain was shaken up. He wasn't being nasty, he was just so shaken to know that he was talking to the brother of one of his men.…

About a month later, Arvo got a letter from home saying that his father had died from a heart attack. Then the campaign started in France, after D-Day, and the twin brother was burned badly in a tank. He went back to Walter Reed Hospital by air in a basket; he was burned from head to foot. His mother died from a heart attack. So Arvo got home, and he wrote to me in January of 1946, and he said, 'I'm back in the Army. There's nothing for me to stay home for. My parents are gone, my brother is dead. My other brother, we don't know what's going to happen to him, he's still in Walter Reed Hospital. The farm is sold. There's no reason for me to stay here at all.' So he went back in. He got married and asked for an assignment in Tokyo. That story is like *Saving Private Ryan*, in a smaller way, of course.

Senator Lodge

Another experience I had was when the war was over and we were stationed up on Lake Como, Italy. They had very nice billets for enlisted men, and nice billets across the lake for the officers. So this fella in my outfit, his name was Casey, got notice from home that his father died. They were going to hold the body for five days if he could come home. So, he spoke to the captain, and the captain said, 'I'll see what I can do for you,' but the captain said, 'I can't do it. I got a hold of the chaplain, I got a hold of the Red Cross, I got a hold of the commanding officer,' and he said, 'they're all stalling me.'

So Casey sat there and he was really kind of down in the dumps. He said, 'I'll see if I can get a telegram home and tell them I can't make it.'

'Wait a minute, Casey,' I said. 'Hold on, hold on. Let's get a boat, go across the lake, and go to the officers' club over there. Your senator from Massachusetts is in our outfit. His name is Lodge'—he was a colonel in the IV Corps—'let's go over and see him.'

We got into a boat and we went across the lake, and there was a party going on in the officers' club. The MP at the door said, 'Hey, listen, we can't let you in,' and I said, 'Wait a minute,' and I told him the story about his father. 'Get Senator Lodge out here, just for a minute.' He went and got him out, and Senator Lodge was a Lt. Colonel, and we told him the story, and he said, 'What's your name?'

'John Casey.'

And he said, 'Casey, I'll be with you first thing in the morning.'

First thing in the morning, he came across the lake, and he said, 'There's a truck waiting for you to take you to Genoa, there's a plane going back to the States. You just stay there, and we'll discharge you from there.'

So Casey said to me, 'Thanks for the suggestion! What can I do for you?'

'You can do one thing. Make sure you have a nickel in your pocket, and call my mother when you get to the States and tell her I'm okay.' And he did. But that's something I never forgot because it really—I don't know how Senator Lodge came to my mind, this guy was from Boston. I said, 'Look, Casey, he's your Senator, come on, let him work for you.' And it happened. It worked!

After the war, Mr. Battillo stayed in Italy an extra six months to complete the illustrations and production of 'The Final Campaign Across Northwest Italy,' the official record of the last campaign in Italy. He managed art and production departments for IBM Corporation. He also took up painting and wrote and illustrated historical articles for national special interest magazines and newspapers, with a specialty in the Civil War. His paintings reside in many collections, including the

Gettysburg battlefield and the New York State Military Museum. He passed away in 2009 at the age of 92.

*Rock climbing at Camp Hale, Colorado.
Credit: U.S. Army photograph, Public Domain.*

PART TWO

MOUNTAIN SOLDIERS

'The (Germans) held all the high ground, and one felt like he was in the bottom of a bowl with the enemy sitting on two-thirds of the rim looking down upon you. There was about as much concealment as a goldfish would have in a bowl.'–10th Mountain Division soldier[25]

The general said to one of the battalion commanders, 'I want you to take Riva Ridge tomorrow night. Go out and scout how you're going to do it. You guys are a bunch of hotshots, you're skiers and mountain climbers, find a way on top of that ridge!'–10th Mountain Division soldier

CHAPTER ELEVEN

Mountain Men

The Champlain Valley, in the shadow of the Adirondack Mountains between New York and Vermont, lies just to the east of the region that was christened 'Hometown, USA' in *Look Magazine's* idyllic portrayal of patriotic life on the home front during World War II. This fertile lakeshore valley, coupled with the Hudson River valley just to its south, was an almost unbroken stretch of water linking New York City with Canada. For centuries, native warriors traveled the 'Great Warpath' to go to war with their traditional enemies to the north. The French and British both constructed rival forts and launched invasions in both directions in the North American Theater of their mid-eighteenth-century quest for world empire; indeed, this was where Robert Rogers and his famous Rangers commenced their operations. Twenty years after that, British general John Burgoyne launched a textbook invasion from Canada southwards along this natural warpath, designing to divide and conquer the rebellious colonies once and for all, only to be stopped at the high ground near Saratoga in 1777. A similar British raid followed before the Revolution was out, and a generation and a half later, British warships again appeared on the lake in the War of 1812. After that, the guns in the region finally fell silent. Though the Civil War and World War I would call more boys away from the region, agricultural and industrial pursuits along the 400-mile stretch of the geologic superhighway thrived until the coming of the Great Depression.

*

Across the ocean in the fall of 1931, in a sprawling factory-hangar in southeastern Germany, construction began on a massive project dubbed LZ-129 just as the Great Depression was plunging into new depths. A little over a year later, a brand-new government was voted into power in Germany with a platform of vague and sinister promises to redress grievances and solve Germany's economic and political woes. Seeing the propaganda value in cutting-edge projects like this, the Nazi government capitalized on the opportunity to pump money into what would become a showpiece, a symbol of resurging German pride and might. Five years in the making, the LZ-129—now dubbed 'HINDENBURG' after the former president and World War I hero—was three times as long as its future successor in transatlantic commercial air travel, the Boeing 747. Her dimensions were comparable to that other largest passenger vessel of its own time, the Titanic.

The Hindenburg's first appearance in the German skies in March 1936 was heralded by the sound of rolling thunder from her diesel engines. With bursting pride, Germans glimpsed what first looked like a giant gray cigar, growing louder and larger as it approached, Nazi flags with black swastikas now clearly emblazoned on her massive tailfins. A portent of burgeoning German power now roared overhead in the first of several maiden test flights that doubled as 'victory laps' over the recently re-militarized German Rhineland. In

Berlin, the Hindenburg and her sister airship, the LZ-130 Graf Zeppelin, drowned out the traffic noises in the busy streets below, where the finishing touches for the 1936 Berlin Olympic Summer Games were being completed.

Heads turned skyward again a few months later when the Hindenburg made its way down the Champlain Valley on her fourth transatlantic journey that year, this time making headlines by completing the passage from Frankfurt, Germany, to Lakehurst, New Jersey, in just over 50 hours, a new speed record. Farm families and camp visitors along the Lake Champlain shoreline were awoken at the sound of 'a fleet of airplanes' as it passed just 400 feet above the lake. Near Ticonderoga, New York, a reporter wrote, 'Silhouetted against a moonlit, star-flecked sky, the zeppelin created a thrilling, almost awe-inspiring sight.' And almost as soon as she had passed overhead at the speed of a car traveling down a modern interstate, she was gone. The world's first transatlantic commercial airship, this shining example of German engineering and excellence, would fly over Olympic Stadium to cheering crowds in Berlin exactly a month later, on August 1, 1936, and cross the Atlantic a record thirteen times before the year was out. And just more than a year after her debut, this harbinger of the New World Order would lie smoldering in ashes by the Jersey shore, her naked skeleton twisted and still hot to the touch.[26]

*

Four years after the appearance of the Hindenburg over the Champlain Valley, in front of a crackling fire in an inn in Manchester, Vermont, a forty-year-old World War I veteran and skiing enthusiast named Charles Minot Dole led a discussion with a handful of the nation's top skiers. In early 1936, Dole had been injured while skiing an icy peak just to the north; his skiing companion that day got him to the doctor after much difficulty getting him off the mountain. Not long after, that same friend hit a tree on a slope, breaking his ribs and puncturing his lungs, and he died because medical assistance was not readily available. Dole and members of his ski club vowed to do something about it, and the National Ski Patrol was born, an organization of trained volunteers and expert skiers who could render first aid and keep the ski areas safer as the fledgling sport expanded rapidly in the Northeast.[27]

Given the 1939 Nazi invasion of Poland and the start of World War II, here by the fireside the talk turned to war preparation. A fellow ski racer and friend had just returned from duty as a military observer on the Russo-Finnish war front, where the Finns on skis and clad in white had been dealing out remarkable hit-and-run blows against the much larger Soviet invader on the frozen, wooded terrain of the Karelian Isthmus.[28] Although they would ultimately lose the war, Finnish fighters and the Arctic cold also left 200,000 Russians dead, whereas the Finns lost just 20,000 in comparison. Vastly outnumbered, their only advantages were their knowledge of the inhospitable wooded terrain and their specialized winter training on skis. It was an inspiring example to the leadership of the National Ski Patrol, and they were quick to recognize it was time to face up to some very sobering facts: the Axis powers—Germany, incorporated Austria, and Italy—had produced more Olympian medalists in the alpine sports than their Allied counterparts, by far. Europeans had been mountaineering and skiing for hundreds of years, fighting at altitudes little known to American military men. Germany already had three mountain divisions and, by war's end, was on her way to fourteen. America had none.[29] It was time for the United States to raise a mountain division of their own.

Dole pointed out that not very far away from where they were sitting, invaders had come down the St. Lawrence River into the Champlain Valley more than once in history. If the Germans were to attack the United States, why wouldn't one of their spearheads be the same as that route taken by the giant zeppelin soaring overhead not so long ago? It was a natural conclusion, and America at the moment had no alpine units to defend the Adirondack Mountains and this northern gateway to the United States. But there had been an important American precedent—hadn't Major Robert Rogers and his hit-and-run Ranger companies of the French and Indian War days struck terror in the heart of the French empire in North America from these very mountains, living outdoors in extreme conditions, in all seasons? And wouldn't young outdoor enthusiasts and skiers, all potential draftees, jump at the opportunity to emulate them as mountain troops?

He knew what to do. By the fall of 1940, the National Ski Patrol had maneuvered their way past the War Department's initial bureaucratic brush-off and buttonholed none other than Army Chief of Staff General George C. Marshall himself. On November 15, 1941, the 87th Infantry Regiment was activated at Fort Lewis in Washington State. Three weeks later, the United States was in World War II.[30] It was here, and it was real, ready or not.

*

The fighting force, eventually known as the 10th Mountain Division, would train hard for this new specialized type of warfare. Near Thanksgiving, 1944, it finally got the call, the last of sixty-three U.S. Army divisions to be sent to the European Theater. It would spearhead the closing push in Italy into the Po Valley north of Rome and Florence in the winter/spring of 1945, with the Fifth Army's all-black 92nd Division on its left and the Brazilian Expeditionary Force on its right.[31] Though it would spend less than four months in combat, it would suffer ten percent losses and garner acclaim for helping bring the Italian Campaign to a conclusion.

CHAPTER TWELVE

The Medic

Frederick Vetter was born on June 17, 1925, in Glens Falls, New York. After completing high school in 1943, he went into the service and found himself in Italy with the 10th Mountain Division as a medic. 'There was plenty of apprehension. When you've seen mortar fire and artillery fire coming in on you, you never know when it's going to strike. And you know that you probably are being watched, even though you're only a small group, and that would draw fire. And there was nothing sacred about the medical Red Cross helmet and armband.... our first casualty that we took off of the mountain was our own leader. Which rather shook us, you know?' Later, he would recall the feeling near the end: 'I said to myself, if this thing goes on two or three more weeks, I'm either going to be wounded or I'm going to be killed. Just had that sense about it.' He sat for this interview in 2004 at the age of 78.

Frederick J. Vetter

[I was in high school when Pearl Harbor happened and] I remember distinctly what I was doing. My father and I were taking a hike up in the woods in the mountains behind Chestertown. There wasn't any snow on the ground even though it was December, which was unusual. And we came out of the woods, came down onto what we called the North Road, and a man came out, a friend of ours, and said, 'You haven't heard, but the country's been attacked at Pearl Harbor.' And that's in the afternoon, December 7. We were shocked, and I think all of the people were in shock.

I graduated from high school in 1943, entered the service shortly thereafter. I had made plans, because believe it or not, the National Ski Patrol System was recruiting at that time for recruits for the mountain troops, which the media called the ski troops, though they were actually mountain troops. They were given a contract by the U.S.

government to recruit, the only time it's ever happened, and probably the last time it'll ever happen. And so I got wind of it—I thought of myself as a skier and an outdoors person. And you had to have three letters of recommendation with your application, and usually it was either your priest or your minister, your high school principal, your coach, or some person of that nature. I had my three letters of recommendation, sent it in, and got accepted, so I did enlist a few days after graduation, and shortly after, I was on my way.

I was fortunate. I wasn't sent to a southern camp to take my basic training, but we were sent directly to Camp Hale, Colorado, where the mountain troops were training. And I was put in a company, and there were probably eight or 10 recruits like myself, very raw recruits. And that's where we got our basic training, with the company.

The mountain troops were in existence in 1941; the first recruit came on board out in Fort Lewis, Washington. And the story goes, he was from Dartmouth. He arrived at the gate at Fort Lewis. He said, 'I'm to report to the mountain troops.' And the sergeant on the gate was puzzled. Never heard of it. And questioned him further, and he called the office, got an answer back, and he said, 'Well, young fella, you *are* the mountain troops.' [*Laughs*] And that was when it happened, 1941, I believe a day after Pearl Harbor.

I got my basic training, and I was sent immediately out into the field where the battalion that I was in was on bivouac. And we were out there probably for the better part of a month. As far as the training went, it was basic rifleman training. We did a lot of calisthenics. I never remember that we were made to jog like the modern army does. We did a lot of hiking, and hard hiking. And it was particularly hard because we were at an altitude of at least 9,500 feet, right there at camp. And you had to be acclimatized to it.

Mountain Equipment

Our equipment was very good. They had really done their homework for those days on getting specialized equipment. We had good packs, the army rucksacks that you've probably seen, with the steel frame. Used to see thousands of them in surplus shops after the war. That was a good pack.

And we had a double sleeping bag, down sleeping bags for the wintertime. We had a jacket, which was called a mountain jacket, which was far and above anything that the rest of the army had at that time. We also trained in snowshoes, though I never had to use any, thank heavens. The heavy weapons people had to use snowshoes. In other words, people in mortar crew, heavy machine gun sections, they used snowshoes. Detested them! But they're better than nothing, right? But the riflemen and so forth, they used skis. The skis were seven feet long, white, better quality, far and above anything that we had ever seen as civilians. They were long, but they were just used as a means to get [from place to place]. We had [winter camouflaged] whites that you pulled on over your trousers. We had plenty of good underwear for those days. They didn't know about the polar fleece then; we had wool.

We were carrying probably upwards of 90 pounds in the rucksack, and we had a mountain tent. One person would carry a mountain tent, which was like a pup tent, only it was far and above better than anything like a pup tent. It was fairly lightweight, and it was completely enclosed, and you could stay out 35, 40 degrees below zero temperatures in one of these. And many times, incidentally, we didn't use the tents because it was dry in the winter usually, and if we were out in the field we would go out and cut boughs with machetes. We'd make a depression in the snow, getting down fairly close to ground level, make a nice bed of boughs, put our sleeping bags on top of those, and hit the sack. It worked out quite well. If it was snowing hard, we'd use the mountain tents. Each two men would have a gasoline stove, which one person would have to carry a little container of white gas for. It was like a buddy system; there were usually two to a foxhole or a depression or a tent. We had good, nice wool ski socks and good ski boots. Better than anything we'd had up to that time, so we thought we had great equipment. By today's standard, it's laughable, perhaps. But the army, and with the help of a lot of interested civilians, had done their homework on our equipment. Weapons were standard issue, rifle, bayonet. The artillery was attached, and they were all pack mule companies. And they used a 75-millimeter howitzer, which was broken down, and it took eight large army mules to carry one artillery piece. They were small guns, but very effective. So we had a lot of mules attached to us, and as far as transport goes, they used pack animals for that too.

In my case I came in July of 1943, and I was there until the following June. Other people had come in a lot earlier. As I say, the mountain troops were formed, the first companies and battalion, was formed in Fort Lewis, Washington, in 1941, '42, and trained out there, and then eventually Camp Hale was established and built in record time. And they moved this first regiment, the 87th Mountain Infantry, to Camp Hale, and those people cadred [into] the two other regiments, the 85th and the 86th. The 87th Regiment was taken and sent to Kiska in the Aleutians, and that's where they found no Japs at all; the Japanese had evacuated Kiska. This was a few months after the battle of Attu, which was a little further out in the chain. And the War Department had anticipated at least 65 or 70 percent casualties for the 87th Regiment. They found the Japanese had escaped through the navy blockade and evacuated about two weeks before they invaded. So, they now had four regiments, because they had started the 90th Regiment, which I was in, to replace the 87th [which was expected to be devastated]. They figured there would be nothing left of the 87th—they would bring back what they could and put them into the other regiments. So the 90th was left hanging, and eventually they were disbanded and I was put into the 86th Regiment. And I can recall that it was a matter of more conditioning; the hikes would be longer, more strenuous. We would be out in the field for longer periods, night and day. And that went on all winter long, '43 and '44. And at the time, it seemed rather senseless to us. We were griping and bitching. But with good reason—they knew what they were doing; we were feeling our way. And then March of 1944, the entire division—that's three regiments of infantry and three battalions of pack artillery and the whole shebang—was out for between three and four weeks in the mountains, for observers from the War Department. They wanted to find out if after all this training and expenditure of money they had mountain troops. And basically, we came through and had proved our worth, at least as far as maneuvering went. But that was tough. First night we were out, it was minus 35 degrees during the night, and we didn't have too much shelter.

*

After that they moved us. The army, in its wisdom, decided that the setup that they had didn't have enough firepower, so we were sent to Texas and reorganized into different-sized squads. They took the heavy weapons away from each company, put them into a [specialized] heavy weapons company, so basically, we had the organization of a flatland division. And they sent us from Colorado in June down to Texas. That was quite a job to get used to that. It was hot, from being nice and cool up in Colorado. And then I think it was in November that they got the word to send us to Italy. Combat.

We'd never been on a troop ship before. We were fortunate by that time that the German U-boats had been pretty much driven from the Atlantic. We were extremely fortunate. And I can remember going up on deck in the morning at sunrise and seeing the coast of North Africa emerging. By that afternoon we had gone through the Strait of Gibraltar. It was a nice, sunny day; this was just before Christmas, 1944. We all recognized the Rock and were quite enthralled by that. Within a couple of days, we had arrived in Naples harbor; Naples was still pretty well beat up, and we were taken to a holding area, a camp if you will. Soon we were sent up the coast to Leghorn, or Legorno. We probably moved out faster than anyone had anticipated, because the German army at that time put on a small offensive north of Florence, and there weren't many troops in reserve up there; they were scrounging for anybody they could find. And we were brand new, and were available, so we were sent up quite quickly.

They gave us maybe a couple of weeks to get our new equipment, get our land legs back under us, and to familiarize ourselves with Jeeps. We didn't have much motorized equipment and we had left the mules behind—they were probably two months behind us, being shipped over. We were sent up into an area that was pretty static that winter, anyway. The Germans were in front of us, and occasionally they would put patrols out, so they could be around us at any time, but they didn't want to stir things up at that time. We were probably sending out more patrols and getting people used to being in a combat situation, so we were fortunate to be able to be brought into it gradually. We had very little of our specialized equipment with us; it never caught up with us, which was sad, in a way.

*

A Red Cross

I got into the medics probably because I knew Sergeant Draper, Art Draper, who was the first sergeant of the 3rd Battalion-Medical Detachment. I had known him because he had lived [nearby at home]. In fact, he had given me the papers to get into the mountain troops. He was well liked, very able, and very respected. So that's probably why I gravitated toward the medics; he was like a mentor for me. Eventually I was put in as a litter bearer. And as it proved out, within a couple of days after we really got into combat, I had to take over and head this group of five or six people, so a bit of responsibility was thrust upon me in a short time.

There was plenty of apprehension. When you've seen mortar fire and artillery fire coming in on you, you never know when it's going to strike. And you know that you probably are being watched, even though you're only a small group, and that would draw fire. And there was nothing sacred about the medical Red Cross helmet and armband. And there were instances where they had a Red Cross flag if we had to go out into a battlefield and pick up a man, but we never had one that I can recall. I don't know if we were even aware, in our unit, that such a thing could be used, but occasionally a group would go out with that, waving it, and pick up the man, and a German sniper would go after them, you know?

Officers

I always felt that officers, both commissioned and non-commissioned, were superior, and I still do. Most of our non-com officers came up through the ranks, were volunteers. Many of them got to be tech sergeants and so on, and they were picked out and they were sent to OCS. And many of them came back to us after they became 2nd lieutenants, so we had a wonderful group, by and large, of non-coms, and officers. Most of the battalion officers probably had been ROTC people, but they were not just sent to the mountain troops, they volunteered for the mountain troops, and many of them came from states like Montana, Idaho, and the state of Washington. They were mountain people. And we had some outstanding battalion commanders. The commanding general of the 10th Mountain was a terrific man, General Hays. He had been a Medal of Honor winner in World War I, and he had a sixth sense about the capabilities of the enemy, and he knew just how to keep pushing, and when not to. He saved us a lot of casualties. And they said he had a terrific temper; he could be very, very angry if things weren't going the way he thought they should be. They said it was not easy to be around him.

The Climb on Riva Ridge

Our battalion itself was not involved in the climb on Riva Ridge, but perhaps you've heard of that. It was the 1st Battalion of the 86th plus F

Company out of the 2nd Battalion. And that was probably the only time that mountain skills were utilized to their fullest extent, and that was quite a feat. It was done at night, and with raw troops, so to speak. They had had a little bit of patrol activity but had never been in a major battle to that time. And to put them into a nighttime situation—this ridge was about 1,600 feet from the base to the top. Very rugged, a very steep slope, and rocky. It was in the wintertime, February 18 I think it was, in 1945. And it was an escarpment that overlooked the valley where the Americans were. On top, the Germans held this ridge, and they had observation posts looking out over all of this area, including Mount Belvedere off to the right.

The Americans had tried to take Mount Belvedere three times before, in November and early December, previous to us getting there. And each time they had gained the summit, they were driven off by counterattacks. One of the keys was that the Germans had observation posts on top of Mount Belvedere, from Riva Ridge. So when the mission was given to the 10th Mountain to take Mount Belvedere, Hays, the commanding general, insisted that he first had to take Riva Ridge. And that was the key to taking Belvedere.

Anyway, they did go up. [Rock climbing had been part of our basic training.] A full battalion, there'd probably be 800 to 900 men, fully loaded with all their equipment, had to climb this Riva Ridge. And they had done a lot of scouting and they were not discovered, which was very fortunate; some of the scouting was done at night and some during the day. They established about three or four routes that could be done, up the ridge. In places they had fixed ropes. And that was tricky, when you had to put in pitons, the little pieces of spiked metal to hold these ropes. And they were pretty clever about that. They had their hammers, and they muffled them with cloth, putting in the pitons. They had those in the worst spots, where they had the fixed ropes. They gathered about a day or two earlier, going in at night through this valley into a number of small villages, and staying hidden during the day. And they started up at night, and they gained the summit, some of them by two in the morning, three o'clock in the morning; they were all on the top by the time dawn came. And the Germans had never figured that any large group would ever come up that cliff! That was their mistake. If they had defended it, as they probably should have, it would have been a different story, but these attack team groups—and they went up in three or four different groups—were not discovered until well after dawn. And the Germans were asleep behind the ridge! And our men attacked and took care of the ones that were up there, but the Germans soon came in and counterattacked.

A brutal fight for the five-mile ridge had begun.

And they drove it off but were counterattacked up there for about two or three days of heavy fighting. The Germans had a couple of battalions of their mountain troops in reserve, and they sent them off to counterattack, fully expecting to drive off the Americans, because they had always been able to 'pull the fat out of the fire' before. And this time they couldn't. Riva Ridge was secured, and then another nighttime attack took place on Belvedere, a day or two after Riva was taken; now the Germans didn't have the observation post for artillery fire anymore. It was truly a noteworthy piece of work, if you will.

*

Mount della Torraccia

[I was slightly wounded with shrapnel] on the end of this whole series of mountains, which had to be taken, a place called Mount della Torraccia. One of our battalions had attacked that; it was the last objective of the attack, and they were beaten up by the time they got there, all cut up. And I've read accounts of that, and it's too bad that they couldn't have been reinforced before, but they really took a walloping there.

The Germans were not about to let their last toehold on the ridges slip away. One soldier of the 86th's 3rd Battalion later recalled, 'Only about thirty percent of our men made it to the top. The rest were either killed or wounded by mines or mortars. Once we got to the top, we were told to dig in. The Germans were counterattacking and firing right in on us. It was very frightening.'[32]

Our battalion was sent in to relieve them and to take the mountain, which we did. And that's where I became involved. The night before the attack started on Mount della Torraccia, we had a new leader of our little group of litter bearers, and within the first ten minutes of the attack, he was hit and killed. And so our first casualty that we took off of the mountain was our own leader. Which rather shook us, you know?

By default, I had to take over the group. That morning, we were going out and looking for some of our wounded in this valley, and it was a clear, sunny day, and I'm sure that we weren't dispersed enough, and the Germans still had observation from the top of the mountain, della Torraccia, which I don't think I realized. Probably a lot of people didn't. And they put some artillery fire on us, and one man was badly wounded, one of my group, and I got just ticked in the shoulder. It was taken care of with a band-aid; I was extremely fortunate. But I can remember the concussion of the shell after it exploded. I was right up in the air, sort of flat out, and dropped. So again, we had to take back our own wounded, out of our own group.

We weren't batting very well. But we kept working after that, you know. We corpsmen would take care of a person if he was wounded, and then get him back to our battalion aid station as quickly as we could. And I always figured, if we could get them back to our first aid station where our battalion surgeon and technicians were, plasma and blood and so forth, they had a very good chance of making it. But you got tired. It was strenuous work. We tried to have four men on a stretcher or a litter, and after going up and down these hills and mountains, you just got tuckered out.

We were usually probably about 1,500 or 2,000 feet [from the front lines]. [Sometimes] they were carried by prisoners back to a collecting company, or sometimes you could get a Jeep out there to take them back. They were very ingenious with making different ways of carrying two or three litters on a small Jeep. And that was a big help.

We were very fortunate because we had a commanding general who wanted to have his troops to be rested, [if possible]. If we were on the line for maybe four, five, six, seven days, he'd send in another battalion, so we could go back and get rested up, and then go into a reserve position, which was relatively safe, and then move up again. That was through March into April. And then they had the final offensive in Italy, which we didn't realize was going to be the final offensive; at that time we were fortunate, our battalion didn't have to go in on the initial attack, but the 10th Mountain did make the initial attack, and took some horrendous losses to crack the prepared German defensive lines in that area along Highway 64.

In the final offensive, the 10th Mountain would be charged with opening the highways to the north, the hillsides and mountaintops of which the Germans had fortified with mines, pillboxes, machine guns, and deadly 88s that could target a single person coming from miles away. The journalist Martha Gellhorn wrote that the German position seemed so intractable that she became physically ill thinking about men being thrown into combat against it.[33]

Eventually they got through in about four or five days, and our battalion was a breakaway battalion and carried the ball. And we caught it then, too. But that brought us to the edge of the Apennine Mountains, the northern edge, and then came the Po Valley, which is probably about 100 miles wide, a beautiful, lovely agricultural area. By that time the German army was in disarray, disorganized, and the Americans, the Allies, had complete control of the air and they raised hell with them. And eventually we got across the Po River and up into [an area with] formidable mountains [ahead of us]. And that's where the war ended. Thank heavens it did, at that time. We had taken a lot of losses. We had lost a lot of our officers and non-coms by that time, and I sensed that—even as a kid, you know, I sensed we were not as effective as we once had been. Didn't take long. And I had the feeling myself, I said, if this thing goes on two or three more weeks, I'm either going to be wounded or I'm going to be killed. Just had that sense about it.

And when we heard that the war had ended, [we felt] disbelief, and relief. And we were very subdued. There wasn't any yelling or screaming. It was just quiet. We appreciated the quiet, basically. I guess we didn't want to break the charm of the thing.

*

We had some occupation duty. Our battalion had to go up to a juncture of the Swiss-Austrian-Italian border, a beautiful mountain valley, to try to stop the surrendered German troops from getting back into Austria and Germany. So we had a good deal up there. Nobody was getting hurt, and the medics, there wasn't much for us to do, so we did a lot of climbing of the peaks around there. And did a lot of sightseeing, with our own two feet. After that we were pulled back down into the Po Valley and sent over to the Yugoslav border, where the Yugoslavian partisans were trying to take more Italian territory after the war had ended; we were sent into that area, and again no one got hurt. Good duty in there; we were there probably three, four weeks, more as a show of force. And we started up in that area, I can recall, we started climbing schools, and some of us went up into Austria and had set up a climbing school up in some of the mountains there. Who better to occupy the alpine regions after the war than mountain troops? But the Army saw it differently. Since we had been the last to come into combat, we were going to be the first to be sent back to the United

States for redeployment to fight in the invasion of Japan itself. And we were very, very fortunate that the war ended when it did with Japan, because I believe it was in mid-ocean going back that the bombs were dropped on the two cities in Japan. We were incredulous that anything like that could happen. And maybe there's a chance that this is going to end this thing sooner than we anticipated. And it was. They brought us home and they sent us back immediately out on furlough. And I was home when the war ended with Japan.

*

I was discharged in late November of '45, as I recall. [I took advantage of the G.I. Bill and] I had four years at St. Lawrence University. With the war, we certainly had to mature a little more quickly. I do know one thing, for instance, and this is probably trivial, but once I got to St. Lawrence—in those days fraternities were big up there—you had to kowtow to the upperclassmen to become even considered in the fraternity. And I just couldn't see it! I suppose I'd been in a different fraternity before that came around, you know? And so I had matured. I rebelled against that situation.

The only thing I've ever joined is the 10th Mountain's association of their veterans; I've always been active in that. I found it very interesting. Made a lot of good friends, people I'd never seen before. Well, we had something in common. [We] had volunteered, and we made our own bed and slept in it.

Mr. Vetter died at his home in the Adirondacks in 2007; he was 82 years old.

CHAPTER THIRTEEN

The BAR Man

Carl F. Newton was born in 1925 in Lockport, the western part of New York State. 'I had three years of high school. Instead of staying and graduating, I volunteered for the draft.' He went on to experience the savage fighting on Riva Ridge: 'A German hand grenade landed right in front of me, one of those potato mashers. I picked it up and threw it back, and it never did go off; it was a dud, thank goodness.' A Bronze Star recipient, he returned home after the war to finish high school, trying to pick up where he had left off. 'I sure was an odd duck as far as the rest of the kids. They didn't know how to act around me and the teachers, they didn't know what to do with me either. [Chuckles] And I really didn't know how to act around them, either...'

Carl Newton

When Pearl Harbor happened, I was home; my mother heard it on the radio and told me about the Japanese bombing. I didn't even know, I never heard of Pearl Harbor. I didn't know where it was, but I was very, very concerned when I found out it was [part of] the United States.

I wound up in the tank corps in Fort Knox, Kentucky. During one of the interviews, this officer told me about the various opportunities for volunteering. He said, 'You can volunteer for the ski troops or the paratroops.'

I said, 'Ski troops? Tell me about the ski troops.'

He said, 'Well, are you a skier?'

I said, 'Well, somewhat.' I did start skiing when I was five years old, had my first pair of skis when I was six. I wasn't a great skier, because we didn't have great hills in Lockport. We were right on the escarpment; we had a good hill in the backyard that we skied on.

I didn't think any more of it. About a week later, the first sergeant called my name. He said, 'Report to the orderly room.' I was pretty much a screwup, so I thought I was in real trouble, so I went to the orderly room and he said, 'You've been transferred to Camp Hale, Colorado, in the ski troops.'

This was a Wednesday. He said, 'Report to the orderly room every day and we'll find something for you to do, and on Monday you're going to ship out.'

I said, 'How 'bout a three-day pass?'

He said, 'Okay,' and he gave me a three-day pass and I got on the train and went home to Lockport.

I came back on Monday and they gave me a great long strip of tickets and shipped me to Colorado. I arrived in Denver on Sunday night. The guys were just going back from weekend passes. And they said, 'What are you doing here?'

I said, 'I'm going to be in the 10th Mountain.'

'Oh,' he said, 'you poor son of a gun. You're crazy to join this outfit.'

Training

Anyway, I got to Camp Hale that night. It was just zero degrees and three feet of snow on the ground. I was in the 90th. When the 87th went to

Kiska they formed the 90th Regiment. When the 87th came back they broke up the 90th. I went to the 86th and stayed in C Company, 86th Regiment, all through the war. It was a good outfit.

[We were given specialized training.] We were out on skis or snowshoes all winter. We'd go out on Monday and train in the mountains and then come back on Friday. We spent three weeks up in a ski resort called Cooper Hill, and they had a T-bar lift—in fact, it was the first T-bar lift in the country. We had intensive ski training by some professional instructors; my instructor was a famous Austrian named Friedl Pfeifer and he was a downhill champion.[34] We learned to snowplow with packs on our back and that type of thing. We had plenty of practice because we were out on skis almost all the time.

[Our winter equipment] was well tested on Mount Rainier earlier by a group of 10th Mountain people when they were stationed out in California at Fort Lewis, so I felt for the most part it was very

---

[34] *Friedl Pfeifer* (1911-1995) - A native of Austria, Pfeifer emigrated to the U.S. After Pearl Harbor, he enlisted in the Army, training 10th Mountain Division soldiers in skiing and mountain maneuvering at Camp Hale. He was wounded in Italy but returned to help build Aspen, Colorado, as a ski resort after WWII.

good. We had parkas that were white on one side and OD on the other. They had a windbreak hood with fur on them; we always took the fur off because our breath would freeze on the fur and it was uncomfortable. We used that when we were training. Then when we came into the bivouac at night we had a jacket called a pile jacket that had buttons, but they're larger with large button holes so I suppose you could button them with your mitts on. And we had what we called 'bunny boots,' they were felt boots. We took our ski boots off and put on our bunny boots. At night when we got in our sleeping bags, we had double sleeping bags; the inside bag came up to your neck and the outer bag had a hood on it. And we would put all our ski boots and all our extra clothing inside the outer bag because it would freeze up at night, and if your ski boots were frozen you couldn't get them on; you could be court martialed, because you wouldn't be any good with ski boots you couldn't get on. That was important.

I never got cold in the sleeping bag except once we were caught in a blizzard up on a treeless mountain, up above the tree line. And we built a wall out of snow blocks for a windbreak, but I was uncomfortable all night. The next day we dug a snow cave, and three of us stayed in that snow cave for two or three days until the blizzard blew out. But the problem with that was that was on a cornice—that's where the wind blows over the top and builds snow up on the other side. We were able to dig a good-sized snow cave there, but one of the guys was a cigar smoker. His name was Abe Tatum, he was from Oklahoma via California. He was trying to light a cigar and he couldn't keep the match lit. And it finally dawned on us that we didn't have enough oxygen, so we dug our way out! After that we had a ski pole up above and we'd jiggle the ski pole so that we'd get oxygen there. If you die from lack of oxygen, you don't even realize it; you just go unconscious. They say it's a good way to go if you have to go.

*

[After training in Colorado, we went right from the mountains into Texas.] For the first week or two, all we did was lie on our bunks and sweat, go take a shower, and then go back and lie in our bunks. They didn't make us do anything. Later on, they started taking us out for short hikes in the evening after dark, when it was cooler. Eventually we did a lot of training at night, but then we also started training during the day. One week we had to jog 5 miles with full equipment in a certain length of time, the next week we had to go 7 miles with full equipment, and then the next week we went 25 miles in the Texas sand. At night we'd start out at maybe seven o'clock and get back in the morning and have the day off.

[One night] they grabbed me for duty and took us to the railroad siding and had us try to lead mules back to wherever they were keeping them in the paddock. Most guys couldn't handle mules. The mules would start running and the guys would hang on for a while and ski on the feet and then let go. Later on we would see these mules, we'd be out on a hike somewhere and we'd see mules tagging along with an Army tattoo on their neck and a little piece of rope hanging. But I got my mule back because I had some experience with leading animals, and I was one of the few that got the mule back to the paddock.

The mules were used for pack artillery and also for equipment. I don't know how they got overseas, but they did arrive in Italy. We saw some; they were all being used by the Italians. They would bring us food; I remember one time we had a mattress cover full of dates that was on a mule's back. They brought it up to the company area and threw the mattress cover down. And then the Italian hopped back on the mule and sat there crosslegged and rode that mule back to wherever he came from. They were very good mule handlers.

*

I arrived in Naples on the 23rd of December. On Christmas Day they gave us a turkey dinner, canned turkey, and everyone got diarrhea. We were on boxcars and that was a pretty tough situation, it was one of those 40 and 8s. And it actually said on there, 40 men or 8 horses.

We went from there to Pisa. And we were stationed outside of Pisa for a couple days. I saw the Leaning Tower in the moonlight the first time. Then from there, they took us by truck north to where [the drivers] had to turn the lights off on the truck. We got off and hiked 14 miles in the snow up to Lizzano. It was a very, very difficult hike. It was probably one of the toughest that I ever made because I was carrying extra mortar shells, plus all my equipment; I didn't think I could take another step or carry another thing by the time I got to Lizzano.

They assigned us to a little pensione and we were at the school in town. Lined up along the sidewalk to the school were all kinds of equipment and rations of stuff. We got back down to this little pensione and every single guy had a can of something to carry, can of coffee or a can of peaches. We did not want to carry anything, but we all did.

Originally I carried an M1. Then later on, because I'm fairly good-sized, they made me a BAR man.[35] And that weapon weighed 20 pounds empty; you had to be big and strong. Each clip of ammunition weighed a pound. Later, I lugged that thing up Riva Ridge. In fact, when I became squad leader, I kept the BAR, even though then I probably would have carried a carbine or an M1. The BAR was a very delicate instrument as far as maintenance went. It had to be absolutely clean or

---

[35] *BAR*- Browning automatic rifle, a .30 caliber heavy machine gun.

it wouldn't fire. But I never had any trouble with my weapon; it worked well all the time. It was a very accurate weapon for the firepower. While we were in Lizzano, we were billeted in a little pensione with partisans.[36] This partisan brought me a BAR that somebody had run over with a truck, and we hammered and pried and messed with it, got it so it would shoot one single shot. We took it outside to try it out. And he aimed it up in the air and shot off the telephone wire. How many times could you do that? But it would only shoot one shot at a time, so it wasn't worth it, that's for sure.

First Action on Riva Ridge

We had artillery fire when we were up in Lizzano, but it was kind of an 'iffy' thing. If they shot one, we'd shoot 10 or 12 shells back at them, so we didn't get too much artillery fire. I went on night patrol on snowshoes one night; there was quite a bit of snow there. I guess there were a few skis, but we didn't have any, so we went on snowshoes and we were going to do an ambush patrol,

---

[36] *pensione*- a small hotel or boarding house in Italy.

because the Germans had been ambushing some of our patrols and so we were going to try and get some of them. Well, on the way out there was a stream, and it was probably six feet wide, maybe a little bit more. The guys were running, jumping across the stream. I ran, and just as I went to jump, I stepped on my snowshoe and I went flat into the water, so I had to lie out there in the snow with wet gear for a while. We didn't encounter any Germans on that patrol. So, I never got shot at until I got on Riva Ridge.

Well, of course we climbed it at night. We had to cross a stream with a temporary log bridge on the way up, and we couldn't see anything, couldn't really know what was going on. There were fixed ropes here and there on the real steep parts. I remember a guy said, 'Oh, I lost my helmet,' and we heard a little clink way down.

I said, 'Oh my God, where are we?' Well, we got up on top of Riva Ridge, and it was foggy, and so we were well covered. The Germans were all in bunkers. Some of the guys went down and woke them up with a rifle pointed at them; we captured a lot of them. In fact, I captured a guy, he surrendered really, running down across this hill on top of the ridge. He was dressed in white like we were and I thought it was one of our guys. Well, he got maybe 100 feet from me and he dropped his pistol belt and threw his rifle down, put his hands up, and I realized it was a German. He said to me, 'Got an American cigarette?' He spoke pretty good English. He said he'd been freezing his feet off up there for three months and he was glad to get out of there, because all they did was observe. They were artillery observers. They didn't have any artillery, they would just call it back to the artillery emplacements, and they would shoot, so every time we did much of anything, they would throw a shell at us.

Counterattacked

We could have captured all of them easily, except that one of the guys in the company took a potshot with his sniper rifle at a [German] relief column coming up and alerted them. They turned around and went back down, then that night we got a counter-attack and one of our squads was separated from the rest of the company out on a nose of the ridge. We lost quite a few people there, wounded and killed. So, we had to retake that the next day.

Fred Schuler was pinned down in a foxhole halfway between this platoon and the company, and with his white helmet with a red cross up there made it a good target; they were shooting at him too. Then we had a running, screaming assault to retake that position and I got a [bullet] crease across the back of my helmet, just above my ear on one side. [Another bullet] hit my arm and I turned around and looked at the guy behind me, because I thought he threw something at me to get my attention or something, but it was a bullet. A German hand grenade landed right in front of me, one of those potato mashers. I picked it up and threw it back, and it never did go off; it was a dud, thank goodness.

I had quite a few close calls. Later on, I was running across a potato field outside of Sassomolare; we lost a lot of people in that assault. A bullet went through my helmet, through my wool cap, through my hair, and out the back end, but it never touched me. I wish I could have kept that helmet, but you used the helmet for everything, and it wasn't that good with a hole in it, so I threw it away. It would have been a good souvenir to have.

Up in Riva Ridge, after that assault, it was a very difficult night, because there were wounded Germans out in front of us. One guy was screaming that he was freezing to death and wanted us to help him. One of the guys in my squad, my assistant gunner on the BAR, had been educated in Switzerland as a young kid and he understood German. And he said, 'He's freezing to death, we have to go out and help him.' We did, and the squad leader interrogated [the German]; he was a captain, but he was shot up really bad and he didn't make it.

And that was [part of] the trouble we had, we couldn't get our own wounded off [the mountain] until later when they built a tramway to take our wounded people down on the tram. Paul Petzoldt, the famous mountaineer, was assigned to build that tramway.[37] There was a huge rock at the bottom just across the stream where we started, and

---

[37] *Paul Petzoldt (1908-1999)*- accomplished mountaineer, making his first ascent of the Grand Teton at the age of 16. In 1938 he was a member of the first American team to attempt a climb on K2. During the war, he pioneered medical evacuation techniques to soldiers in the 10th Mountain Division. He went on to establish the National Outdoor Leadership School in 1965.

they anchored the cable there and then ran the cable up the mountain. Then they fastened the litters to the cable to run them down; it was a fun ride if you weren't wounded. We had to walk down. See, Riva Ridge was very steep from the American side. On the other side, it was gradual, and the Germans could actually drive up there. It wasn't easy going, but they could get up there. Of course, they could just hike out. But they never expected anybody could climb from the other way, so they didn't man any positions at night. We were lucky there, because they could have rolled rocks down and knocked us off the mountain. It would have been absolutely [like] shooting fish in a barrel, because [the terrain] was so difficult. There weren't any trees at that time. Now, when we went back in '95, it was all second-growth trees. [Back then], the Italians had stripped the mountain of wood for fire.

[I received the Bronze Star] at Sassomolare. That's where I got the bullet hole in my helmet. Our squad was going across this field and there was a machine gun in this house, up in the town. [The Germans] had good field of fire and we lost

[Bill Crookshank], who got severely wounded; he wound up in the hospital for about three years. They never expected him to make it, but he did. He has his one arm, but it is somewhat useless. Two people in my squad were killed. When I saw them go down, I went out from where we were pinned down to try and see if I could help, but when I got out there, I found out they were both dead. So that's what I got the Bronze Star for.

The Artillery Observer

From Sassomolare we went over to Grande d'Aiano, and we were there for quite a while. We received a tremendous amount of artillery fire; every day we would get artillery fire, especially around dinnertime, in the early evening. The artillery observer of our side came up; our foxholes were dug on the forward slope—we had dug a trench between our foxhole and the back so we wouldn't have to expose ourselves on the ridge coming and going to our foxholes. And this artillery observer came up, with his map in a plastic envelope, and it's shining in the sun and his binoculars are hanging around his neck [*gestures to his chest area*] ... It was a sunny day, and I'm sure he was just advertising [to the Germans] that he was there, and then he got in our foxhole. I was in there with our squad leader; I was assistant squad leader at that time, because Bill Crookshank was in the hospital. And he started calling fire from our foxhole! [*Makes incredulous expression, shakes head*] He was calling artillery fire in on the Germans, who were down in the valley. And whew, they reciprocated with a big bombardment, we got an awful bombardment! We had a tree burst right over our hole—it killed my squad leader and practically blew the leg off this artillery observer! I got one little piece of shrapnel in my leg, and that was all. I dug that out myself, but the guy in the foxhole next to me was riddled. He had a bandolier of ammunition hanging up, and somehow that concussion set that off. And it just riddled him, killed him. And another guy had both knees... [*Pauses, looks down*] He was sitting in a trench with his knees exposed, he got both his knees... [*Trails off, pauses*] I never did hear what happened to him. Boy, I wish I had followed through on that, but I never did—I had so many other things to worry about after the war.

[The Germans] knew where our artillery observer was. They knew exactly where he was. Yes. We cussed that guy. But that's how I became squad leader—by attrition.

We had a well. There was a house up there on Grande d' Aiano and the Germans polluted it. Almost everybody in the company got hepatitis. I wound up in the hospital for three months, and that's where I was all through the rest of the war, whereas Fred had to slog all the way up through the Po Valley. Fred was up learning how to climb glaciers and I was in the hospital; I missed all that. At that time, [the doctors] were very concerned about [liver damage], so they did keep us in the hospital for a long time.

I got out of the hospital after the war was over. We were up in the Trieste area at that time, because Tito was threatening to retake Trieste.[38] But we didn't have anything to do. We had a really great time. We'd get up and have morning formation, and then we'd be free the rest of the day. We went hiking. We went trout fishing in a nice

---

[38] *Tito was threatening to retake Trieste-* Josip Broz Tito (1892-1980), Communist partisan leader during World War II and dictator of Yugoslavia, active in Yugoslavian politics until his death in 1980.

stream. Boy, that was a beautiful area, steep mountains and narrow valleys. In fact, it was a winter resort. In the hotel there they had a climbing wall in the gym; now climbing walls are really popular. Those were steel [rungs], a bit like staples in various routes up this wall for your hands and feet.

*

'The Little Things'

I was discharged in December '45; I got out in December, just before Christmas. I went to work for Harrison Radiator, part of General Motors at Lockport. I worked 5:00 to 1:30 a.m., I was the custodian of the general offices. Then I went to high school in the morning and took the required courses. [Having been in the military and in the war], I sure was an odd duck as far as the rest of the kids. They didn't know how to act around me and the teachers, they didn't know what to do with me either. [*Chuckles*] And I really didn't know how to act around them, either. It was a pretty easy thing to finish high school. Later I went to college on the G.I. Bill.

After they broke up the 10th, they shipped us all over and I wound up down in St. Louis at the Fort Jefferson Barracks. I was the chaplain's assistant. My job was to work in the separation center. When a group got discharged, I would take their discharges and follow them out into the street and form them up into some semblance of good formation and give the guy a signal and he'd put on the 'Stars and Stripes Forever' tape. I'd march them down to the Polk Theater and then I'd introduce the chaplain... and hand the discharge to the chaplain. He would shake their hands. After they all got discharged then I'd march them down to get the bus. Well, some of them, you know... they were out, they weren't about to take any orders from me. [*Laughs*] But some of them, after being in the service for quite a while, they couldn't help but do it...

*

I think [the war] had a tremendous effect on my outlook on life. I feel the training was something that it's too bad every young man can't go through, because I think it gives you a sense of patriotism, but also the feeling of, 'Don't sweat the little things.' It was a difficult thing, but I'm glad I did it.

Mr. Newton died in 2010 at the age of 85.

CHAPTER FOURTEEN

The Squad Leader

Arthur Thompson was born into a family of railroaders on the shores of Lake Champlain in the shadow of the Adirondack Mountains. He was excited to join the Army, and at 18, became a machine gun squad leader in the 10th Mountain Division. A seat at the local drugstore was where his war began and ended: 'I was at home on furlough, and I was in the drug store, sitting on a stool, when they dropped the second bomb. I was sitting on that same stool in that same drug store on December 7, 1941, when the Japs bombed Pearl Harbor and started the war. I had gone full circle.'

After the war, he furthered his education, going on to become a superintendent of schools. 'I used the G.I. Bill, probably the greatest law that the United States Congress ever passed. Life has been good. My best buddy *was left in Italy and I often wonder what would have happened if he had lived as I had been able to.'*

Arthur Thompson

I was born on April 5, 1925, and I was born in Port Henry, New York, which is on the banks of Lake Champlain. When I went in the service, I was a fresh 18-year-old boy who had graduated from high school the previous June. I went back to school and post-graduated because I was anxious to go in the service but couldn't because the Army was only taking 18-year-olds at that point. I could have gone in the Navy but I wasn't interested in the Navy. I was interested in the Army because during the late '30s, I was very intrigued with the Russian-Finnish war when the ski troopers in the Finnish army were very active. In Port Henry, I was probably one of the only two or three who skied. I used to enjoy skiing through the woods above our house and make-believing I was a ski trooper. My ambition was to be a ski trooper. Later on, when I decided to join, the National Ski Patrol was doing the recruiting for the ski troops of the United States Army. What they were looking for were skiers to develop a ski division out in Colorado at Camp Hale—that's where the training center was.

I enlisted in the Army Reserve, which you could do at age 17. One month after my birthday in April of 1943, I was called to active duty and went to report at Camp Upton, New York, which was the processing center. After several days of processing, I was put on a troop train with a lot of other people, and went to Fort McClellan, Alabama, where I did my basic training. Basic training lasted for 16 weeks. At the end of the 16 weeks we were called out in the company street. The first sergeant read off the list of the soldiers from our unit who would be on the troop train the next morning to go to Fort Ord, California, and deployment to the Pacific as replacements. Low and behold, my name was on that list.

I have to tell you, I was a little bit excited about it. When the formation was dismissed, I walked into the orderly room and said to the first sergeant, 'I can't be on that list. I have a letter here that said I'm going to Camp Hale, Colorado, where the ski troops are training. This letter says that's where I'm supposed to go'.

The first sergeant's reply was, 'Soldier, you'll go where you're told you're going to go.'

With that, the company commander was in his office. He said, 'First sergeant, what's going on?'

The first sergeant said, 'Well, Private Thompson thinks he's going to the ski troops and we've got him on the list to go to Fort Ord, California.'

They dismissed me, and the next morning, when the group fell out to go to Fort Ord, California, the first sergeant said, 'Private Thompson, go back to the barracks.'

I sat in the barracks for five days. At the end of five days, lo and behold, the first sergeant came down and he said, 'Here are your orders. You're going to Camp Hale, Colorado.'

And so I was put on a train all by myself and went from Fort McClellan, Alabama, to Camp Hale, Colorado, where we trained for the next year and a few months in mountain warfare and ski patrol. It was the beginning of the activation of the 10th Mountain Division, which was the only ski mountain division in the United States Army in World War II.

Because I was a skier and had skied, you had to pass a special test to determine that you were qualified to be a ski trooper. We were issued, of course, skis and parkas and ski boots and poles. After you passed that test, you were taken on ski marches where you had ruck sacks, which were special to our division. We didn't have a pack like the regular infantry people had. We had a ruck sack, which carried 90 pounds of equipment. If you couldn't ski with 90 pounds of equipment on your back, they soon found another job for you.

I qualified as a machine gunner. At the point where our company, F Company of the 86th Mountain Infantry Regiment, was formed, I was the youngest in our machine gun squad. They asked me if I would like to be the sergeant of the squad. As an 18-year-old kid, just turning 19, I became a sergeant. I was a machine gun squad leader for the entire time from that point on.

At the end of our training in Camp Hale, we went down to Camp Swift, Texas, where all kinds of rumors, as the Army always has, came across about the fact that we weren't going to be trained, or we weren't going to fight as a mountain division, but we were going to be retrained as a flat land division, and we were going to just be put wherever they needed such a division.

In the meantime, the war in Italy had gotten to the north Apennines and they reached a stalemate. They were in the Apennine Mountains, and General Clark, who was the Commander of the Fifth Army in Italy, told General Marshall, or told someone in the War Department, that they needed some special troops. The 10th Mountain Division was put on troop trains, sent to Fort Patrick Henry, Virginia, at Norfolk, put on several ships. We were on the *SS Argentina*, the 86th Mountain Infantry, and we spent eleven days going from Norfolk, Virginia, to Naples, Italy; we were the first regiment [in the division] out, and we were the first regiment to reach Naples. The trip was very exciting because we had no escorts. Of course, those of us that didn't like the water anyway, were concerned about where the submarines were and when they were going to come and get us. But nothing happened. The *USS Argentina* was now a troop ship. It went straight through Gibraltar and straight to Naples. One ship. No escorts at all. The rest of the division followed in a convoy. I guess it was because the *Argentina* was a faster ship and they figured it didn't need to have an escort.

We arrived in Naples, Italy, on Christmas Eve in 1944. Being just 19, my best friend and I and a couple of other fellas decided that Christmas Eve in Naples, Italy, [was going to be memorable]. We found a wine cellar and we all proceeded to get very sick. I had never had anything alcoholic to drink before that, and until my youngest son graduated from college, I didn't have any anymore.

The next day they put us on a cattle boat and shipped us from Naples up to Leghorn. Leghorn was the port just below the Apennines in that area. They took us off the boat. Needless to say, that was a rough, rough ride for us because we weren't feeling too good.

They took us off the boat and trucked us up to an encampment area near the Leaning Tower of Pisa. That's where we had our first casualties. One of the fellas was walking guard duty along the railroad tracks and he stepped on a mine. Two or three fellas ran to help him and they stepped on other mines, so we had two or three fellas killed at that point. A few days later, we went on the front lines, the first regiment of the division on front line. We were in a stalemate position where they were just breaking us in. I was able to go on one patrol and we ran into a German bunker and had a firefight. That was our baptism from the standpoint of what combat was all about.

Riva Ridge and Mount Belvedere

We were there for eight or ten days. The rest of the division caught up with us and they put us on the front at that location, which was toward the western end of the north Apennine Mountains. The stalemate was caused by the Germans having control of Mount Belvedere, which was the prominent point in the Apennine line. They were able to control the roads going into Bologna from the Mount Belvedere area. They had observation posts on Riva Ridge, which was to the west of Mount Belvedere. Anybody that tried to take Mount Belvedere ran into a difficult situation because the observers at Riva Ridge were able to pour the artillery down on them.

Our general said to the division, 'You guys were trained to be mountain soldiers. Now you're going to be mountain soldiers.' The First Battalion of our 86th Regiment and F Company, which was the company I was in, was assigned to take the ridge; F Company was to protect the left flank of the 1st Battalion.

We started up that ridge. It was about a 1,500-foot ridge, and we started up at 9:00 at night and reached the top of the ridge just as daylight broke in the morning and attacked and drove the Germans off that ridge. They had two or three counterattacks, which we repulsed; we secured the ridge. Once we secured the ridge, the main force then started the battle up Mount Belvedere. Two days later, we took Mount Belvedere.

When Belvedere was secured, F Company came down off the ridge and joined the rest of our 2nd Battalion, and we went around on the east side of Mount Belvedere and were attacking there until the next stop. We were stopped for a few weeks and regrouped and then started the final push out into the Po Valley. At that point, several weeks before we reached the Po Valley, my best friend was killed when a mortar landed a direct hit on his foxhole. He was the platoon messenger, and he and the platoon sergeant were killed. Around the same time, I had some pieces of shrapnel from another situation, so I was back in the hospital in Florence for a while and was awarded the Purple Heart. I then came back up and joined the regiment and our company, just as we broke out of the Apennines into the Po Valley.

The Po Valley

They put a task force together, which was led by the 86th Mountain Infantry Regiment. We sped across the Po Valley hoping to cut the Germans off before they got to the highways that went up into the Brenner Pass and back into Germany. We got to the Po Valley way ahead of any of our amphibious vehicles or any boats that we had, so we went across the Po River in little rubber boats with five or six fellas to a boat, paddling like hell. The current was stiff, so we ended up half a mile downstream, but we were able to get across the river and establish a foothold. The pontoon people came up and eventually got the bridges across and the whole rest of the division came.

At one time, the 10th Mountain Division task force I was with was 65 miles ahead of the rest of the front in Italy. We were exposed on both flanks. We were exposed behind us as well, except for the supply line that was coming up with us. We got into Verona two days before the rest of the division caught up. From Verona, General Hays, who was a tremendous tactician, said to General Clark and the boys back in the headquarters, 'We can get to the Brenner Pass. And if we can get to the Brenner Pass, we can cut off everything that comes out of Italy going back to Germany, except those that go the other routes.' General Hays was a Medal of Honor recipient in World War I, and he was our commanding general all the way through.

We took off again and went up along Lake Garda. There was a highway on both sides. On the west side of Lake Garda, Mussolini had his big palace, summer estate. We were on the right-hand highway going along Lake Garda. Lake Garda, on the eastern side, had seven tunnels along the lake.

When we got to the first tunnel the Germans had an 88mm gun in the tunnel. At that point, F Company was in the lead. As we came up over the hill, the first shots were fired from the tunnel and we realized that we were in trouble. I was awarded a Bronze Star there because I directed artillery fire into the tunnel. Finally, the Germans pulled the 88 back and went back on toward Torbole at the other end of the tunnel.

They then put some of the 87th Regiment in ducks.[39] They went across the lake and captured Mussolini's summer place and were trying to cut off the Germans coming up the road on that side.

As we were going up the lake, we got in the duck, just ahead of the first tunnel, and we landed about the fifth tunnel up, so we had to go through the last couple of tunnels. As we were going up the lake, we could see the 88 shells landing in the

---

[39] *They then put some of the 87th Regiment in ducks–* The DUKW was a six-wheel-drive amphibious vehicle; Mr. Thompson clarified: 'A duck is an amphibious vehicle that carries troops. They used a lot of them in the South Pacific. It was a transportation group that was attached to us at the time that we were going across the Po Valley. They were used later on, going across the river before they got the bridge up. They weren't like landing craft. They didn't have a front that went down. You climbed over the side. They were wheeled vehicles. They were big, probably about a platoon, 40 men or so.'

water. For a guy who doesn't like water, it was a harrowing experience.

We landed, and as we went through the sixth tunnel, we discovered that one of our shells had hit that tunnel and the Germans that were in there were really annihilated. We were walking over bodies through that sixth tunnel until we got to the seventh.

War's End

We got to the town of Torbole. Our assistant division commander was Bill Darby, who was the head of Darby's Rangers in World War II. The Rangers were no longer being utilized as such, and so they gave Colonel Darby a command as the assistant division commander of our division with the idea that he would become a general, eventually become commander of his own division. General Darby was killed at Torbole shortly before the war was over.

From Torbole we went up to Garda, which was at the end of the lake. We were four miles above Garda on the road going into the Brenner Pass when the war was over; we had thought we were going to get all the way to the Brenner Pass. When the Germans in Italy surrendered, they wanted General Hays to be the general who accepted the surrender because he was the general that ran that mountain division, which caused them all their problems. So we all felt honored for General Hays.

The war was over but they were having problems over in Yugoslavia. The man who [would become] the dictator in Yugoslavia, Tito, was anxious to take over the free city of Trieste. The Allies sent the 10th Mountain Division up there to make sure that he didn't get the city. We were there for probably three or four weeks before we were replaced by soldiers of the 32nd Division. We were trucked back to Leghorn, where we got on ships and came back to the United States with the idea that the 10th Mountain Division was going to be going to the Pacific and was going to be involved in the invasion of Japan.

While we were on the ocean coming back the first atomic bomb was dropped. When I got home, we went into Norfolk, Virginia, again. They sent us up to Fort Dixon. From there we went home on a 30-day furlough with the idea that we'd then report back to Camp Carson, Colorado, and be retrained and then go to the Pacific. I was at home on furlough, and I was in the drug store, sitting on a stool, when they dropped the second bomb. I was sitting on that same stool in that same drug store on December 7, 1941, when the Japs bombed Pearl Harbor and started the war. I had gone full circle.

*

I went to Camp Carson and immediately they sent us back home for another 30 days because the war was over; they didn't know what to do with us. So I went back home for a second 30-day leave, went back to Camp Carson, got discharged, and then came back to Port Henry.

*

I think the 10th Mountain Division influenced that [determination to go onto higher education] because our company commander was later the Governor of the State of Massachusetts, Francis Sargent. The 10th was an all-volunteer outfit, and as such, we had college kids all over the place who were skiers, rock climbers, and mountain climbers. We had a lot of forest rangers, we had a lot of real classy people. At one time the 10th Mountain Division was reported to have had the highest IQ in the United States Army. I believe they did because all of the platoon sergeants had had two or three years of college. All the officers were college graduates. They were all quality people. Eisenhower at one point was reported to have said, 'I can't use that Ivy League crowd in Europe.' I don't know if he said that, but that was one of the comments that was made.

[When I heard about the second atomic bomb, I felt] pure elation because we knew that if we were going to be in on the invasion of Japan, the expectation was for something like 70 to 80 percent casualties. That would probably mean that our division was going to be used somewhere where the cliffs were, or the mountains were, in the entrance to Tokyo. We later found out that we were scheduled to be in reserve and would be landed after the initial landing. When the war was over and they deactivated our division at Camp Carson, General Hays had a division review. He called the entire division—at that point, we weren't very many more than eight or nine thousand because a lot of them had already been discharged—and showed us the map of the invasion, what was going to happen, and so forth. I was most relieved at that point. I'd done what I had to do and it was time for me to go on to college.

My family were all railroaders. I used the G.I. Bill, probably the greatest law that the United States Congress ever passed. I think the G.I. Bill should be available for everybody who ever served in service; I probably never would have gone to college if it hadn't been for World War II and the G.I. Bill. I became a schoolteacher and eventually became a superintendent of schools and was able to be the superintendent of schools in Lake Placid for 18 years. One of my dreams as a young kid was to someday live in Lake Placid. We spent 40 years of our life there, with all of our kids graduating from the school there. Life has been good. My best buddy was left in Italy and I often wonder what would have happened if he had lived as I had been able to.

*

I belong to the American Legion, but my allegiance has been with the 10th Mountain. I have been very active since the war in the 10th Mountain Division Association, in fact was the President of the New York State chapter and National Vice President at one point. When they activated the 10th Mountain Division in 1985 up at Fort Drum, it was the most modern military installation in the world, but nobody had ever made any provisions for anything at the main gate; most posts across the country had a monument of some kind at the main gate. I was asked to serve as chairman of a committee that raised $115,000, and we put a monument at the main gate at Fort Drum. I consider that my contribution to today's 10th Mountain Division, which is the division that just came home from Afghanistan. They've been the most deployed division in the United States Army in this last 15 years.

We have a reunion every three years. I've been back to Italy twice. The first time my wife went with me, and the second time my son went with me. I was able to show both of them what we had done while we were over there.

Arthur Thompson passed away at the age of 89 in December 2014.

CHAPTER FIFTEEN

The Platoon Leader

Harold J. Wusterbarth

Harold J. Wusterbarth was born on June 12, 1920. Before the war, he had been a student at Bentley School of Accounting in Boston, and then worked for General Electric in Schenectady, New York, which was big on defense; the American Locomotive Alco Plant produced tracked vehicles there. 'But I wasn't involved in that. I was an accountant, which is not very romantic when it comes to the military, and it also meant I wasn't going to get a deferment. Accountants came cheap.' [Laughs]

Mr. Wusterbarth was involved in the assault on Riva Ridge and Mount Belvedere. After settling into a defensive position, he was led across a field by a sergeant and stepped on a landmine. 'I weighed 140 pounds; if you're going to step on a mine, don't be too heavy. I still have my foot; it's messed up, but they were able to patch me up. Took two years, but I walked in here today without a cane.' A recipient of the Bronze Star and Purple Heart, he was nearing his 88th birthday when he sat for this interview in 2008.

While I worked at General Electric I had fallen in love with the Adirondacks. Coming from Connecticut, we had mountains, but nothing to match the Adirondacks. So, it was a love affair with the Adirondacks, and I had been up climbing mountains on that weekend and on the way home, somebody turned the car radio on and that's when I heard about Pearl Harbor. The reaction from most of us was, 'Where the heck is Pearl Harbor?' [*Chuckles*]

I enlisted.

The head of the National Ski Patrol was a guy by the name of Dole, no relationship to the senator, Robert Dole, who incidentally was in the same regiment as I was, eventually. This guy's name was Minny Dole, Minot Dole, and he was convinced that America was going to get into the war. This was in 1939 or 1940; Germans had some mountain infantry troops, America didn't, so he convinced George Marshall, Chief of Staff, that America should have some mountain ski troops. And Marshall said, 'Where would I get them?' Well, every hill and ski center was manned by National Ski Patrol people. So, for the first time, the Army used civilians to find the skiers, soldiers for the Army; so that was the beginning of it, and word went out that anybody who was a skier and who was interested could apply to the National Ski Patrol, which had an office down in New York City. You had to get three letters of recommendation. I got my three letters together, and though I had never had a skiing lesson in my life, [I would soon be] associating with some real hotshots in Colorado, even though I was way out of their class. But I loved skiing and I said, 'Gee, this is a big deal. I ski, and Uncle Sam wants me, and I get to do my patriotic act, and they're going to pay me!' Now this is the story that is recounted by a lot of guys—we had the romantic idea that we were going to be 'shooshing' down slopes, you know, killing the enemy at the bottom, which shows how naive we were, you know; the Germans didn't defend at the bottom, they defended at the top. But that's how I got in.

I was in the 2nd Battalion in the first regiment of the 10th Mountain Division being formed up, the 87th, fairly soon after Pearl Harbor. I went to Fort Lewis, Washington, first while they were building Camp Hale for ski troop training in Colorado near Leadville and Vail, Colorado. The barracks were pretty much complete. We had a lot of snow starting in December, the mountain part of the Rocky Mountains, and I don't recall that we had any lack of snow until springtime. We soon discovered this romantic idea of Alpine downhill skiing wasn't what they were going to feed us; first of all, the packs we trained with contained more junk than any of us really needed—mountain tents, three days' ration of food, the skis themselves, a rucksack, and a double-down sleeping bag. Some of this stuff we discarded early because with 80 or 90 pounds on our backs, we weren't pretty mobile. [*Chuckles*] Plus, of course, we also had our M1 rifles, and some of the guys in the mortar squad had to carry the baseplate, the tube, and the bipod. And also some of them were assigned the snowshoes, which they hated. Any skier looked with disdain on those who had snowshoes. [*Laughs*] [The mortar squads] had such heavy stuff to carry, snowshoes just seemed to be the logical solution, and incidentally, when we got into combat, we never used skis, outside of a patrol or two. They weren't practical. You're crawling up the mountain, not 'shoosing' down.

We had more training probably than any other infantry outfit. This was basically an infantry outfit, so we had squad training. I started out as a private. Incidentally, the pay when I went in was Depression pay. Twenty-one dollars a month, which I think comes out to seventy cents a day. Shortly after, Congress upped the private's pay to fifty bucks, and I moved from corporal, which I think was sixty-six dollars a month. Eventually, I went to Officer Candidate School, and pay was a lot better.

Mules

I stayed away from those mules, they were deadly! I'd rather face the enemy than those mules! The muleskinners, as they're called, had a way of taming them. They would put their elbow against the mule's ribs and they'd give them one of these. [*Thrusts elbows out*] The mule would give out a 'foosh' and go down on its knees. People knew to stay away from them. Stand in front and they'd bite you, to the side they'd step on you, and I don't have to tell you what they'd do if you're behind them. [*Laughs*] They were very dangerous for a guy that didn't know how to handle them. Those muleskinners would swear all kinds of things, and the mules understood swearing, I guess. In Colorado I was assigned a job to train some of these muleskinners. They were from the mountains of West Virginia, they never saw skis before. They would swear at those skis the same way they'd swear at those mules. Eventually I taught them the basics of skiing and they got a kick out of it.

*

We already had basic training in Fort Lewis, Washington, and one of the transitions was that

Fort Lewis was about 100 feet above sea level, on Puget Sound, and Camp Hale was 9,000 feet. The first thing we discovered was that we weren't in as good shape as we thought because we were all wheezing, and it took a couple of days to get acclimated to the thinner mountain air. And we just continued to do training. The training was the same kind of infantry training that anyone would expect. I learned weapons. I could take an M1 apart in the dark, BAR, Browning Automatic Rifle; I knew my weapons. Not so much mortars and machine guns, but I became a BAR squad leader. BAR, Browning Automatic Rifle, was kind of a combination of M1 rifle, which you could shoot one round at a time, or an automatic weapon, twenty rounds in a magazine which went from the bottom.

The area around Camp Hale is all mountain. There's nothing to 'practice' attack; there's no cities, no towns, except Leadville, and that was off limits, and we were told there were bad ladies that were there that weren't good for our morals. [*Chuckles*] So we'd attack a simulated farmhouse; it was good training because eventually we did that very thing!

You asked me if I ever had a problem with my weapons. In combat I was a platoon leader, 35 guys, 1st lieutenant, and since I wasn't supposed to be laying down a base of fire, I had a carbine. A carbine is a small version of an M1 rifle, but it's frailer. Well, the first time we were on a patrol, there was snow on the ground, this was Italy. I stupidly got snow in the barrel. And I said to myself, I didn't know it, 'I've come a long way, I've had a lot of training, I ought to hit that house with a few rounds out of my carbine.' I pulled the trigger and there was a funny popping noise; it wasn't the way it's supposed to sound. I looked halfway down the barrel and there was a bulge, like a snake having swallowed a rodent. So here I am on my first patrol, first time in combat, and my carbine's got a bulge in it! I got a weapon that doesn't work! I was crawling forward, moving to one squad at a time towards the farmhouse; I'm heading straight for a foxhole. And when we hit this farmhouse, there was a machine gun that opened up, and our two scouts got hit, and I was heading for this foxhole. I looked over the edge, and there's the German, with his machine gun down in his foxhole; he'd heard all this firing, and decided this was an appropriate time to become a prisoner of war, and he was smart enough to bring the machine gun down in the foxhole, otherwise he would have gotten a grenade, because that's the way you took out a machine gun. After that, I was careful about getting snow in a carbine.

In June of '43, our group of about 3,000 guys moved out of Camp Hale to Fort Ord near Monterey Bay in California for amphibious training. [We practiced] moving off the assault ship, down the net, into the landing craft. The tricky part is going over the side, the gunwales of the ship, down a cargo net, and you're warned 'don't do this,' [*raises both of his fists up, knuckles to the ceiling*] 'do this,' [*turns his fists outward*], because the guy above you might be 200 pounds with an 80-pound pack and you'll get your hands crushed, so it doesn't take long before you realize that's the way to do it. Now it's tricky to get to the landing craft if the sea is rough because the landing craft is banging against the ship and going up and down.

Anyway, it was a nice, calm day; we went over the side of the ship and into the landing craft. There were about 20 to 30 landing craft all lined up, going in a circle, until all of them were loaded, and then they got in a line and hit the beach at the same time. We hit the beach, went down the ramp, and we didn't even get our feet wet! Hey, this is a piece of cake! [*Chuckles*] Don't think that it is.

*

Attu and Kiska

A month or two later we're off the coast of Kiska in the Aleutians, way out in the end of the Aleutian chain. That's incidentally why we had the amphibious training. To backtrack a bit, at the Battle of Midway the Japanese tried to divert our attention and landed troops on Attu and Kiska, which are the last two islands in the western chain of the Aleutians. There's a thousand-mile line of islands, and the western part is almost to Asia, and that's where the Japanese had landed. They thought that they could pull our navy out of Pearl Harbor to take these islands back. We were going to hit the shore, the beach of Kiska, but there's no beach, it's just all rocks. And there's eternal fog, rain, so the coxswains are all lined up and they can barely see each other, but they can't see where they're going to go. So nobody landed on the shore where they were supposed to. The coast guard would have two guys piloting. One guy is supposed to throw out a sea anchor right before he gets to shore, so if he gets hung up on [a rock], he can winch his way in. So it was a real, real messed up landing. Attu had been a bloody affair with a banzai charge at the end, and probably 6,000 Japanese troops died for their emperor. We were all geared up for the worst in Kiska, and it took us a week to figure out that there were no Japanese on this island. We got into firefights with ourselves. [We did not have a single line on Kiska]; our flanks were hanging in air and there was a big space between us and the company next to us. That first night, these green troops sized [the situation] up for the worst and somebody started firing at something moving, and pretty soon we were firing at each other. We had a lieutenant by the name of Wilfred Funk, his family owned the Funk and Wagnalls outfit, and he was the one that was killed when trying to defend the battalion CP. Later on, you try to explain this and you can't explain it. Friendly fire—they didn't call it that then, but that's what it amounted to. We lost about twelve guys in our regiment, because the first night, nobody knew where the other guys were. When we got to combat in Italy, the same thing happened all over again.

We were there for five months; it was the most miserable place to be, though I think I'd rather have had that than the jungle of New Guinea, where you got a lot of squirmy things. There was no life on Kiska. Fog, rain, gale winds came off the Bering Sea. It was picturesque in the beginning, but there were 35,000 troops eventually on Kiska; our regiment was just 3,000. There were some Canadian troops and a lot of American troops, and as soon as we started mogging around on that island, it turned the tundra into a big mudhole. There was an extinct volcano at one end of the island and a lot of volcanic ash, powdery stuff. It was bad enough when there was just grass on the top, but as soon as you start churning up that tundra grass, you're into mud, and 35,000 guys can make a big mudhole in a short time on a small island. So that was the way we lived, and because of the great gale winds, we finally got the green pyramidal tents, and the first thing we had to do was dig down so only the roof of the tent was showing, because the first time the guys pitched them, they went to sea! [*Laughs*] If we didn't dig down, the tent couldn't stay up. The unfortunate part was that the deeper in the mud you went, the more water you got. They finally gave us Army cots, which was a real luxury. And I should tell you about the stove that they finally dropped off about a month later. It looked like an aluminum beer keg. It had a little door in the front. They gave us a four-inch pipe, and an adapter at the peak. Now, there's no wood, trees on Kiska, just nothing! They dumped bags of the powdery bituminous coal. We had all we wanted, provided we would head down to the docks and lug it up. We were way up in the hills at this point.

They wanted to bring us back to Colorado, but it was five months before they got a ship available to evacuate us. The Pacific was such a big ocean, and shipping was scarce. Finally, the ship did arrive around December. We landed in Ketchikan,

Alaska, which is the southern tip of Alaska. There the Canadian railroad took over and took us to Colorado, where our regiment was the first formed, and now there were two other regiments being formed, the 86th and 85th. Now don't ask me why the Army goes 87, 86, 85—that's the way they do it. So there were two other regiments forming up, and that then consisted of the 10th Mountain Division, so they brought us back because we were a trained regiment and we'd supplement the other two regiments.

Shipping Out

The 10th Mountain Division went to Texas, and we're only there for a short time before we shipped out to the point of embarkation, Newport News, Virginia, in December 1944. I was now a 2nd lieutenant. Now the first time I went up to Kiska, I was a corporal. The enlisted man's version of a troop ship is pretty grim. You're in the hull of the ship, no ventilation, no portholes, very low light, red lamps. The bunks were four high or five high. You had to kind of slide in, and if the guy above you moved around, you got your nose pushed in. I considered it three steps below what those poor immigrants on the *Mayflower* did! Awful! There were a lot of guys topside heaving over the side. After a couple of days, most of us got over that. But now I'm an officer on the *USS West Point,* which was formerly the *USS America,* and I'm getting served in a dining room. I didn't apply for commission to get better service on a troopship, I did it to get more money, but that was kind of a bonus. We had staterooms and there were bunks in the stateroom, but the enlisted men had the same kind of accommodations that I had the first time I went to Kiska. It wasn't such a bad life, but they never told you where you were going. We went through the Strait of Gibraltar; by then we knew we were heading for Italy, just a single ship by then, [not in a convoy]. The German U-boat mess had apparently been solved. We'd been carrying gas masks all the time. The first thing we did as we came off the ship, they told us to pile up our gas masks on the dock, you don't need gas masks; I don't know what they did with all those gas masks. They were pretty sure the Germans weren't going to use gas, doesn't work much in the mountains anyway.

Now we're in Italy. We got in there late; it took two years to go from Sicily all the way up the boot of Italy. We were welcomed; the Germans had distributed little pamphlets that said, 'Welcome to the 10th Mountain Division. You're going to get some surprises when you get into combat, you're going to get slaughtered.' Well, we didn't pay any attention to that. It was really the other way around.

We had early patrol duty way out in the mountains. The lines were probably ten miles apart. And that's where I had my first experience with a patrol. The G2 [Intelligence] Division said we'd like to interview some prisoners. That was a brilliant idea, but they didn't go get the prisoners. Out of 150 platoons in the 10th Mountain Division, I'm the one that's selected to go take some prisoners. You don't argue, you do what you're told.

So we moved against the farmhouse and in the fog [as we set out]. This wasn't Kiska fog, but a snow field with a certain kind of warm climate generates fog. Now we're on the top side of a farmhouse which was built on the side of a slope. The fog had lifted and we could see what we're doing, but I only had two squads and one squad was back at the trailhead.

We're above the farmhouse firing in the windows. I said, 'You two guys come with me.' We jump down off this parapet onto the patio. I said, 'I'm going to lob a grenade.' This is the first time I've fired a live grenade; we practiced over and over with dummy grenades, you know, 'Stand! Pull pin! Prepare to throw! Throw!' You do that in training, and you say, 'This is boring,' but in combat, sometimes you get excited and you forget to pull the pin! [*Chuckles*] This time I didn't, in went the grenade, there's an explosion, and I said, 'You two guys bang in the door, I'll be right behind you.' So that's what we did. Now the scene is kind of interesting, it could have been out of a Hollywood movie. Hanging from the rafter is the carcass of a black, hairy goat, partly butchered. There's a fire going, and on the roughhewn table are five plates. We apparently had interrupted their lunch. There's nobody around, though. Out on the patio, there's a dead German. How did I know he was dead? He had a hole in his head. One of our guys firing had caught him; he was in the wrong place at the wrong time. What about the three other guys? I can claim the first prisoner in kind of a bizarre way, here's a dead one, there are five plates, the other guys must be someplace. I'm going over the dead German's body to get papers; this is the first time I've ever touched a dead guy. Without even telling them, the guys knew their stuff, even when being new to combat; they went to the basement and there were some goats in that basement. They went in, pushed the goats away, and down in the straw are three other Germans. They were trying to con their way out of it. So now we've got four prisoners, we had two casualties. The first and second scout were hit by that machine gun. The second scout was able to walk out, but the first scout was hit in the leg. It was bad news, he died that night. We had the four Germans carry down the wounded guy on a stretcher. They were very cooperative, they knew they were PoWs and they knew it was not the time to get surly. I said, 'Let's get out of here,' because I didn't know what contact the German patrol had and I didn't know how far we were from the main German force; we got out of there fast. That was my first combat experience.

We got the combat infantry badge from that. Later I got a Bronze Star, and then a Purple Heart, because I tangoed with a land mine.

Riva Ridge and Mount Belvedere

The attack on Mount Belvedere was really the first time the Division was committed. Other guys from the 10th Mountain Division have the same story, but everybody has a little bit of a different experience. The general, General Hays, knew that we could take Mount Belvedere, but there was a mountain, Riva Ridge, close by that commanded artillery on Mount Belvedere. You could take Mount Belvedere, but you wouldn't stay there. Kind of like the situation with Fort Ticonderoga and Mount Defiance.[40] You can take Ticonderoga, but you can't hold it. The general said to one of the battalion commanders, 'I want you to take Riva Ridge tomorrow night. Go out and scout how you're going to do it.' Riva Ridge is a sheer cliff,

---

[40] *the situation with Fort Ticonderoga and Mount Defiance-* Mount Defiance overlooks Fort Ticonderoga on Lake Champlain; during the American Revolution, British General John Burgoyne's army forced the Americans to abandon the fort in 1777 by scaling the height and bombarding their position.

not quite vertical, but almost. The Germans didn't even put outposts on that side because it was obvious you couldn't get up. The battalion commander came back to the general and said, 'There's no way to get up that thing.' The general said, and we've heard this at reunions, 'Now you guys are a bunch of hotshots, you're skiers and mountain climbers, find a way on top of that ridge!' They went back, and yes, maybe there were a couple places where they might be able to do it. They did it the next night, got all the way up without being discovered by the Germans. The Germans had some artillery and soldiers up there, but they weren't worried about Riva Ridge. The next morning, some of the Germans were relieving the guys on top, and they were waving, and our guys were waving back! [*Laughs*] As soon as these guys got within rifle shot, they discovered they had lost Riva Ridge. Although there were some casualties, we held on to Riva Ridge. At that point the engineers put up a cable to take the wounded down and supplies up. There was a cable car arrangement put in the next day. In the meantime, while that battalion was taking the rest of Riva Ridge, the rest of the Division moved fairly close to the base of the ridge in big trucks. Then we marched in under the cover of night. We were in the trees at the base of Mount Belvedere with the instruction of no extra noise and no movement. We stayed there all day. During the day they assembled all the officers and told us how we were going to take Mount Belvedere. There were maybe 40 or 50 guys, mostly 2nd lieutenants, that assembled. There were machine guns all over the front of Mount Belvedere. It had been taken twice before, once by Brazilian troops and once by American troops, but they couldn't hang on to it. They explained that Riva Ridge was taken, so that wouldn't be a problem, but there were a bunch of machine guns there.

'We are Going to be Slaughtered'

We're going to go into a night attack. Night attack? You wouldn't have any contact with each other, and single file, which means if the line breaks, you don't know where you are. Well, if the line breaks and you don't know where you are, the goal is to keep going up. Okay, so much for that.

But what about friendly fire? We're going to be in the dark and we're loaded with all kinds of weapons. No, you're going to clear your piece. That's army talk for you're going to take all the rounds from your BARs and rifles. Not loaded, so nobody's going to be shooting. You're going to know who the enemy is because they're going to be shooting at you! That sounded like a hare-brained idea to some of us. We never had a training session where we attacked a mountain in the dark with no ammunition!

We went back to our areas. I had to explain this to the guys. All I could think of was the Charge of the Light Brigade, 'Ours is not to reason why/ours is but to do and die.' But orders are orders.

[We got to the top], and soon we were under fire, and we just went around the guys that were firing. Pretty soon the Germans firing the machine guns realized, 'Hey, there are Americans above, on either side, and below,' and they surrendered, but not before we took some casualties, because there were minefields we had to go through. I didn't get caught in that minefield. And we held it. Incidentally, that wasn't the end of the day. We were on top of the mountain by dawn, but Mount Belvedere was connected by lesser mountains that went off to the northeast, and we had to take that along with Mount Belvedere. It was like a Fort Benning exercise at this point. One company would move up and get shot up, then the battalion commander would move another company through. Then a platoon, the company commander would move one platoon up, and when they got shot up, another platoon would go through. I was the last platoon to be assigned and there was a stopping point—at the end of this [string] of mountains, I had half a platoon left. My platoon sergeant had been killed, a couple of guys had to take prisoners back, and a couple of guys just drifted off. In fact, I went back because the company CP told me to come back for instructions, and I saw two of my guys. They were so scared they were behind a tree with their back to the tree shivering. I said, 'Hey, guys, you're in trouble. You get back to your squad right now.' They did, and I never brought it up. I was a little sympathetic to them because I was scared stiff too!

[*Chuckles*] But officers aren't supposed to get scared.

At the end of the day I had just about half of a platoon, and I was heading in a defensive position and I said, 'These Germans are going to counterattack, they never give up without a counterattack.' I said, 'We are going to be slaughtered.' Well just then, a whole company of guys, about 180 men—I think it was K Company—their officer said, 'We're here to relieve you.' Boy, was I relieved! [*Chuckles*] I took my guys and we trudged back. We hadn't eaten all day and the company cook prepared a hot meal for us. Now Army chow is not all that great, but a hot meal after that experience [was memorable].

The Minefield

Right after Belvedere, we went into a defensive position. We were in Tuscany, in the northwest corner of Italy. There were more mountains to take. The first sergeant knew where this area was. We were going to drop our kitchen equipment, our supplies, our ammunition, and our packs, and I was assigned with some officers to see where we were going to drop our packs. [A sergeant] led this little collection single file. There's the battalion CP here, [*gestures*] a road here, and the sergeant, instead of going across the path diagonally, cut across this field. That field was a minefield. [*Chuckles*] He missed all the mines, and I'm right behind him and I didn't miss them, I stepped on one. Now, I don't know whether I'm lucky or unlucky. I can say I'm lucky I got wounded that way because the next day I could have been killed, because we were going into an attack. Also, I was wearing shoe packs, which are rubber bottoms, leather tops. I had two felt inner soles in the shoe pack and was wearing two pairs of cotton socks. That kept me warm and it kept me dry; I didn't wear all that stuff because I thought I was going to step on a mine, but in fact it cushioned some of it. Also, I weighed 140 pounds; if you're going to step on a mine, don't be too heavy. I was lucky too because [just then] an ambulance went by. They stopped the ambulance and they loaded me in and I got prompt medical attention. I'm also thankful for the guy who invented penicillin; at the end of the war there was plenty of it. I must have had five gallons of penicillin pumped into me! Every six hours for about three months, the nurse would come around and give me a shot of penicillin. I still have my foot; it's messed up, but they were able to patch me up. Took two years, but I walked in here today without a cane.

I was no hero, I was a dumb bunny who walked into a minefield! The real heroes are the medics. Since we were near the battalion CP, there were a couple of medics standing there. They came in the minefield to get me out! They didn't know where the rest of the mines were. Now that takes guts! Doesn't take guts to stumble into a minefield, but it takes guts to go into a minefield and evacuate. In many of the reunions I tried to find out who they were and I never was successful. My guess is some of them probably got killed the way I could have been.

*

We were in a tent hospital, like a MASH unit, only it was an early version of it.[41] The reason they used tent hospitals was to keep moving it forward. The closer you were to where you got wounded,

---

[41] *like a MASH unit*-Mobile Army Surgical Hospital

the better chance you had of getting a break. [Senator Bob Dole] was in the same regiment, he had the same job I did. I was hit about a month before the end of the war, and he was hit about two weeks before the end of the war. It's not clear whether it was shrapnel or machine gun bullets, but his right shoulder was really messed up. I'm quite sure we were in the same officers' ward. Second lieutenants were good casualties, a lot of us were casualties. I didn't know him, but when he was running for president he appeared at one of the reunions and we met him. I wouldn't say he was a buddy, but I fantasize that he was probably in the next bed in the hospital. Could have been, but I don't know that. Anyway, most of us weren't in a sociable mood in the hospital.

I went from a tent hospital to a general hospital in Italy, but it was fully equipped. They patched us up enough, so the next step is get you home. Do they want to get you home for your morale? No, it's a logistical problem. They've got to keep moving the guys because there are more wounded coming through. There are two ways of getting home. You can get on a hospital ship out of Italy, or you can fly out of Northern Africa, to the Azores, to the Bahamas, to Miami. I consider myself lucky. That's the way I got back to the States. That's over the water, but I read later that not one plane ever went down, because it was short hops, and the DC-6, I think it was, was a workhorse. It could land anyplace, had no complications. It wasn't a fancy plane but it was dependable. The Azores, incidentally, belonged to Portugal. Portugal was neutral, but I think we convinced them that they weren't that neutral, so we took over the island.

They want to get you closer to where your home is. I first landed in Fort Dix, New Jersey, but then they said, 'No, we want you to go to Framingham, Massachusetts, for plastic surgery.' So I had some plastic surgery that took some skin from my right leg and put it on my left leg. They did some amazing things, but most of my surgery was orthopedic. My care was excellent. I had a colonel at Framingham who was an orthopedic surgeon who came out of the Shriners Hospital, and boy, he knew his stuff. Every time he'd come by to check me or before an operation, he'd have half a dozen young doctors. They were getting the real dope from a guy who knew what he was doing. I had excellent care all the way through. Prompt medical attention when I first got wounded, those two medics.

It took two years [to recuperate], and the nice part about it was as soon as I was ambulatory, they didn't want me around the hospital. I spent a lot of my furloughs back in Schenectady. I was on crutches, but I could get on a train and get picked up by my wife, who was praying for me. I have a question about whether the prayers did any good, but she claims that's why I got home. [*Laughs*]

Shoes

Eventually I was at the stage for orthopedic shoes, and they had an interesting system. A lot of guys stepped on mines and they had foot problems. They had me stand in a tray of little tiny ball bearings, very tiny. I'd put my weight on them, and then they'd put on a magnet and freeze those ball bearings to the shape of your foot. Then they made a plaster cast of that. They gave me two pairs of shoes and told me that's all the shoes that I would get. I had a disability pension and they gave me the name of a guy in Albany and he made my shoes from then on. Every time he'd make one pair, I'd tell him, make two pairs. He was older than I was, I figured someday he's not going to be around. Eventually, when I stopped getting shoes, I think I had about a dozen pairs of shoes. I think I have eight pairs of shoes now, I think they should last me. I'm eighty-eight. What I didn't account for is that I'm not going to be walking as much as I did, so I can go beyond one hundred years old if I have to. I had the guy make me a pair of high shoes, so I was able to put cable bindings on cross-country skis, so I was able to cross-country ski for a long time. One day, I went down this little hill, and I said, 'Hey, I'm still pretty good!' I got to the bottom and stopped, and I promptly fell over backwards. I said, 'Wusterbarth, your skiing days are over!' [*Laughs*] When you fall down when you're standing still, you've had it. But anyway, we've had a great life. Let's see, four kids, eight grandkids, and now we're up to the fifth great-grandchild, who we just saw a couple of days ago. Life is good.

Mr. Wusterbarth passed away at the age of 95 in 2015.

CHAPTER SIXTEEN

The Cannoneer

William Millette was born on August 8, 1925, in Oneonta, New York. He attended Christian Brothers Academy but was forced to graduate early in three years due to the draft quotas. He was drafted into the Army in 1944 and became an artilleryman as part of a task force with the 86th Infantry Regiment of the 10th Mountain Division. 'When we jumped off on April 14, our orders were to go like hell, pell-mell, and not to let anything stop us, get over the Po River and seal the Brenner Pass to prevent the Germans from getting back in there. At that time, there was a great deal of concern that if the Germans got back into those mountains, we'd be ten years digging them out.' He gave this interview in 2004 at the age of 78.

William A. Millette

I received basic training at Fort Sill, Oklahoma, in the pack artillery. Pack artillery is a special arm of the army's artillery. Their weapon is the 75-millimeter pack howitzer, which can be broken down and disassembled into ten individual pieces and mounted and carried by six army mules. To qualify to get into the pack artillery, when you went through the reception center at Fort Sill, a sergeant stood at the top of the line and measured everybody going through. Anyone 5'10" or taller went in the pack artillery. Everyone less than that went to the regular artillery.

It was very strenuous training. Our PT was ongoing constantly to keep us in top physical shape. As I recall, the only time we ever rode was the time that the trucks picked us up at the train and the time the trucks took us back to the train when we left Sill. After our second or third week of basic training, we never walked less than 14 miles a day.

Basically, in a pack artillery section, there are 13 people. There was a chief of section and six cannoneers and six mule handlers. It took approximately a minute to disassemble that howitzer and pack it onto a mule or take it off the mule and assemble it. We could have that howitzer off a mule in less than a minute, ready to fire. That's a well-trained crew. Due to the type of our training and the type of weapon we're training on and the potential for where we would be serving, we had to qualify in all types of weapons, because most of the pack artillery battalions were then serving in the South Pacific. Most of them, a lot of them, were the Merrill's Marauders.[42]

I finished my basic training, was sent to Camp Carson, Colorado, and assigned to the 613th Pack Artillery Battalion. Fortunately for me, when I got to Carson, the 613th had already shipped out to the West Coast, heading for the South Pacific. At that time, they didn't know what to do with us. After about two or three days of doing nothing, they sent us over to a place called Cheyenne Mountain at Camp Carson for rock climbing. We got our shipping orders to go to Camp Hale, Colorado, with the 10th Mountain Division.

---

[42] *Merrill's Marauders-* specialized Army force that conducted deep-penetration missions behind Japanese lines in the China-Burma-India Theater of Operations.

While at Carson, while we're rock climbing, as each day progressed and we ascended higher into the rocks and so forth and looked down, I was not particularly happy with what I saw below me. Upon our return to our barracks, there was a big bulletin issuing a call for immediate volunteers for the airborne.

I said to this one fella from Chicago, 'I've had enough of this rock climbing.' We went over and volunteered to join the paratroopers. Took our physical, passed with flying colors. We're all set. Unfortunately, at that time, we got shipping orders to go to the 10th Mountain. Got to the 10th Mountain, informed the sergeant at wherever we were at, some headquarters, that we wouldn't be staying with the 10th Mountain. We were going to go in the airborne. We were very politely but firmly informed that our days in the airborne were over—'You're now in the 10th Mountain and you're going to stay here.' That was it.

Then, we went from Camp Hale to Camp Swift, Texas, for flat land training, the main purpose being that the difference in altitudes from firing weapons and mortars and artillery at 11,000 and

12,000 feet elevation is a lot different from firing at ground level. Your ballistics are a lot different. We had to be trained for that.

We also had to be proficient in some skiing and be able to move around in the snow, because many times, we had to [break a path] for the mules going through the snow. Sometimes the snow was crusted and it would eat into their skin. Snowshoes were [necessary] and we had to be proficient in using them.

*

The 10th was made up of three mountain infantry regiments, the 85th, the 86th, and 87th mountain infantry regiments. These were supported by the 604th, the 605th, and the 616th pack artillery battalions into regimental combat teams.

We left the United States in December of '44. We got over there early January. [Our destination was] Naples, which we didn't know at the time until we got on board the *USS Meigs*. I asked one of the crew members where we were heading. He said this, and I always remember his remark. He said, 'This tub has been nowhere but Naples.' We knew we were heading for Italy.

We got to Italy. We disembarked, walked down the quay, and got on an LCI.[43] The LCI was supposed to take us up the coast of Leghorn. On our way up, we had a tremendous storm in the Mediterranean. I might add that an awful lot of our guys were seasick. It was unbelievable. The storm was so bad that the fantail back where the latrine was cracked right in half! We had to turn around and put into port.

We went into a staging area around Pisa Lucca, where we had to get the howitzers and get cleaned up and oriented. Then, we were trucked up to a place called Lizzano in Belvedere, where we put our weapons in and began our firing missions prior to the infantry assault on Belvedere and Riva Ridge. Then, we went from there up through the campaign with the rest of the division.

My particular assignment, while I was not assigned to a particular gun section as a cannoneer or whatever, was as a security person with a BAR to provide perimeter security for the battery. That meant being out two, three, 400 yards in front of them to intercept enemy patrols and that type of

---

[43] *got on an LCI-* Landing Craft, Infantry

thing. Also, to provide security for our forward observers in the observation point. As a result, I was up on the OP when we supported the 86th when they went up the Riva Ridge, to provide security for our forward observers. We had incidents where the Germans counterattacked and sought out weak spots. I loved the BAR, contrary to a lot of people, who hated it. The only reason I could think they hated it, they didn't know how to handle it or they didn't maintain it, or keep it clean. I kept mine immaculate at all times. I never had a problem with it, [but the bipod] got an early death. [*Laughs*]

*

Pack Mules

We had 5,000 mules in our division. It was basically our organic transportation. I know every artillery battalion had a service battery. That was where the shoers were and the saddle makers; these guys were really good. The mules carried their own food. On those mules, they had what they call a Phillips pack saddle. They were common for every mule and they had a rack, an adapter on the top of the saddle, which was to put different parts of the howitzer on, plus carrying hay, oats, and grain and that type of thing or water, ammunition, whatever.

At that time, they had nothing but the best of leather. Civilians couldn't get leather. These guys had the best leather you could get. The mules shied [when the cannon was fired]. They're very sensitive to noise and so forth. But believe me when I tell you, there is nothing on this God's earth as ornery as a Missouri mule. They are intelligent. They're hard. They're tough. A mule is a lot smarter than a horse will ever be. I've seen them do stuff that was unbelievable. I had one take off on me and I'm holding the holds and I can't hold them. He ran me up towards a tree; he ran so close to that tree, I had to let go of the halter. They're just bad news. I've been kicked by one. We had a stable sergeant, a Southern boy from South Carolina. Mules were his specialty. He said, 'I don't want to see you boys smoking.' He got some of the guys' chewing tobacco, me included. I chewed tobacco until I was cleaning out the hoof of one of our mules. He just drew back that hoof and kicked me square in the butt and sent me flying. When he did that, I swallowed the cud. I'll tell you. I was sick for two days. [*Laughs*] That was one amusing incident about the mules, but they were an amazing animal. They're sure-footed and just as nice as any horse. They're really, really tough.

Obviously, they weren't the only ones we had. The Italian Alpini did a lot of service for the 10th.[44] In fact, they had an Alpini mountain company pack unit attached to each regiment. All the regiments in their service companies had pack platoons and used mules. They had to; that's the only way they could get ammunition and water up in the mountains. The problem was that although we were a pack artillery and trained with mules, we didn't get our own mules. In fact, we were one of a very few units, the only unit that I know of, that used the mules when we jumped off on April 14 on our final offensive out of the Apennines. Our G.I. mules were big animals. These were a little bit smaller.

---

[44] *Italian Alpini*- an elite mountain warfare troops of the Italian Army.

When we jumped off on April 14, we were part of a task force with the 86th Infantry. Our orders were to go like hell, pell-mell, and not to let anything stop us, get over the Po River and seal the Brenner Pass to prevent the Germans from getting back in there. At that time, there was a great deal of concern that if the Germans got back into those mountains, we'd be ten years digging them out.

*

The Tunnels

Our combat ended on May 2, 1945. Today is the anniversary of one of our big campaigns, April 30th, up on Lago di Garda in Northern Italy, when our battery went in on an amphibious assault in DUKWs to go around blowing out tunnels on the lake to support our infantry. We disassembled the howitzers, put them on the DUKWs with the ammunition, and went up the lake. Then, when the DUKWs pulled into a disembark area, where we were under fire, we hand-carried those pieces up a steep embankment onto the road.

Lago di Garda is a very beautiful lake. In fact, Mussolini had one of his palaces up there. The road was built right into the side of the mountain and a series of five or six tunnels. The Germans, in their retreat, blew some of these tunnels to halt our progress. As a result, we had to go around them in DUKWs to support our infantry. In fact, the Germans had a couple of 88s up at the head up in Torbole that were firing into our troops. We went up and we duked them out. This is where I got my Bronze Star, and we duked them out, then knocked the 88s out.

Some of our infantry were actually trapped up there because, even if they had to, they couldn't get back down because the tunnels were blowing up behind them. The Germans, in their haste to blow these tunnels, had prematurely blown one and trapped one of their own trucks full of engineers. I think there were 15 or 20 German soldiers in that truck that were killed.

Lago del Predil

Then, our infantry went into Torbole. We went in behind them. The war ended [in Italy] on May 2.

We were there for a little while up in Torbole. Then, we got orders to move to the east coast; they were having some problems in Trieste with the Yugoslavians. The Yugoslavs moved into Trieste and claimed that port city as their own, which was an Italian city. We had orders to go across the top of Italy to Trieste, which we did.

We were over there with the British. Finally, the British conned the Yugoslavs into surrendering. They invited them into a huge soccer field. These guys were armed right to the teeth. The British colonel invited them to lay down their arms. The war was over. 'Go home to your farms, your homes, and leave your weapons here.' When he said that, the Yugos became a little restless. Then—and I always remember the colonel saying this, he had an interpreter—'If you chose not to lay down your weapons, look behind you or around you.' The place was completely surrounded with British and American troops with automatic weapons. They got the message and dropped their weapons and filed out.

We went up into a little place called Lago del Predil, right in the corner of Yugoslavia, Austria, and Italy. Beautiful little valley, and there we were. We stayed on occupation until we came home. We visited over and over and got a chance to go over to Austria, do some skiing, did a lot of road work, exercising; life was good then.

[On one of our excursions], we came across huge, huge caverns, with doors, I don't know, 15-feet wide probably. [These huge chambers] were dug into the mountain. Fortunately, we had engineers with us; we probed them for mines and booby traps. The first one we went into was a cavern loaded with brand-new Pratt-Whitney airplane engines from Ohio; I remember they were made in Ohio somewhere. Another of the big caverns we went into was just loaded with kegs of German beer, German brandy, and champagne that you would not believe. Fortunately, our division people got the trucks and we got that stuff out of there before one of the other divisions from southern France was to come up to meet us in the Brenner Pass. As a result, when we went up into Predil, everybody got a huge ration of champagne, brandy, and whatever. We had a good time. [*Laughs*]

Civilians

We had some contact with the Italian people. Our relations, as far as I know, were excellent. I know we were in one position, and there's a little farmhouse down to our right. We watched this woman come out every once in a while; we were there for a while. She came out, obviously very, very pregnant, and that's the first time I ever realized how the Italians made spaghetti; they rolled it out. They brought it out and laid it over the clothes line, and that's where there's a loop in it to dry.

She had her baby while she was there, our medics were there to help her and so forth. The biggest problem we had was with the children, the kids. God! They were just so poor, it was unbelievable. As a result, you had to watch your equipment, because they would come in and take whatever they could get. They were just completely poverty-stricken. When we finished [our missions], our mess sections were in operation, we were getting hot food and so forth. They'd stand at the end of the mess line and take your scraps any way they could get them. Coffee, they'd take coffee. They were begging for cigarettes and candy and so forth.

They were not above taking something if you laid it down; if it had any value, it would be gone.

I had a very fortunate experience. When we were in Predil, we used to bring our clothing up to the Italian family up in the northern end of the lake. When we got ready to leave, they invited three of us up to have a farewell dinner on a Sunday. I think it was a 12 or 13-course dinner. My God, they had pasta, they had all kinds of stuff. One of the items they had, which I didn't recognize at first, was snails in sauce. They treated us very well. Obviously, they did our washing, our clothes, and so forth, which we paid for. That was a nice experience for them. They were very nice people.

[The war in Italy was over], but the war was still going on in the Pacific. We were informed that since we were actually the last division to arrive in Italy, we were going to be redeployed to the United States, refitted, and shipped to the Pacific. I have the plans. I came by some plans some years ago of our position in the final assault on Japan.

Another interesting point about our unit's artillery that was top secret at that time was that they shipped all of our artillery to the Greeks to use in their army. We sent something like 20 or 24 of our artillerymen along with them to train the Greek army in their use. The Greeks were fighting for their independence against the communists in Greece. They were having a real battle; they asked for help. Officially, President Roosevelt, being the liberal that he was, thought he could control Joe Stalin and didn't want to offend the communists. That never came out. It was never made public until many years later.

When we found out we were heading for the South Pacific to go heading for Japan, [it was tough]. When [the war in the Pacific ended], we were very relieved that we had survived, as obviously a lot of our guys did not. There were some bittersweet moments. We had our memorial services and that type of thing. In our division association, we had many, many annual, semi-annual meetings and so forth. We chat personally. We have never, ever, ever forgotten these people who we lost over there; there's a huge cemetery in Florence where they're buried. We have the division association that goes back to Italy every two or three years, and it's always a stop at the Florence cemetery. We have a memorial service. Whenever we gather the group, they're always remembered. And I think World War II made me appreciate more of what life is all about.

Mr. Millette passed away at the age of 92 in 2017.

EPILOGUE

'Live by the sword, die by the sword.' In Berlin on April 30, Hitler committed suicide as Soviet forces closed in on the Führerbunker. On May 2, 1945, the fighting in Italy finally ended with the German surrender; the rest of the German forces in Europe capitulated by May 8, the official date of the Allied victory in Europe. Soldier celebrations were muted, however, as all knew that a war still had to be won against Japan, whose soldiers showed no sign of giving up anytime soon as the battle for Okinawa raged on and invasion planners added American ETO forces into the calculus of war. Many American soldiers, sailors, and airmen were in transit to their new destinations when word came of the atomic bombs and Japan's surrender; like the bombing at Pearl Harbor four and a half years earlier, and the sudden death of the commander in chief on the cusp of victory, few veterans would forget where they were, and how they felt, when the news of the end of World War II was formally announced following the official surrender of Japan on September 2, 1945.

*

In every town in the nation, like those of Hometown, USA, markers appeared in the following years, some simple, some complex and ornate. But the men and women who fought came home to a world in flux, a world that they helped to save and, in doing so, create anew. Life would never be the same. And they did not talk about what happened 'over there.' So many had had the experience of war. And so many who had not would never understand, nor would they want to hear about it. It was time to move on, get married, go to college, find a job, or complete high school. It was time to raise families, to put the children down for the night, and sometimes just to linger in the darkness at the bedroom door, as the minutes ticked by, in silent contemplation of what it all meant. The children would grow up, in many instances not knowing anything about Father's war, perhaps puzzled by sobs in the night, or Mother's gentle insistence on a terrible anniversary for a day out of the house without him, or the troubled behavior in the home. The years slipped away; new generations unfolded, oblivious; old friends passed. A phone call and a faraway voice from a different time and place might jolt loose a cascade of memories, two men talking excitedly for hours long into the night. Grandchildren with school projects to complete might begin with a question or two, and an unconscious realization was made manifest in elder households across the nation:

What I did, what we all did back then, was important after all. Maybe my buddies did not die in vain. At least I hope it was all worth something. And maybe I should share my story, before it's too late. Maybe I should remember, so that my friends are not forgotten. Maybe it is time for someone besides me to remember them, long after I am gone myself.

In the words of Susie Stevens-Harvey, who lost her brother in Vietnam and advocates for all those still missing in action, or prisoners of war:

*'Dying for freedom isn't the worst that could happen.
Being forgotten is.*

***

THE THINGS OUR FATHERS SAW ®

SERIES:

VOICES OF THE PACIFIC THEATER

WAR IN THE AIR: GREAT DEPRESSION TO COMBAT

WAR IN THE AIR: COMBAT, CAPTIVITY, REUNION

UP THE BLOODY BOOT- WAR IN ITALY

D-DAY AND BEYOND

THE BULGE AND BEYOND

ACROSS THE RHINE

ON TO TOKYO

HOMEFRONT/WOMEN AT WAR

CHINA, BURMA, INDIA

***

IF YOU LIKED THIS BOOK, you'll love hearing more from the World War II generation in my other books. On the following pages you can see some samples, and I can let you know as soon as the new books are out and offer you exclusive discounts on some material. Just sign up at matthewrozellbooks.com

Some of my readers may like to know that all of my books are **directly available from the author, with collector's sets which can be autographed** in paperback and hardcover. They are popular gifts for that 'hard-to-buy-for' guy or gal on your list.

Visit my shop at matthewrozellbooks.com for details.

Thank you for reading!

I hope you found this book interesting and informative; I sure learned a lot researching and writing it. What follows are some descriptions of my other books.

Find them all at matthewrozellbooks.com.

The Things Our Fathers Saw: The Untold Stories of the World War II Generation from Hometown, USA-Voices of the Pacific Theater

Volume 1 of The Things Our Fathers Saw® series started with my first book on the oral history of the men and women who served in the Pacific Theater of the war. *"The telephone rings on the hospital floor, and they tell you it is your mother, the phone call you have been dreading. You've lost part of your face to a Japanese sniper on Okinawa, and after many surgeries, the doctor has finally told you that at 19, you will never see again. The pain and shock is one thing. But now you have to tell her, from 5000 miles away."*

— *"So I had a hard two months, I guess. I kept mostly to myself. I wouldn't talk to people. I tried to figure out what the hell I was going to do when I got home. How was I going to tell my mother this? You know what I mean?"* — **WWII Marine veteran**

But you don't have to start with this book—I constructed them so that you can pick up any of the series books and start anywhere—but it's up to you.

The Things Our Fathers Saw—The Untold Stories of the World War II Generation-Volume II: War in the Air—From the Great Depression to Combat

Volume 2 in the series deal with the Air War in the European Theater of the war. I had a lot of friends in the heavy bombers; they tell you all about what it was like to grow up during the Great Depression as the clouds of war gathered, going off to the service, and into the skies over Europe, sharing stories of both funny and heartbreaking, and all riveting and intense. An audio version is also available.

— "I spent a lot of time in hospitals. I had a lot of trouble reconciling how my mother died [of a cerebral hemorrhage] from the telegram she opened, announcing I was [shot down and] 'missing in action.' I didn't explain to her the fact that 'missing in action' is not necessarily 'killed in action.' You know? I didn't even think about that. How do you think you feel when you find out you killed your mother?" — **B-24 bombardier**

— *"I was in the hospital with a flak wound. The next mission, the entire crew was killed. The thing that haunts me is that I can't put a face to the guy who was a replacement. He was an eighteen-year-old Jewish kid named Henry Vogelstein from Brooklyn. It was his first and last mission. He made his only mission with a crew of strangers." —B-24* **navigator**

— *"The German fighters picked us. I told the guys, 'Keep your eyes open, we are about to be hit!' I saw about six or eight feet go off my left wing. I rang the 'bail-out' signal, and I reached out and grabbed the co-pilot out of his seat. I felt the airplane climbing, and I thought to myself, 'If this thing stalls out, and starts falling down backwards, no one is going to get out...'" —B-17* **pilot**

The Things Our Fathers Saw—The Untold Stories of the World War II Generation-Volume III: War in the Air—Combat, Captivity, and Reunion

Volume 3 is about the Air War again, and this time I have some of my friends who were fighter pilots, including a Tuskegee Airman who had to deal with racism back home, on top of defeating fascism in Europe. There is also the story of my B-17 crew friends, sitting around a table and telling about the day they were all shot down over Germany, and how they survived the prisoner-of-war experience in the last year of the war. An audio version is also available.

—"*After the first mission Colonel Davis told us, 'From now on you are going to go with the bombers all the way through the mission to the target.' It didn't always work, but that was our mission—we kept the Germans off the bombers. At first they didn't want us, but toward the end, they started asking for us as an escort, because we protected them to* *and from the missions." —**Tuskegee Airman, WWII***

— "[Someone in the PoW camp] said, 'Look down there at the main gate!', and the American flag was flying! We went berserk, we just went berserk! We were looking at the goon tower and there's no goons there, there are Americans up there! And we saw the American flag, I mean—to this day I start to well up when I see the flag."

*—**Former prisoner of war, WWII***

— "I got back into my turret. Fellas, the turret wasn't there anymore. That German fighter who had been eyeing me came in and he hit his 20mm gun, took the top of that Plexiglas and tore it right off!

*Now we're defenseless. The planes ahead of us have been shot down, we're lumbering along at 180 miles an hour, and these fighters were just [warming up] for target practice." —**B-17 Turret Gunner***

The Things Our Fathers Saw—The Untold Stories of the World War II Generation-Volume V: 'D-Day and Beyond'—The War in France

Volume 5 in this series will take you from the bloody beach at Omaha through the hedgerow country of Normandy and beyond, American veterans of World War II--Army engineers and infantrymen, Coast Guardsmen and Navy sailors, tank gunners and glider pilots--sit down with you across the kitchen table and talk about what they saw and experienced, tales they may have never told anyone before.

— *"I had a vision, if you want to call it that. At my home, the mailman would walk up towards the front porch, and I saw it just as clear as if he's standing beside me—I see his blue jacket and the blue cap and the leather mailbag. Here he goes up to the house, but he doesn't turn. He goes right up the front steps.*

This happened so fast, probably a matter of seconds, but the first thing that came to mind, that's the way my folks would find out what happened to me.

The next thing I know, I kind of come to, and I'm in the push-up mode. I'm half up out of the underwater depression, and I'm trying to figure out what the hell happened to those prone figures on the beach, and all of a sudden, I realized I'm in amongst those bodies!" —Army demolition engineer, Omaha Beach, D-Day

— *"My last mission was the Bastogne mission. We were being towed, we're approaching Bastogne, and I see a cloud of flak, anti-aircraft fire. I said to myself, 'I'm not going to make it.' There were a couple of groups ahead of us, so now the anti-aircraft batteries are zeroing in. Every time a new group came over, they kept zeroing in. My outfit had, I think, 95% casualties." —Glider pilot, D-Day and Beyond*

— *"I was fighting in the hedgerows for five days; it was murder. But psychologically, we were the best troops in the world. There was nobody like us; I had all the training that they could give us, but nothing prepares you for some things.*

You know, in my platoon, the assistant platoon leader got shot right through the head, right through the helmet, dead, right there in front of me. That affects you, doesn't it?" —Paratrooper, D-Day and Beyond

ALSO FROM MATTHEW ROZELL

~SOON TO BE A DOCUMENTARY MINI-SERIES~

"What healing this has given to the survivors and military men!"-Reviewer

FROM THE ABC WORLD NEWS 'PERSON OF THE WEEK'

A TRAIN NEAR MAGDEBURG

THE HOLOCAUST, AND THE REUNITING OF THE SURVIVORS AND SOLDIERS, 70 YEARS ON

–Featuring testimony from 15 American liberators and over 30 Holocaust survivors
–500 pages-extensive notes and bibliographical references

BOOK ONE—THE HOLOCAUST
BOOK TWO—THE AMERICANS
BOOK THREE—LIBERATION

BOOK FOUR—REUNION

THE HOLOCAUST *was a watershed event in history. In this book, Matthew Rozell reconstructs a lost chapter—the liberation of a 'death train' deep in the heart of Nazi Germany in the closing days of World War II. Drawing on never-before published eye-witness accounts, survivor testimony, and wartime reports and letters, Rozell brings to life the incredible true stories behind the iconic 1945 liberation photographs taken by the soldiers who were there. He weaves together a chronology of the Holocaust as it unfolds across Europe, and goes back to literally retrace the steps of the survivors and the American soldiers who freed them. Rozell's work results in joyful reunions on three continents, seven decades later. He offers his unique perspective on the lessons of the Holocaust for future generations, and the impact that one person can make.*

A selection of comments left by reviewers:

"**Extraordinary research** into an event which needed to be told. I have read many books about the Holocaust and visited various museums but had not heard reference to this train previously. The fact that people involved were able to connect, support and help heal each other emotionally was amazing."

"**The story of the end of the Holocaust and the Nazi regime** told from a very different and precise angle. First-hand accounts from Jewish survivors and the US soldiers that secured their freedom. Gripping."

"**Mr. Rozell travels 'back to the future'** of people who were not promised a tomorrow; neither the prisoners nor the troops knew what horrors the next moment would bring. He captures the parallel experience of soldiers fighting ruthless Nazism and the ruthless treatment of Jewish prisoners."

"**If you have any trepidation** about reading a book on the Holocaust, this review is for you. [Matthew Rozell] masterfully conveys the individual stories of those featured in the book in a manner that does not leave the reader with a sense of despair, but rather a sense of purpose."

"**Could not put this book down**--I just finished reading *A Train Near Magdeburg*. Tears fell as I read pages and I smiled through others. I wish I could articulate the emotions that accompanied me through the stories of these beautiful people."

"**Everyone should read this book**, detailing the amazing bond that formed between Holocaust survivors likely on their way to death in one last concentration camp as WWII was about to end, and a small number of American soldiers that happened upon the stopped train and liberated the victims. The lifelong friendships that resulted between the survivors and their liberators is a testament to compassion and goodness. It is amazing that the author is not Jewish but a "reluctant" history teacher who ultimately becomes a Holocaust scholar. This is a great book."

ABOUT THE AUTHOR

Photo Credit: Joan K. Lentini; May 2017.

Matthew Rozell is an award-winning history teacher, author, speaker, and blogger on the topic of the most cataclysmic events in the history of mankind—World War II and the Holocaust. Rozell has been featured as the 'ABC World News Person of the Week' and has had his work as a teacher filmed for the CBS Evening News, NBC Learn, the Israeli Broadcast Authority, the United States Holocaust Memorial Museum, and the New York State United Teachers. He writes on the power of teaching and the importance of the study of history at TeachingHistoryMatters.com, and you can 'Like' his Facebook author page at MatthewRozellBooks for updates.

Mr. Rozell is a sought-after speaker on World War II, the Holocaust, and history education, motivating and inspiring his audiences with the lessons of the past. Visit MatthewRozell.com for availability/details.

About this Book/ Acknowledgements

*

A note on historiographical style and convention: to enhance accuracy, consistency, and readability, I corrected punctuation and spelling and sometimes even place names, but only after extensive research. I did take the liberty of occasionally condensing the speaker's voice, eliminating side tangents or incidental information not relevant to the matter at hand. Sometimes two or more interviews with the same person were combined for readability and narrative flow. All of the words of the subjects, however, are essentially their own.

Additionally, I chose to utilize footnotes and endnotes where I deemed them appropriate, directing readers who wish to learn more to my sources, notes, and side commentary. I hope that they do not detract from the flow of the narrative.

*

First, I wish to acknowledge the hundreds of students who passed through my classes and who forged the bonds with the World War II generation. I promised you these books someday, and now that many of you are yourselves parents, you can tell your children this book is for them. Who says young people are indifferent to the past? Here is evidence to the contrary. The Hudson Falls Central School District and my former colleagues have my deep appreciation for supporting this endeavor and recognizing its significance throughout the years.

Naturally this work would not have been possible had it not been for the willingness of the veterans to share their stories for posterity. All of the veterans who were interviewed for this book had the foresight to complete release forms granting access to their stories, and for us to share the information with the New York State Military Museum's Veterans Oral History Project, where copies of most of the interviews reside. Wayne

Clarke and Mike Russert of the NYSMMVOP were instrumental in cultivating this relationship with my classes over the years and are responsible for some of the interviews in this book as well. Please see the 'Source Notes.'

For this book, I would especially like to thank my old friend Captain Jim Sedore and his wife Elise of the Carolina Dive Center for inviting me to a remote Caribbean island for a disciplined two-week sprint in hammering out the narrative; when it was time to close the laptop, Jim mandated a few Toña cervezas, several hands of seaside euchre, and late-night 'Name That Tune' sessions on his balcony overlooking the cove. It was also a clearing of the mind with new friends who felt like family, especially pig roast virtuoso Dr. Theo and his lovely wife Dr. Beth, who pumped me up with antihistamines when my leg swelled up and stitched Theo's thumb when the meat cleaver went awry. Sometimes you need distractions after the day's work is done, and Jim has helped keep me sane for decades. And thank you, Elise, for putting up with us!

I dedicated this book especially to the memory of Al Havens and Skip Gordon. They were lifelong friends with each other who I did not get to be acquainted with until much later in life. Not old enough for World War II themselves, they knew many of the subjects of my books and eagerly awaited each volume, always the first in line. And both men recently passed at home, Al with his grandson reading Vol. 2 to him, and Skip this past winter with his daughter reading Vol. 3 aloud. This one is for you, guys. I hope your old friends gave you comfort, and that you met them again.

As always, I would be remiss if I did not recall the profound influence of my late mother and father, Mary and Tony Rozell, both cutting-edge educators and proud early supporters of my career. To my younger siblings Mary, Ned, Nora, and Drew, all accomplished writers and authors, thank you for your encouragement as well. Final and deepest appreciations go to my wife Laura and our children, Emma, Ned, and Mary. Thank you for indulging the old man as he attempted to bring to life the stories he collected as a young one.

NOTES

[1] Miller, Donald. *The Story of World War II*. New York: Simon & Schuster, 2001. 215.
[2] Atkinson, Rick. *An Army at Dawn: The War in North Africa, 1942-1943, Volume One of the Liberation Trilogy*. Henry Holt and Co., 2002. 2.
[3] Snow, Richard. *A Nation at War With Itself*. The Wall Street Journal. April 19, 2016. www.wsj.com/articles/a-nation-at-war-with-itself-1461104812.
[4] Miller, Donald. *The Story of World War II*. New York: Simon & Schuster, 2001. 163.
[5] Miller, Donald. *The Story of World War II*. New York: Simon & Schuster, 2001. 164.
[6] The National World War II Museum. *Operation Husky: The Allied Invasion of Sicily*. July 12, 2017. https://www.nationalww2museum.org/war/articles/operation-husky-allied-invasion-sicily
[7] Jenkins, McKay. *The Last Ridge: The Epic Story of America's First Mountain Soldiers and the Assault on Hitler's Europe*. New York: Random House, 2003. 73
[8] Jenkins, McKay. *The Last Ridge: The Epic Story of America's First Mountain Soldiers and the Assault on Hitler's Europe*. New York: Random House, 2003. 75
[9] MacDonald, Charles B. *The Mighty Endeavor: American Armed Forces in the European Theater in World War II*. Endeavour Press, 2015. Location 3270.
[10] Global Security.org. *Gustav Line*.www.globalsecurity.org/military/world/europe/de-gustav.htm

[11] *World War II: Time-Life Books History of the Second World War.* New York: Prentice Hall, 1989. 239.

[12] Hull, Michael D. *U.S. Army Rangers in World War II.* Warfare History Network, April 7, 2017. http://warfarehistorynetwork.com/daily/wwii/u-s-army-rangers-in-world-war-ii.

[13] Hull, Michael D. *U.S. Army Rangers in World War II.* Warfare History Network, April 7, 2017. http://warfarehistorynetwork.com/daily/wwii/u-s-army-rangers-in-world-war-ii.

[14] Atkinson, Rick. *An Army at Dawn: The War in North Africa, 1942-1943, Volume One of the Liberation Trilogy.* Henry Holt and Co., 2002. 330.

[15] Hull, Michael D. *U.S. Army Rangers in World War II.* Warfare History Network, April 7, 2017. http://warfarehistorynetwork.com/daily/wwii/u-s-army-rangers-in-world-war-ii.

[16] Atkinson, Rick. *The Day of Battle: The War in Sicily and Italy, 1943-1944, Volume Two of the Liberation Trilogy.* Henry Holt and Co., 2007. 210.

[17] Hull, Michael D. *U.S. Army Rangers in World War II.* Warfare History Network, April 7, 2017. http://warfarehistorynetwork.com/daily/wwii/u-s-army-rangers-in-world-war-ii.

[18] Atkinson, Rick. *The Day of Battle: The War in Sicily and Italy, 1943-1944, Volume Two of the Liberation Trilogy.* Henry Holt and Co., 2007. 396.

[19] Hull, Michael D. *U.S. Army Rangers in World War II.* Warfare History Network, April 7, 2017. http://warfarehistorynetwork.com/daily/wwii/u-s-army-rangers-in-world-war-ii.

[20] Atkinson, Rick. *The Day of Battle: The War in Sicily and Italy, 1943-1944, Volume Two of the Liberation Trilogy.* Henry Holt and Co., 2007. 396.

[21] Walter F. Nye, quoted in Hull, Michael D. *U.S. Army Rangers in World War II.* Warfare History Network, April 7, 2017. http://warfarehistorynetwork.com/daily/wwii/u-s-army-rangers-in-world-war-ii.

[22] Brown, John Sloan. *Draftee Division: The 88th Infantry Division in World War II.* Lexington, KY: University Press of Kentucky, 1986. 147.

²³ Schultz, Duane. *Rage over the Rapido.* HistoryNet.com. Jan. 8,2012. http://www.historynet.com/rage-over-the-rapido.htm

²⁴ Paltzer, Seth. *The Dogs of War: The U.S. Army's Use of Canines in WWII.* https://armyhistory.org/the-dogs-of-war-the-u-s-armys-use-of-canines-in-wwii/.

²⁵Kennedy, Michelle. *Bootprints in History: Mountaineers take the Ridge.* U.S. Army, February 19, 2015. www.army.mil/article/143088/bootprints_in_history_mountaineers_take_the_ridge

²⁶ Reports on the Hindenburg's Champlain Valley July 1, 1936 appearance from Gooley, Lawrence P. *Hindenburg: When Dirigibles Roamed North Country Skies.* Adirondack Almanack, July 10, 2002. https://www.adirondackalmanack.com/2012/07/hindenburg-when-dirigibles-roamed-north-country-skies.html

²⁷ Obituary of Charles Minot Dole. The New York Times, March 16, 1976.

²⁸ Jenkins, McKay. *The Last Ridge: The Epic Story of America's First Mountain Soldiers and the Assault on Hitler's Europe.* New York: Random House, 2003. 14.

²⁹ Jenkins, McKay. *The Last Ridge: The Epic Story of America's First Mountain Soldiers and the Assault on Hitler's Europe.* New York: Random House, 2003. 17.

³⁰ Jenkins, McKay. *The Last Ridge: The Epic Story of America's First Mountain Soldiers and the Assault on Hitler's Europe.* New York: Random House, 2003. 33.

³¹ Whitlock, Flint. *The 10th Mountain Division: Taking the Po Valley During War in Italy.* Warfare History Network, July 10, 2017. http://warfarehistorynetwork.com/daily/wwii/the-10th-mountain-division-taking-the-po-valley-during-war-in-italy.

³² Thomas O'Neill, quoted in Baumgardner, Randy W. *Tenth Mountain Division.* Turner Publishing Company, 2013. 31.

³³ Jenkins, McKay. *The Last Ridge: The Epic Story of America's First Mountain Soldiers and the Assault on Hitler's Europe.* New York: Random House, 2003. 6.

—THE INTERVIEWS—

Source Notes: **Peter Deeb.** Interviewed by Robert von Hasseln and Michael Aikey, February 21, 2001, Buffalo, NY. Deposited at NYS Military Museum.

Source Notes: **Edwin Israel.** Interviewed by Matthew Rozell, July 24, 2003, Queensbury, NY. Deposited at NYS Military Museum.

Source Notes: **Thomas Collins.** Interviewed by Catherine Heil, January 2, 2004, Glens Falls, NY. Deposited at NYS Military Museum.

Source Notes: **James Brady.** Interviewed by Matthew Rozell, June 22, 2003, Fort Ann, NY. Deposited at NYS Military Museum.

Source Notes: **Elizabeth Brady.** Interviewed by Matthew Rozell, June 22, 2003, Fort Ann, NY. Deposited at NYS Military Museum.

Source Notes: **Harold Erdrich.** Interviewed by Robert von Hasseln and Michael Aikey, February 27, 2001, Freeport, NY. Deposited at NYS Military Museum.

Source Notes: **Fred Crockett.** Interviewed by Michael Russert and Wayne Clarke, April 30, 2007, Cazenovia, NY. Deposited at NYS Military Museum.

Source Notes: **Floyd Dumas.** Interviewed by Michael Russert and Wayne Clarke, December 14, 2007, Saratoga Springs, NY. Transcribed by Paige Mager. Also several classroom interviews with Matthew Rozell, Hudson Falls, NY, and unpublished narrative. Deposited at NYS Military Museum.

Source Notes: **Abbott Wiley.** Interviewed by Wayne Clarke, February 19, 2013, Valley Falls, NY. Deposited at NYS Military Museum.

Source Notes: **Anthony Battillo.** Interviewed by Michael Russert and Wayne Clarke, April 15, 2002, Hyde Park, NY. Deposited at NYS Military Museum.

Source Notes: **Frederick Vetter.** Interviewed by Michael Russert and Wayne Clarke, February 23, 2004, Glens Falls, NY. Deposited at NYS Military Museum.

Source Notes: **Carl Newton.** Interviewed by Michael Russert and Wayne Clarke, May 18, 2004, Johnson City, NY. Deposited at NYS Military Museum.

Source Notes: **Arthur Thompson.** Interviewed by Michael Russert, November 20, 2002, Saratoga Springs, NY. Deposited at NYS Military Museum.

Source Notes: **Harold Wusterbarth.** Interviewed by Michael Russert and Wayne Clarke, April 8, 2008, Saratoga Springs, NY. Deposited at NYS Military Museum. Transcribed by Kazashi McLaughlin.

Source Notes: **William Millette.** Interviewed by Michael Russert and Wayne Clarke, April 30, 2004, Latham, NY. Deposited at NYS Military Museum.

www.ingramcontent.com/pod-product-compliance
Lightning Source LLC
Chambersburg PA
CBHW070042080526
44586CB00013B/888